The Right to Privacy in Texas

The Right to Privacy in Texas

From Common Law Origins to 21st Century Protections

John C. Domino

LEXINGTON BOOKS
Lanham • Boulder • New York • London

Published by Lexington Books
An imprint of The Rowman & Littlefield Publishing Group, Inc.
4501 Forbes Boulevard, Suite 200, Lanham, Maryland 20706
www.rowman.com

86-90 Paul Street, London EC2A 4NE

British Library Cataloguing in Publication Information Available

Library of Congress Cataloging-in-Publication Data

Names: Domino, John C., author.
Title: The right to privacy in Texas : from common law origins to 21st century protections / John C. Domino.
Description: Lanham : Lexington Books, 2024. | Includes bibliographical references and index.
Identifiers: LCCN 2024004492 (print) | LCCN 2024004493 (ebook) | ISBN 9781666933116 (cloth) | ISBN 9781666933123 (ebook)
Subjects: LCSH: Privacy, Right of--Texas. | Privacy, Right of--United States. | Torts–Texas.
Classification: LCC KFT1397.P7 D66 2024 (print) | LCC KFT1397.P7 (ebook) | DDC 342.76408/58–dc23/eng/20240205
LC record available at https://lccn.loc.gov/2024004492\
LC ebook record available at https://lccn.loc.gov/2024004493

I dedicate this book to my children Nicholas and Chloe

Contents

Acknowledgments

This book would not have been possible without the support of the faculty and students at Sam Houston State University. In addition, over the years, the Texas Supreme Court Historical Society has provided me with numerous opportunities to publish my research in their excellent journal and to learn from many scholars and members of the bench and bar who know far more than I about Texas legal history. The Society also generously supported this project by funding the Texas State Historical Association's Larry McNeill Research Fellowship in Texas Legal History.

Introduction

The Right to Privacy in Texas

> "[T]he right to be free from the unwarranted appropriation or exploitation of one's personality, the publicizing of one's private affairs with which the public has no legitimate concern, or the wrongful intrusion into one's private activities in such manner as to outrage or cause mental suffering, shame or humiliation to a person of ordinary sensibilities."
>
> —Texas Supreme Court Justice James Gray Denton in *Billings v. Atkinson*[1]

As this passage from the Texas Supreme Court's ruling in *Billings v. Atkinson*[2] illustrates, the right to privacy reflects a fundamental human need to be free from intrusion into the most personal and intimate matters. Encompassing much more than the "right to be let alone" from eavesdropping and wiretapping, privacy protects reputation and self-identity, and it gives us control over the personal information that we choose to disclose and guards against the theft of our name, likeness, and identity. *Billings* was the first case in which a Texas court adopted the right to privacy based on common law principles and state constitutional provisions. As Justice Denton wrote in the opinion, by eavesdropping on Billings's conversation, the telephone company invaded the right to privacy, henceforth establishing that "an unwarranted invasion of the right to privacy constitutes a legal injury for which a remedy will be granted."[3] Other privacy decisions followed *Billings*, building upon common law doctrines and provisions of the Texas constitution to provide the basis for the right to privacy. This book, *The Right to Privacy in Texas: From Common Law Origins to Twenty-First-Century Protections*, examines the origins, evolution, and scope (as well as limitations) of privacy law in Texas based primarily on the rulings of the state's courts and, to a lesser degree, on the statutory protection enacted by the state legislature.

Common law is law that is derived from judicial decisions instead of statutes. Courts in the United States originally followed legal rules and concepts that were based on the English common law until the American legal system was able to create its own common law rules either from precedent or by analogy to comparable areas of law. Until the late nineteenth century, there was no important body of statutory law in the United States. Common law courts had jurisdiction in the area of property, torts, wills, and contracts, and they often defined crimes such as murder, manslaughter, arson, robbery, larceny, and rape. Slowly, the common law evolved through judicial decisions and statutory law, although some concepts and principles remained unaltered. State legislatures codify common law rules and doctrines handed down from state courts to give the rule or doctrine permanence, or to expand or narrow scope of the common law.[4]

DEFINING PRIVACY

The definition and precise scope of the right to privacy can be elusive. Privacy law is far more complex than most people can imagine, consisting of numerous legal doctrines, state court decisions, statutory protections, and constitutional provisions. At its most fundamental, it is the right to be let alone, free from intrusion or interference. Privacy protects a broad concept of personhood—it allows for a cause of action for intentional or willful invasion of one's person and home; it protects against intrusion into solitude, seclusion, and the most private and intimate matters. Invasion of privacy extends to entering a home without permission, surveillance and wiretapping, video recording of sexual acts and sharing the recording without consent to third parties, to conversations in private as well as public places when there is a reasonable expectation to keep conversations private. Further, privacy allows a person to recover damages resulting from the unwanted public disclosure of private information and from the misappropriation of a person's name, likeness, or reputation for commercial gain or the value associated with self-identity. There is also a distinction between a normative, or moral, definition and a legal one. One might argue that there *ought* to be a right to privacy without there necessarily being an actual legal or constitutional right.

A legal right to privacy is a relatively new idea, both in Texas and in the United States. Of course, the desire for privacy—to have a private sphere of life separate from the public sphere of one's life—has always existed in human society as far as we know. The term "privacy" commonly appeared in legal complaints in court filings as far back as the 1600s, but the right to privacy as a legal doctrine as we have come to know it today emerges in its earliest form as recently as the late nineteenth century and even then, it was not well defined.

The origin of the right to privacy as a cause of action in the United States is attributed to the first published argument for a broader common law protection by two Boston lawyers, Samuel Warren[5] and Louis Brandeis,[6] in a famous essay published in the *Harvard Law Review* in 1890.[7] As discussed at length in chapter 1, the article is arguably the most well-known and often-cited law review article in American legal history, remaining one of the most trenchant articulations of the interests warranting protection by a privacy right. Their essay has been cited in thousands of state and federal privacy cases. Warren and Brandeis argued that existing common law doctrines at that time already contained the necessary elements for what they believed to be a broader, more comprehensive right of privacy—a "right to be let alone."[8] This right extends to the right to remain a private person, to protect oneself from being photographed, and from having one's private affairs written about by the press. The right to privacy, therefore, prohibits any disclosure of information that is *not* of public interest; it protects persons "whose affairs the community has no legitimate concern, from being dragged into an undesirable and undesired publicity."[9]

Privacy also means different things to different people. For some, privacy is informational privacy—control over electronic communication, online activities, and financial, medical, or academic records. For others, privacy protects against the prying eyes of the state or physical intrusion or trespass. And still others believe that the right to privacy extends to sexual intimacy, lifestyle choices, and matters of reproduction or abortion.

Another way of looking at privacy is the relative degree to which a person has the power to control what is disclosed about them. A celebrity or social media "influencer" who spends all day broadcasting provocative images of themself along with highly personal health or financial information on social media ironically might at the same time be shocked and appalled by being surreptitiously photographed or recorded by a stranger at their favorite coffee shop or gym. They want to set the terms of what information is disclosed—to control their image presented to the world, if you will. Does this hypothetical celebrity have a reasonable expectation of privacy? The reasonable expectation of privacy doctrine, applied in civil as well as the more familiar Fourth Amendment search and seizure context, depends not only on our subjective expectation of the degree of privacy we believe we deserve but also on society's judgment of what we claim to be reasonable. A person's expectation that they should live in perfect secrecy and anonymity, free from prying eyes or ears might be desirable, but in the internet era of human history it is not reasonable to suppose that strangers, businesses, and the government will *not* know their age, gender, address, value of their home, occupation, and what they look like. If a person is engaged in malfeasance—particularly in a public place—they may have no expectation of privacy whatsoever. However, under privacy law it is reasonable to assume that a person has an expectation of privacy in a locker room, a changing room in a department store, or in an email or text message to one's closest confidants. Less certain is the assumption that privacy protects a person's right to live a lifestyle that flouts all contemporary social norms or harms other human beings.

One need not focus solely on court opinions and legal scholarship to gauge support for the right to privacy. Shortly after the Supreme Court reversed *Roe v. Wade*[10] in the *Dobbs*[11] ruling in 2022—in which several justices expressed skepticism about an implied right to privacy in *Griswold v. Connecticut*[12]—Americans were asked in a 2023 poll which constitutional right is the most threatened. By ten percentage points, they responded that among our rights, privacy is more "threatened" than it is "secured," that it is more "threatened" than either equal protection under law or freedom from unreasonable searches and seizures.[13] Further, 65 percent of respondents agreed with the proposition that the Constitution contains a right to privacy, with little difference across party lines.[14] When asked about *Griswold*, the 1965 case which safeguarded a couple's constitutional right to use contraception, over 80 percent agreed that the Court should uphold this right, with similar strength of support among Democrats (78 percent), Republicans (80 percent), and Independents (81 percent).[15] A total of 79 percent of Americans say they agree that "both married and unmarried couples have a constitutional right to buy and use contraceptives without government restriction."[16]

Regarding the rights of LGBT persons, a 2023 poll found 69 percent of Americans surveyed support *Lawrence v. Texas*,[17] the 2003 privacy ruling that banned sodomy laws that punish people for engaging in homosexual conduct. Support for the ruling was similar across the partisan spectrum, with Democrats (68 percent), Republicans (62 percent), and Independents (74 percent) agreeing with Court's ruling.[18] The poll also raised the question of marital privacy in *Loving v. Virginia*[19] (1967) and *Obergefell v. Hodges*[20] (2015). Support for the Supreme Court's decision in *Loving*, which held that states may not ban interracial marriages is overwhelmingly strong: 81 percent of Americans surveyed believe that states should not have the power to prevent two people of different races from marrying. Support for the ruling was similar across the partisan spectrum, with Democrats (79 percent), Republicans (81 percent), and Independents (83 percent) agreeing with Court's ruling.[21]

Public opinion is more divided on *Obergefell*, the Court's 2015 ruling that there is a constitutional right of same-sex couples to get married. A total of 54 percent of respondents believe states should be required to continue acknowledging same-sex marriages, while 46 percent believe that states should be permitted to refuse to recognize such marriages. Self-identified

Democrats (66 percent) are twice as likely as Republicans (31 percent) to support requiring states to continue to recognize same-sex marriages.[22]

In the area of informational privacy, concern about online data privacy is at an all-time high. Of the 74 percent of adults in the United States who use Google, 35 percent of users are very concerned about invasion of privacy when using that search engine. Of the roughly 60 percent of Americans who have a Facebook page, 43 percent are very concerned about their privacy being invaded.[23] Americans understand that they willingly give up a degree of privacy everyday by using apps and shopping online, but individuals prefer legislation rather than self-regulation as the main way of protecting their privacy. A total of 83 percent of Americans believe that Congress should pass national data privacy legislation and that both federal and state lawmakers bear responsibility for protecting privacy.[24] According to polls, 62 percent of Americans believe their online and offline activities are being tracked and monitored by companies and the government. And over 80 percent believe that they have little or no control over data being collected by businesses and the government. Roughly 60 percent state that it is impossible "to go through daily life without having data collected about them by companies or the government."[25] Some 64 percent of Americans say their social media activity is not very or not at all secure, and 50 percent believe their private text conversations lack security.[26] About 70 percent of Americans think their smartphone or other devices are listening in on their conversations without their knowledge or consent.[27] We will review Texas public opinion polls on matters such as contraceptives, abortion, and rights of LGBT persons in chapter 4.

STATE COURTS AND THE RIGHT TO PRIVACY

Conventional wisdom emphasizes the role of the US Supreme Court as the primary actor in protecting the right to privacy: state courts are believed to play a subsidiary role in the protection and expansion of individual rights. As innovators in the area of personal rights, state appellate courts have far-reaching impact on American society, often acting as laboratories of constitutional law. State supreme court decisions are often precursors of "landmark" US Supreme Court decisions. There are relatively few US Supreme Court privacy rulings compared to the vast corpus of privacy jurisprudence in the fifty states. US Supreme Court Justice William J. Brennan observed in 1966 that:

> The composite work of the courts in the fifty states probably has greater significance in measuring how well America attains the ideal of equal justice for

> all. The state courts of all levels must annually hand down literally millions of decisions which determine the vital issues of life, liberty, and property.[28]

Brennan also wrote in a frequently cited 1977 law review article, "State Constitutions and the Protection of Individual Rights,"[29] that "state courts no less than federal are and ought to be the guardians of our liberties," by extending protections and by going beyond those required by the US Supreme Court's interpretation of federal law. Brennan argued that we should not be reticent to look to a state's constitution for more protection of individual rights than that which is guaranteed by the federal constitution. Texas judges have the discretion to analyze and resolve disputes from either the standpoint of the state precedent, federal precedent, or some combination of the two. Indeed, the US Supreme Court has ruled that when a state supreme court decides a case on "an adequate and independent state ground" alone, the Court will not subject the ruling of the state court to judicial review.[30] This approach to judicial interpretation—where a state court looks primarily at the state constitution and laws to resolve disputes—has been referred to as the primacy model of state judicial decision making.[31]

PURPOSE AND ORGANIZATION OF THE BOOK

This book reflects Justice Brennan's sentiment about the importance of state courts by examining the state court rulings that serve as the foundation for privacy jurisprudence in the Lone Star State. It documents the extent to which fundamental privacy interests are protected by state court decisions. Analyzing a large corpus of state court privacy decisions over a period of more than six decades, this book explores and documents the origins and development of the right to privacy in Texas, beginning when the state's courts had not yet recognized the common law tort doctrines that allow recovery for intrusion into the private affairs of individuals and culminating with the Texas Supreme Court and lower state appellate courts adopting a robust right to privacy in groundbreaking cases.

Readers other than legal scholars and practitioners here in Texas might find that the origin of the right to privacy in Texas is an unlikely one. The right did not instantly spring forth from US Supreme Court cases like *Griswold* and *Roe* but evolved slowly on a state-by-state basis from the common law tort doctrines beginning in the late nineteenth century. Civil cases consist of legal disputes between two private parties, such as lawsuits brought for defamation, breach of contract, negligence, property disputes, and, of course, invasion of privacy. Legal remedies for privacy violations can also be found in state statutes that provide criminal as well as civil penalties, such as the Texas

Wiretap Act or various informational privacy or consumer protection laws. In rare instances, the reasonable expectation of privacy doctrine, which is derived largely from criminal search and seizure law, will be applied in civil cases, such as when a surreptitious recording is made in the workplace or in a locker room. Although the book does acknowledge the Fourth Amendment origin of the reasonable expectation of privacy doctrine—because of its influence on the evolution of privacy law—the massive body of criminal search and seizure law in Texas, however, falls outside of the scope of this book. Search and seizure caselaw in Texas relies largely on the application of the Fourth Amendment of the US Constitution by the US Supreme Court and federal courts. Again, the focus here is on civil cases decided by state courts. Criminal law deals with the actions of persons that are offenses against society, even though the immediate victim is an individual. When the government conducts an unreasonable search or criminalizes intimate sexual conduct between two adults, privacy as a civil liberty is invoked as a safeguard against the government's actions.

Because most Americans equate the phrase "right to privacy" with the rulings of the US Supreme Court and see Texas as ground zero for abortion politics and the battle for reproductive and LGBT rights, it is important for readers to understand that this book is *not* about abortion politics or US Supreme Court decisions regarding contraception, abortion, or same-sex marriage. As important as those topics are, the focus of this book is on the decisions of Texas courts that address injuries resulting from civil violations of the right to privacy. While matters of abortion, reproductive rights, and issues related to the LGBT community deserve our rapt attention in light of recent dramatic legislative restrictions on abortion in the state, the focus here is legal history and caselaw rather than politics. Since, however, it would be remiss to ignore a trend on the US Supreme Court that appears to be retreating from its commitment to federal constitutional privacy protection—as evidenced by an ongoing discussion of unenumerated rights and the shortcomings of substantive due process in cases such as *Dobbs v. Jackson*[32]—the final chapter will address these matters as they relate to the scope and limits of privacy protection here in Texas. If the US Supreme Court does go silent on the question of privacy, individuals will need to pursue their privacy claims in Texas courts under common law doctrines, state constitutional provisions, and statutory protections.

Following this introductory chapter, chapter 1 provides a foundational discussion of the origins of the right to privacy under the common law and US Constitution. We examine the major doctrines adopted by the courts of other states in the nation as early as 1900, over seventy years before Texas recognized privacy as an independent right, and analyze select US Supreme

Court rulings that have been central to the articulation of the principles and doctrines underpinning our understanding of the right to privacy.

Chapter 2 contains the central or core discussion of the book: the analysis of Texas appellate court privacy rulings based on tort doctrines and constitutional provisions. These rulings have had the most profound impact on the origins and development of the right to privacy in Texas. They contain the most substantive discussion and explication of the scope and nature of the right to privacy. The basis of the right to privacy in Texas are four common law tort doctrines that were originally adopted by state courts outside of Texas in the early to mid-twentieth century: (1) intrusion or invasion into a person's private affairs, seclusion, or solitude; (2) public disclosure of private information; (3) appropriation of name of likeness for value or commercial gain; and (4) disclosure of false communication about a person, or what came to be known as the "false light" doctrine. These four tort doctrines in aggregate form an independent right to privacy in Texas (tort law is a body of law dealing with wrongful acts, injuries, or violations of a rights by a private person or entity, other than a breach of contract). Further, the Texas Supreme Court has held that although the Texas Constitution does not contain an express guarantee of a right to privacy, the state's constitution *does* contain an implied right to privacy found in the protections of the Texas Bill of Rights against arbitrary deprivation of life and liberty.

Chapter 3 examines the state's statutory privacy protections. The chapter is organized in the form of an analysis of the scope and limitations of the privacy interests protected by state statutes. Many of the older common law and constitutional remedies discussed in previous chapters have been codified into law. Statutory protections include civil and criminal remedies for matters such as wiretapping and the unlawful interception of intimate visual and recorded images, the use of spyware and tracking devices, identity theft and consumer privacy, the use of drones to spy and snoop, cybercrime, and student records and data.

Chapter 4 begins with a brief recap of the previous chapters from the standpoint of the definition and scope of the right to privacy. It then offers an assessment of the degree to which the right protects Texans in the second decade of the twenty-first century. A number of questions are raised. What fundamental interests are protected by the right to privacy in Texas? What are the strengths and weaknesses of this body of law? For example, does it fall short in areas such as reproductive rights in light of the US Supreme Court's reversal of *Roe* and possible retreat from other federal privacy rulings? Now that abortion is no longer a constitutional right, what impact will legislative restrictions on abortion and abortion-related activities, such as travel or medical services, have on privacy? What recourse will LGBT persons have in the face of an onslaught of legislative measures aimed at regulating their public and private lives?

NOTES

1. *Billings v. Atkinson*, 489 S.W. 2d 858, 861 (Tex. 1973).
2. Ibid.
3. Ibid.
4. See generally Andrew Forsyth, *Common Law and Natural Law in America* (Cambridge: Cambridge University Press, 2019), 46–69.
5. Samuel D. Warren (1852–1910) was a prominent Boston lawyer and businessman who practiced law with Brandeis.
6. Louis D. Brandeis (1856–1941) practiced law in St. Louis and Boston. He is the author of the famous "Brandeis Brief" and served as a justice on the US Supreme Court from 1916 to 1939.
7. The article can be found by searching most law content or social science databases; or see Samuel D. Warren, and Louis D. Brandeis, *The Right to Privacy*, with an insightful forward by Steven Alan Childress (New Orleans: Quid Pro Books), *Legal Legends Series* (2010).
8. Ibid.
9. Ibid, 214.
10. *Roe v. Wade*, 410 U.S. 113 (1973).
11. *Dobbs v. Jackson Women's Health Organization*, 597 U.S. 215 (2022).
12. *Griswold v. Connecticut*, 381 U.S. 479 (1965).
13. American Civic Life Survey conducted by the Civitas Institute at the University of Texas at Austin (July 2023). The survey found that the rights that a rebelieved to be "most secure" include freedom of religion and the right to bear arms. https://civitas.utexas.edu/wp-content/uploads/2023/06/Civitas-Polling-Memo-06-06-23.pdf.
14. Based on FiveThirtyEight/Ipsos panel survey waves conducted May 26 to June 6, 2022, among a sample of 1,691 adults, and June 27 to July 5, 2022, among a sample of 1,549 adults (drawn from the same panel as the previous poll). Each sample of respondents was weighted to match the general population. Respondents could select up to three issues.
15. SCOTUSPoll, conducted by researchers from Harvard University, Stanford University, and the University of Texas at Austin in 2023 in collaboration with YouGov, gauged American attitudes about major cases in front of the court. It also asked about four landmark Supreme Court cases: *Griswold v. Connecticut* (1965), *Loving v. Virginia* (1967), *Lawrence v. Texas* (2003), and *Obergefell v. Hodges* (2015), https://today.yougov.com/topics/politics/articles-reports/2023/06/09/scotuspoll-2023-supreme-court-landmark-rulings. Majority support for the rulings in these four cases demonstrates widespread endorsement of the following: prohibition of racial discrimination in marriages, the right of couples to use contraception, the decriminalization of homosexual conduct, and the recognition of same-sex marriages. (An Economist/YouGov poll in July 2022 also found majority support for each of *Griswold*,

Lawrence, and *Obergefell*, while using different question wording; another poll conducted the same month found majority support for Congress codifying each of these as law). A 2022 Yahoo News/YouGov poll found that 83 percent of Americans believe that contraceptives ("like birth control pills") should be legal, https://news.yahoo.com/poll-most-americans-will-balk-if-conservatives-challenge-contraception-and-gay-marriage-after-overturning-roe-202215040.html.

16. Yahoo News/YouGov, "Poll: Most Americans will balk if conservatives challenge contraception and gay marriage after overturning Roe," (2022), https://news.yahoo.com/poll-most-americans-will-balk-if-conservatives-challenge-contraception-and-gay-marriage-after-overturning-roe-202215040.html.

17. *Lawrence v. Texas*, 539 U.S. 558 (2003).

18. Taylor Orth and Carl Bialik, "SCOTUSPoll 2023: Views of landmark rulings in Griswold, Loving, Lawrence, and Obergefell," YouGov (June 9, 2023), https://today.yougov.com/politics/articles/45801-scotuspoll-2023-supreme-court-landmark-rulings.

19. *Loving v. Virginia*, 388 U.S. 1 (1967).

20. *Obergefell v. Hodges*, 576 U.S. 644 (2015).

21. Ibid.

22. Ibid.

23. Gallup, April 2018, https://news.gallup.com/poll/232319/facebook-users-privacy-concerns-2011.aspx.

24. Morning Consult, poll conducted April 2021, https://pro.morningconsult.com/instant-intel/state-privacy-congress-priority-poll.

25. Pew Research Center, November 2019, https://www.pewresearch.org/internet/2019/11/15/americans-and-privacy-concerned-confused-and-feeling-lack-of-control-over-their-personal-information/.

26. The Associated Press-NORC Center for Public Affairs Research and MeriTalk (September 16, 2021).

27. Source: Nov. 4-22, 2021, Washington Post-Schar School poll of 1,122 US adults with an error margin of +/– 3.5 percentage points. 2012 results are from the Pew Research Center.

28. William J. Brennan, Jr., "State Supreme Court judge versus United States Supreme Court Justice: A change in function and perspective," *University of Florida Law Review*, 19 (1966): 225–37.

29. William J. Brennan, Jr., "State constitutions and the protection of individual rights," *Harvard Law Review*, 90 (1977): 489, 491.

30. *Michigan v. Long*, 463 U.S. 1032 (1983).

31. See Judith S. Kaye, "Dual constitutionalism in practice and principle," *St John's Law Review*, 61 (1987): 399.

32. *Dobbs v. Jackson Women's Health Organization*, No. 19-1392, 597 U.S. ___ (2022).

Chapter 1

Origins of the Right to Privacy in the United States

The common law right to privacy in Texas is the right to be "let alone," which provides a civil cause of action for unwanted invasions of a person's property, image and reputation, and emotional well-being. This right is based on common law tort doctrines adopted by state courts. A much broader definition of privacy is "privacy as autonomy," understood as the right to choose to engage in personal and intimate acts—such as procreation, contraception, sexual intimacy, and abortion—free from governmental intrusion or regulation. This latter dimension of privacy emerged from the rulings of the US Supreme Court.

As stated in the introduction, the main purpose of this book is to examine the privacy rulings of Texas state courts. Before proceeding to that task, however, this chapter provides a foundational discussion of the origins of the right to privacy traced back to (1) common law doctrines adopted in the states and (2) landmark US Supreme Court decisions. These two bodies of law—common law and constitutional—influence how the bench and bar, legislators, legal scholars, and average Texans understand the right to privacy.

COMMON LAW ORIGINS

The origin of the of the right to privacy in the United States is attributed to the first published argument for a broader common law protection by two Boston lawyers, Samuel Warren[1] and Louis Brandeis[2] in a famous essay published in the *Harvard Law Review* in 1890.[3] This article is arguably the most well-known and often-cited law review article in American legal history, remaining one of the most trenchant articulations of the interests warranting protection by a privacy right. Nearly every court opinion covered in this book—or any other book on privacy—cites Warren and Brandeis's article. Written out of concern about a trend of overzealous journalists prying into the private affairs of prominent families—including Warren's—the authors objected to the highly profitable "yellow journalism" of the day. Victims of surreptitious photography, eavesdropping, and disclosure of private and intimate images and facts deserved access to a legal remedy, the authors argued.[4] The two lawyers believed, as many scholars maintain today, that the established tort of defamation/libel fell short of the protection needed to guard against an intrusive press.

Warren and Brandeis argued that the invasion of privacy constituted an independent tort, or injury, not merely because it violated the space physically inhabited by a person but also one's dignity and identity. Privacy was not merely a property right, such as that which is violated by trespass or theft of creative works, but an incorporeal or personal right, the violation of which adversely affects a person's sense of independence, self-esteem, dignity, and integrity. Based on the privacy interests that extend to "corporeal property," such as one's home, papers, or creative endeavors which produce monetary value, privacy is a right that affords protection of "incorporeal property," such as one's reputation, peace of mind, and the products and processes of the mind.[5] Existing common law doctrines contained the necessary elements for a broader, more comprehensive right of privacy—a "right to be let alone." A new understanding of privacy was necessary in the face of encroaching modernity in the form of recent technologies, a powerful and intrusive press, and rapidly expanding government bureaucracy.

Attesting to the impact of Warren and Brandeis, federal judge and respected legal scholar Richard Posner wrote in an opinion dealing with the disclosure of the medical records of a man living with HIV that the modern legal concept of privacy not only originated with Warren and Brandeis but perhaps they invented a new field of law, as well.[6] Posner stated:

> The concept originated in a famous article by Warren and Brandeis that found latent in a number of areas of the common law, ranging from copyright to trespass, a policy of protecting people against the invasion of their "private space" (not Warren and Brandeis' term) and the involuntary revelation of personal, private facts about them. . . . After a lag, the concept proposed by Warren and Brandeis fructified in a distinct, many-branched tort of invasion of the right to privacy.[7]

The invasion of this right to privacy, wrote Prosser, can occur as a result of electronic eavesdropping or surveillance, the disclosure of information or publicity that casts a person in a false light, the release of the intimate details of a person's life, or the use of a notable person's name or likeness for profit without their consent.[8]

In the 1973 case of *Billings v. Atkinson* (discussed at length in chapter 2) in which the Texas Supreme Court ruled for the first time that the Texas Constitution protects the right to privacy, Justice James Gray Denton[9] stated that it is conventional wisdom that "courts had not prior to Warren and Brandeis's article in 1890 granted relief expressly for invasion of [a]right to privacy." Denton was speaking broadly and not simply in terms of Texas jurisprudence.[10] His sentiments mirror those of most other state court judges in the United States. Other jurists believed that "[p]rior to 1890, if the phrase ['right to privacy'] was used at all it represented, at least logically, an amorphous concept somewhat in the nature of 'the pursuit of happiness,' something to which we had a right; but educing that right to enforceable proportions was not even imagined."[11]

Warren and Brandeis's journal article never languished in academic obscurity like most scholarly publications. Shortly after the article was published, scholars heralded its importance. In 1905, Elbridge L. Adams, a lawyer and publisher, wrote that their article "is one of the most brilliant excursions in the field of theoretical jurisprudence." Adams agreed with the Warren and Brandeis's argument that rapid political, social, and economic changes require us to recognize new rights and new remedies to secure those rights, which the common law, "in its eternal youth, expands to meet."[12] He wrote that there was a developing consensus because of the intrusive and abusive practices of newspapers that the law ought to address not only invasions of a person's property rights but also their privacy rights—a right to be let alone.[13] The law of libel, however, fell short of addressing this problem because it dealt with damage to one's reputation. The right to privacy redresses a "spiritual wrong,—damage to one's own feelings."[14]

Warren and Brandeis may not have been the first to fret about emerging technology having the potential to invade our private spaces—there were many instances in their era in which new cameras with fast shutter speeds and wiretapping technology led to complaints, lawsuits, and legislation—but they were the first to lay the foundation for a body of law or legal doctrines that would address a changing society. They advocated for "elasticity" in the law to deal with changing technology and an increasingly intrusive press of the time. The two forward-thinking men believed that "political, social, and economic changes require the recognition of new rights, and the common law evolves to meet the new demands of society."[15] They continue, "Recent inventions and business methods call attention to the next step which must be taken for the protection of the person, and for securing to the individual what Judge Cooley calls the right 'to be let alone.'"[16]

In short, the scope of privacy protection extends a right under the common law to determine to what extent our thoughts, sentiments, and emotions should be communicated to others by means of words, painting, or music. No one may publish these thoughts or "productions" without consent. This common law right is independent of copyright statutes, the purpose of which is to protect property, or the loss of pecuniary interest or profit in the productions. This is the right we have in corporeal property.

Privacy protects the right to remain a private person, to protect oneself from being photographed or even sketched, from having one's private affairs written about by the press. It prohibits any publication of personal information that is *not* of public interest and protects persons "whose affairs the community has no legitimate concern, from being dragged into an undesirable and undesired publicity."[17] Warren and Brandeis concluded that "[t]he common law has always recognized a man's house as his castle, impregnable" even to legitimate government authority, so why "[s]hall the courts thus close the front entrance to constituted authority, and open wide the back door to idle or prurient curiosity?"[18] One of the more well-known phrases used by Warren and Brandeis warns readers about the specter of "mechanical devices [that] threaten to make good the prediction that 'what is whispered on the closet shall be proclaimed from the housetops.'"[19]

The twenty-first-century reader familiar with a half-century of privacy law may experience a pang of disappointment reading the article by Warren and Brandeis. The lofty language calling for the right to privacy is there, but the authors are calling only for the recognition of legal protection against the public disclosure in the newspapers of private information about the individual that causes embarrassment or emotional distress—a terribly narrow right to privacy by today's standards. Reading between the lines, one can speculate that the authors would have liked to see an even broader right to be let alone, but it was undesirable and undesired publicity that irked them the most. To this end, they cobbled together old court decisions that granted relief to injured parties using the doctrine of defamation, invasion of a property right, and breach of confidence or of an implied contract as the basis of a new right to privacy. The authors were by no means alone in their disdain for journalists' ability to violate privacy using First Amendment press freedoms. The key was to find a countervailing right, a right to be let alone, so that injured individuals could fight back.

Granted, no one dares gainsay the importance of the *Harvard Law Review* article, but it can plausibly be argued that the *idea* of privacy existed long before 1890, in colonial America and before.[20] Early cases recognized privacy as a property right, a physical intrusion in violation of the doctrine of trespass. The adage that "a man's house is his castle" was taken seriously and was adopted in numerous legal and nonlegal situations as early as 1605 in Semayne's case.[21] This common law principle would provide the basis for the Fourth Amendment—enshrining a right against unreasonable governmental intrusions. Search and seizure jurisprudence is said to emanate from the

Fourth Amendment but it was an old English case of *Entick v. Carrington*[22] that provided the guiding precedent for *Boyd v. United States* in 1886, one of the earliest US Supreme Court cases in Fourth Amendment caselaw.[23] Relying on the eighteenth-century *Entick* precedent, the *Boyd* Court embraced the idea that there is an "indefeasible right of personal security, personal liberty and private property" that guards against invasions of the "sanctity of a man's home and privacies of life."[24] In nineteenth-century America, such violations of the "sanctity and inviolability of one's house" were met with both civil and criminal judgments.[25] A resident of a house enjoyed a right to "quiet and peaceable possession" and a place of "family repose."[26] The common law concept of trespass and the Fourth Amendment's prohibition of unreasonable search and seizure were understood to protect the right to privacy against governmental searches as well as invasions by private persons. Private property encompasses the right to exclude others from intruding upon domestic privacy once the rightful occupant of a home shuts the door.[27] As in today's society, the legal occupant was understood as having protections against the unwelcome intrusions of landlords making repairs[28] and the knock of the sheriff sent by creditors.[29] State courts enforced houseguests' "right of quiet occupancy and privacy" when a physician brought an uninvited person into the bedroom of a woman giving birth.[30] The trespass doctrine was an often used remedy for invasions of domestic privacy. Injured parties could recover for property damage, pecuniary loss, as well as "insult, invasion of privacy, and interference with the comfort of . . . the family."[31] Eavesdropping, a common law crime documented in Blackstone's *Commentaries*,[32] was prosecuted in America in the 1800s based on the maxim that no one has a right to "pry into the secrecy of your own house."[33] Trespass was not merely a physical intrusion resulting from an uninvited stranger stomping around your property or entering your home but the freedom from observation, from Peeping Toms peering in through the window. For example, in the late 1800s a New York appeals court ruled that a plaintiff could sue for damages for "loss of privacy" after the defendant railroad company built an elevated train platform that would allow a steady stream of passengers to observe the plaintiff at home.[34]

Today, state and federal statutes protect confidential electronic communications: civil and criminal penalties exist for hacking into computer accounts, accessing medical and education records without consent, or illegally intercepting emails. The concern for privacy in our communications is not a modern one, however. In the nineteenth century, sanctity of the mail was regarded as a central element of privacy. There was legal protection for private letters and measures to keep confidential correspondence protected from prying eyes; it was a criminal offense to "pry into another's business or secrets."[35] Privacy extended to letters sent in the mail even after they were delivered to their rightful recipient under state law.[36] In the 1800s, courts of equity routinely enjoined the publication of private letters even if the letters had no pecuniary value—no value as property per se.[37] Even personal letters produced as evidence in open court received privacy protection from parties in a case, jurors, or onlookers, with judges often reading the letters privately.

Many homeowners who used force to protect their right to privacy were acquitted by the courts. Violent extrajudicial action on the part of homeowners under the idea that "a man's house is his castle" was regarded as an acceptable remedy to unwanted intrusions. In 1890, the same year that Warren and Brandeis published their article, a homeowner's resort to violence as a means of protecting privacy received national press attention. A police officer named John Mahoney forcibly entered, without a search warrant, the home of Thomas Bailey. Bailey shot Mahoney but was acquitted by a Chicago court. A Chicago newspaper wrote:

> "A man's house is his castle"; in it he is supposed to be safe; privacy is sacred in the eyes of civilization, and no individual has the right to violate the privacy of another; ergo, has not the right to enter his house without consent for any purpose whatsoever. . . . The courts have so decided, and a fresh decision by Judge Collins has brought to notice the danger of violation of the principle.[38]

As with the rise of any new technology, the use of the telegraph in the 1840s created new privacy challenges. Unlike letters, written in private and sealed in an envelope by the sender, telegrams were read by the telegraph operators who sent and received them. Those sending communications via telegraph needed to rely on the discretion of the operators. Many courts held that telegraphic correspondence was considered to be as inviolable as mail[39]; the disclosure of the contents of the telegraphs by operators was prohibited by company rules.[40]

Courts in the nineteenth century consistently upheld the doctrine of interspousal communications—what was then known as the "sacred privacy of domestic life."[41] Now regarded as an anachronistic common law rule of evidence reflecting the old notion that a married couple shared a single legal identity; the principle of interspousal immunity was at that time a reflection of the idea that confidential communications between husband and wife should never be revealed in open court. Judges sought to guard against the revelation of embarrassing intimate matters from the courtroom where news reporters—desperate for juicy gossip—sat perched in the gallery like vultures.

So it was that the need for a right to privacy that Warren and Brandeis shared in their famous article did not spring from their personal experiences alone. As the nineteenth century drew to a close, more personal information was being collected by businesses and government than ever before.

Newspapers printed sensational news and gossip. Records of financial matters, taxes owed, and land titles were now available to the public. Not only individuals and corporations who had a legitimate interests in these matters could see this information but, appallingly, idle curiosity seekers or news reporters desperate for a story had access. For most people, but particularly for those with wealth, fame, or notoriety, the availability of personal and financial information—coupled with advances in photography to capture at a distance private moments in time—was infuriating and degrading. Libel law offered a modicum of protection against the disclosure of personal information to the public, but to bring a successful libel action—and provide a disincentive for newspapers to publish personal information—information published had to be proved untruthful or inaccurate. But for men like Warren and Brandeis it was the veracity of the information that made the invasion all the worse. The "whole truth" of their personal lives being published may not have legally defamed them or cast them in a false light, but it simply shone an unwelcome spotlight upon them. Inaccuracies can cause emotional distress and harm to reputation but the fact that the private intimate facts published were accurate could be as bad. Today, for many, this thinking might seem alien: if the information is true then you have not really been harmed. But the fact that the information is available to all—true or not—is an invasion of privacy—disclosing for all to know what we wish to keep secret.[42]

Professor William L. Prosser's body of writing on tort law—including his seminal article, *Privacy*[43]—rivals Warren and Brandeis's article in terms of the evolution of privacy law. Prosser's name and work is cited in nearly every Texas privacy case that is discussed in this book. Building upon Warren and Brandeis's general notion of a right to be let alone, Prosser, a law professor at the University of Minnesota, wrote systematically on the four privacy torts central to this book's discussion of privacy law in Texas. Indeed, civil privacy actions brought in the Texas court system use one or more of these doctrines as a cause of action. Beginning in the 1950s, Prosser's scholarship—which included lectures and treatises[44]—articulated four privacy tort doctrines: (1) intrusion, (2) public disclosure, (3) false light, and (4) appropriation.[45] On his four-part understanding of the right to privacy, Prosser wrote in 1955:

> Most courts now recognize the existence of the right to privacy, which will be protected against interferences which are serious and outrageous, or beyond the limits of common ideas of dangerous conduct. The right has been held to cover intrusions upon the plaintiffs' solitude; publicity given to his name or likeness, or to private information about him; placing him in a false light in the public eye; and the commercial appropriation of elements of his personality.[46]

The first doctrine, intrusion, is perhaps the most important privacy doctrine because while the scope of its coverage is not as specific as the other doctrines it in many ways lays foundation for privacy law. Throughout this book we find that it is not unusual for courts to use "intrusion" of privacy synonymously or interchangeably with "invasion" of privacy. In its late nineteenth-century form, intrusion was instrumental to the development of modern privacy doctrines adopted as a common law remedy for a range of privacy injuries. For instance, in 1881 the Supreme Court of Michigan adopted the intrusion of privacy doctrine in a notable case[47] involving Dr. John H. DeMay, physician, who while administering to a pregnant woman named Alvira Roberts, took an "unprofessional unmarried man" named Alfred Scattergood into her bed chamber. Dr. DeMay defended his decision on the grounds that he asked "young unmarried" Alfred Scattergood to carry an umbrella and other items necessary for his medical practice. Dr. DeMay and Mr. Scattergood had traveled on horseback through the night to the Roberts's modest apartment. The plaintiff and her husband assumed that the physician's friend was a medical associate or medical student and therefore allowed both men to pass into the wife's bedroom on "a dark and stormy night" when Roberts went into labor. At one point the doctor asked Scattergood to hold Roberts's hand during labor contractions. After the baby was born Roberts sued both men for invasion of privacy arguing that had she known that Scattergood was not a medical professional she would not have let him administer to her during childbirth.[48]

The Michigan state supreme court upheld the trial court's ruling for Roberts, stating that the two men indeed committed an "intrusion" upon the privacy of the woman, "indecently, wrongfully, and unlawfully laid hands upon and assaulted her."[49] The court recognized that on this "most sacred" occasion no one had a right to intrude unless invited or because of an emergency, which the court added this was not. The pregnant woman thus had "a legal right to privacy of her apartment" and a right to recover damages after suffering "shame and mortification."[50]

In 1908 an Indiana appellate court adopted the intrusion of privacy doctrine in an action involving eavesdropping through the windows on the private activities in the home.[51] In 1939 a Georgia court ruled that harassment or torment taking place at a person's home can constitute an actionable invasion of privacy if carried out in such a manner as to cause outrage or mental suffering, shame, or humiliation to a person or ordinary sensibilities.[52] Extending beyond physical invasion,[53] intrusion was incrementally broadened to include electronic eavesdropping on private and personal conversations,[54] and comings and goings in one's home. It is an intentional—not negligent—tort analogous to both trespass and battery in protecting personal integrity.[55] As more courts adopted the doctrine, its definition and scope became more capacious. For example, in 1965 the Ohio Supreme Court ruled that the protracted harassment and torment of a person constitutes an invasion of a person's privacy, offering a very broad definition of the right to privacy:

> [E]ach person possesses a right to privacy and may maintain an action for a wrongful invasion thereof. . . . An actionable invasion of the right to privacy is the unwarranted appropriation or exploitation of one's personality, the publishing of one's private affairs with which the public has no legitimate concern, or the wrongful intrusion into one's private activities in such as matter as to outrage or cause mental suffering, shame or humiliation to a persona; of ordinary sensibilities.[56]

By the 1960s, the intrusion doctrine had become a catch-all legal concept for a myriad of privacy actions and was recognized as "an intentional tort analogous to trespass and battery in protection of personal integrity."[57] Most courts recognized then and still today that a person cannot bring a mere *negligent* intrusion of privacy action; the intrusion must be an intentional tort.[58] We will return to the question of intentional versus negligent in Texas privacy cases in chapter 2.

Prosser's second privacy tort, public disclosure of private information, can best be understood as a right to exert control over one's personal information. The issues and questions that fall under its rubric are diverse, ranging from the sharing of candid photos or videos of celebrities to the unauthorized release of medical records. The general intent of the doctrine is to protect a person's self-image and reputation. The plaintiff must suffer from a form of emotional distress from the release of private information to recover damages. One of the earliest adoptions of the public disclosure doctrine was in a 1927 Kentucky case in which the defendant posted a sign in his garage window door announcing to all passersby that his neighbor—the plaintiff in the lawsuit—owed him money for services rendered. The court ruled that public disclosure of private facts about a person, even if true, constitutes an actionable invasion of his privacy.[59] In an early California public disclosure case in 1931, a Hollywood film production company revealed the identity of a retired prostitute who was involved in an infamous murder trial but was now living a quiet and respectable life in obscurity.[60] The court's ruling for the defendant cited Warren and Brandeis's view that privacy protects against embarrassment, damage to self-image and reputation, and the person's relationship with the community in which he or she lives. The decision also cited a provision in the California constitution that guarantees the "inalienable rights' of "enjoying and defending life and liberty; acquiring, possessing, and protecting property; and pursuing and obtaining safety and happiness."[61] In 1940 a California court ruled that a *New Yorker* magazine article about a former "infant prodigy," once famous but now living in obscurity, violated his right to privacy by dissecting the "intimate details of its subject's personal life."[62] However, the court denied relief under the public disclosure doctrine because he had once been a public figure and there was a strong public interest in his current life.[63]

In 1964 the Alabama Supreme Court ruled that unauthorized public disclosure of a candid photograph taken even in a public place constitutes an invasion of privacy because the subject's appearance was changed without her consent. The photo showed the plaintiff with her dress blown up, like the iconic Marilyn Monroe scene, as she was leaving a funhouse at a fair.[64] In public disclosure cases it matters less that information disclosed is true or false or even whether the public sympathizes or mocks you; instead it boils down to the fact that the publicity is a form of intrusion of privacy, as if crowds of people are looking in your window or, in twenty-first-century terms, watching a video of your daily life. Your reputation may be intact, but you have lost whatever anonymity it is possible to maintain.

The third tort doctrine, "false light" invasion of privacy, involves making statements or communicating information that portrays an individual to the public in a false and offensive manner.[65] To be subject to liability for invasion of privacy under this doctrine, the plaintiff must show that the false information is highly offensive to a reasonable person and that the defendant acted recklessly.[66] False light doctrine is different from the tort of public disclosure because it requires some element of untruth, whereas the public disclosure doctrine is applicable regardless of whether the information is true or false. Prosser wrote that the tort made its first appearance in 1816 in England, when an English court enjoined the circulation of a poem of poor quality that was attributed to Lord Byron's hand.[67] Discussion of the doctrine occurred in several cases in the 1940s and 1950s in the United States in which the falsity of information about an individual was held to constitute an invasion of privacy that outweighed the publisher's freedom of the press. Being falsely depicted as a witness to a crime or appearing in a weekly "rogues gallery" of infamous criminals constitute false light invasion of privacy.[68] The injuries sustained can range from economic harm to a ruined marriage. In 1952 a California appellate court ruled for a married couple against the *Ladies Home Journal*[69] after the magazine ran a candid photo of the couple showing affection in their place of business to illustrate a magazine feature about how "love at first sight" is a risky basis for a marriage. In essence, the magazine article suggested that Mr. and Mrs. Gill had the "wrong kind of love." Had the magazine published merely a candid photograph of the couple taken in a public setting without a caption or story then the false light doctrine would not apply. A modern corollary might be a photograph taken at a baseball game that appears on a social media site, with no accompanying comments or commentary. However, if that same photo is posted along with a joke caption or "thought bubble" attributing to the subject a lewd or outrageous thought, a person could plausibly argue that the post depicted them in a false light. The "false light" that shone upon the aggrieved party does not necessarily need to be defamatory—that is, a willful and malicious action that causes harm to reputation—though it must be objectionable to a reasonable person.

Defamation law is related to the evolution of the doctrine of false light invasion of privacy because many of the judicial standards of proof, liability, and damages employed in false light cases overlap the law of libel and slander. In *Norris v. Moskin Stores, Inc.* in 1961, as a mean-spirited strategy to collect a debt a collection agent employed by the creditor made calls to the debtor's family suggesting that the debtor was in an illicit sexual relationship.[70] The Alabama Supreme Court ruled that the false light in which the debtor was placed constituted an invasion of his privacy—an intrusion into the intimate relationship of husband and wife.[71]

The fourth tort doctrine, appropriation of name or likeness, applies to the unauthorized use of a person's name, image, notoriety, or prestige for commercial gain. The doctrine of appropriation differs from the other three privacy doctrines in that it deals with the proprietary nature of the tortious action.[72] In other words, one has a privacy interest in one's name or likeness and invasion of that privacy occurs when that name or likeness is used without consent for commercial or pecuniary gain. Early cases involve an unauthorized use of the plaintiff's name and photograph for the purpose of selling a product or service[73] or the publication of an image without consent in an advertisement.[74] It is not merely the plaintiff's name that is at issue here, but a symbol of a person's identity.[75] This concept of privacy goes beyond protecting a person from a snooping photographer who surreptitiously captures their image though an open window but extends the right to privacy to the unauthorized publication, or theft, of the image. The newly recognized doctrine of appropriation was adopted in a case dealing with the unauthorized erection of a statue of a deceased woman.[76] In 1892 the family of a departed philanthropist, Mary Hamilton Schuyler, sued to enjoin the erection of a statue depicting her to be displayed alongside of Susan B. Anthony at the Columbian Exposition in New York City. The family objected on the grounds that Mrs. Schuyler (apparently not a fan of Susan B. Anthony), if living, would find it to be an invasion of her right to control her image and reputation, citing the theory of privacy appearing in Warren and Brandeis's article. *Schuyler v. Curtis* held that the sculpting and public exhibition of a statute of a deceased woman violated her right to privacy because she was not a public person. Therefore, her relatives, asserting her postmortem right to privacy, was able to obtain an injunction for the unauthorized erection of the statue.[77]

In 1899 the Michigan high court refused to recognize an asserted right to privacy in a case involving the sale of a cigar brand bearing the name of a

Colonel John Atkinson, a deceased lawyer and public official, as long as the use of his name did not constitute a libel.[78] *Atkinson v. Doherty*, still an influential case, can be found in contemporary court opinions and scholarly articles. Many earlier privacy cases are cited in this case, but *Atkinson* addresses only the issue of whether one's right to privacy exists posthumously. There we see the foundations for what we now call the right of publicity, beginning with *Atkinson* when his widow sued to enjoin the production of cigars bearing the name and likeness. However, the action was not based upon a property right in his name and reputation—which is the right to publicity—held by deceased notable persons, but rested on an asserted right to privacy that the Michigan Court was not yet ready to recognize.[79]

Although the early cases had at best a regional impact (mostly in the northeast) on nascent privacy caselaw, two cases that do stand out in the debate over the existence of the right to privacy found a broader audience and are still cited by state courts around the country. The first case is the frequently cited *Roberson v. Rochester Folding Box Company* in 1902,[80] which involved the unauthorized use of a young woman's picture to sell flour. The advertisement next to the picture contained an awful pun about "The Flour of the Family." The young woman, who claimed to be the original subject of the lithograph that appeared in the advertisement, claimed that she had been humiliated by the notoriety caused by the picture. She did not allege defamation of her character or reputation, but an invasion of her right to privacy. Rejecting her argument and denying relief, the New York Court of Appeals went to great lengths to strenuously refute Warren and Brandeis's argument that an independent and very broad right of privacy existed and that the plaintiff was not entitled to protection from the company's conduct. The court based its decision on the grounds of lack of precedent, the purely psychological nature of the alleged privacy violation, the danger to freedom of press, the problem of discerning the line between private and public persons, and the problem of the immense volume of litigation that would ensue if such a right were recognized. The court ruled that the "so-called 'right of privacy' has not as yet found an abiding place in our jurisprudence,"[81] which sounds much like an argument employed by a majority of Texas judges in rejecting early privacy claims. The "Flour of the Family" ruling would prompt a public outcry[82] and ultimately prompt the New York legislature to enact statute making it a tort and misdemeanor to use a portrait or photograph of any person for advertising purposes without that person's written consent.[83]

Another leading privacy opinion handed down in the early twentieth century is *Pavesich v. New England Life Insurance Company*[84] in 1905. The case originated from a set of facts similar to those in *Roberson* but this time involving the unauthorized use of the plaintiff's name and photograph for the purpose of selling life insurance. An advertisement in the *Atlanta Constitution* displayed a photograph of a well-dressed Paolo Pavesich juxtaposed with a photo of an ill-dressed, sickly looking unidentified man. Pavesich's likeness was easily recognizable to his friends, family, and acquaintances. Under Pavesich's photo was a fictitious testimonial lauding the benefits of purchasing life insurance. Above his photo was the caption, "Do it now. The man who did" (referring to the purchase of a life insurance policy). The caption above the likeness of the unhealthy man read "Do it while you can. The man who didn't."[85] There was also a fictious testimonial attributed to Pavesich which read, "In my healthy and productive period of my life I bought insurance in the *New England Mutual Life Insurance Co*. of Boston, Mass., and to-day my family is protected and I am drawing an annual dividend on my paid-up policies." The photo of Pavesich was made from a negative procured by a photographer named J.Q. Adams without the plaintiff's consent. A trial court ruled for the insurance company, but the Supreme Court of Georgia reversed, handing down an opinion that served as an authoritative precedent for decades. The court held that the advertisement constituted a trespass upon Pavesich's right of privacy which was caused by breach of confidence and trust on the part of the photographer, J.Q. Adams and the New England Life Insurance Company. Writing for the majority of the state supreme court, Justice Cobb boldly argued that the absence of a precedent for an asserted right to privacy does not mean that the right does not exist and that this right is derived from the natural law protecting the rights of personal security and liberty; this right enables us to enjoy "life according to the nature, temperament, and lawful desires of the individual."[86] In an exhaustive and often philosophical treatise citing natural law, Roman law's conception of natural law justice, Blackstone's account of the rights of individuals, the common law, and, of course, Warren and Brandeis's article, Cobb wrote an extraordinary account of the origins and scope of the right to privacy. The right to privacy, writes Cobb, "is a right derived from natural law, recognized by the principles of municipal law, and guaranteed to persons in this state both by the Constitution of the United States and of the state of Georgia" although this right predates either document.[87] Roman law recognized that a person had a right "to be let alone" and that right is reflected in the common law. Cobb argued that to enter a home without the permission of the one lawfully residing there, even to serve a summons, was considered and invasion of privacy.[88] This is the foundation of the common law axiom "every man's house is his castle." To be secure from invasion by the public into matters of a private nature is the right to privacy, the violation of which is a tort and entitles a person to recover damages.[89] The publication of the advertisement by the insurance company and a false statement that the person is pleased with the decision to purchase a policy—when in fact no statement was ever made—is libelous, a violation of privacy, and a breach of trust. Furthermore, the creation and publication of the advertisement by the insurance company is not protected by the freedom of speech or the press.[90] The Georgia Court rejected the *Roberson* ruling, agreed with Warren and Brandeis, and recognized the right to privacy. The court also cited *Atkinson* in its opinion. At the time of the influential *Pavesich* ruling state courts around the nation still held conflicting views as to whether the right to privacy actually existed, but *Pavesich* became the leading case for decades to come.[91]

In 1911 a Missouri appellate court held that the unauthorized appropriation and use of a young child's photograph in an advertisement for jewelry constituted a violation of his privacy right and a libelous action.[92] A jewelry company in Kansas City published a photo of a five-year-old child as a part of an advertisement for Elgin watches. Under the photo read the caption: "Papa is going to buy mamma an Egin watch for a present, and someone (I mustn't tell who) is going to buy my big sister a diamond ring. So don't you think you ought to buy me something." The jewelers rejected the privacy and libel action on the grounds that under *Roberson v. Rochester Folding Box Company*[93] one cannot recover for an invasion of privacy unless such injury occurs as a result of an injury to or interference with the use of one's property. The Missouri court rejected this argument and held for the child and his family, concluding that the invasion of privacy extends not only to a violation of a tangible right but to intangible rights as well, such as "[l]ife, liberty, and the pursuit of happiness."[94] Since the quote attributed to the five-year-old that appeared under his photo was false, the child could recover for libel as well. The caption was an utterance of a falsehood, holding the child up as a liar and subjecting him to ridicule.[95]

In a rare invasion of privacy by appropriation case in the 1930s, *Fitzsimmons v. Olinger Mortuary Association*,[96] a state court extended a form of postmortem right to privacy after an "undertaker" published in a newspaper, without the decedent's family's consent, a photograph of a corpse being removed from an airplane as an advertisement for his business.[97] The widow of a notable person named Fitzsimmons recovered damages from a mortuary company for mental suffering after the body of the deceased was photographed and used in an advertisement for the mortuary published in a Denver, Colorado, newspaper.[98] Several years later in 1938 a North Carolina court ruled that a newspaper violated the privacy of a famous popular singer and radio personality when it mistakenly used her photograph in an advertisement for "Melt's Rye and Whole Wheat Bread" rather than that of a well-known exotic dancer whose likeness was intended to be used to tout the slimming effects of the bread.[99]

An important privacy case is *Hinish v. Meier Frank Company*[100] in 1941. An optical company appropriated the name of Hinish, a government employee, and used it in a telegram urging the governor of Oregon to veto a bill that would harm the Meier Frank Company. As a civil service employee, Hinish was prohibited from engaging in political activities and did not consent to using his name. By sending the telegram in his name the company jeopardized Hinish's position and his right to receive his pension upon reaching the age of retirement. In a long and detailed opinion, citing Warren and Brandeis as well as a long litany of nearly every major privacy case from across the United States as of 1941, the Oregon court recognized that this was the first time that the question of "whether there is such a thing in this state as a legal right of privacy" was raised in an Oregon state court. The court recognized the right to privacy and ruled for Mr. Hinish, stating that the defendants "appropriated to themselves for their own purposes, without the plaintiff's consent and against his will, his name, his personality and whatever influence he may have possessed, and injected them into a political controversy in which, as far as appears, he had no interest."[101]

In *Spahn v. Julian Messner, Inc.*,[102] an authoritative case cited by state courts across the country, the New York Court of Appeals held that a fictitious biography of a well-known baseball player—published without his consent—constituted an unauthorized appropriation of his personality for commercial gain. The court rejected the book publisher's argument that in his capacity as a public figure Spahn had no right to privacy. By virtue of being a public figure with national fame Warren Spahn may have given up a degree of privacy because he was a public personality during the years he played baseball—indeed, that was the price of fame. Warren Spahn *was* a public personality, but the court disagreed with the contention that "insofar as his professional career is concerned, he is substantially without the right to privacy." His personality may not be "fictionalized" and appropriated for commercial benefit without his consent in the form of an unauthorized biography.[103] Celebrities and public figures may earn a living by being in the public eye (many are famous simply for being famous) but that does not mean that they are precluded from recovering damages for appropriation of their likeness and fame. Warren and Brandeis would likely consider the misappropriation of Spahn's fame and achievements to financially enrich another as a violation of his "inviolate personality," an affront to his dignity and individuality.

These early court opinions demonstrate not only an effort by state courts to reach a consensus on the definition and scope of privacy doctrine, but the fact that the privacy right that emerged—independent of the US Supreme Court—is robust and comprehensive. There was also frequent cross-pollination or diffusion—that is, judges citing or acknowledging privacy doctrine adoptions in other state court systems. We will return to these doctrines in the discussion of Texas court rulings in chapter 2.

IMPACT OF US SUPREME COURT PRECEDENT

Privacy as Autonomy: Reproductive Rights, Abortion, and Same-Sex Intimacy

The concept of privacy as autonomy serves as the foundation of a distinct body of federal privacy caselaw. Although no Texas court has ever adopted the "privacy as autonomy" doctrine in a state privacy action—as we will see in chapter 2—this concept has nevertheless influenced the debate over the scope and limits of the right in Texas. Privacy as autonomy represents the most comprehensive definition of privacy. Not merely the common law right to be let alone, this doctrine is the basis of a positive liberty—a right to determine for oneself whether to perform a specific act or undergo a particular experience. Thus, while the right to be let alone can be understood as a negative right—to be free from intrusion—privacy as autonomy grants to the person a positive right to make autonomous choices free from limitations.

This expansive theory of privacy has its origins in the US Supreme Court's application of substantive due process found in the Fifth and Fourteenth Amendments. Constitutional interpretation based on substantive due process reasoning has led the Court to "discover" implied or unenumerated rights within the text of the Constitution. *Procedural* due process is the manner in which a law is applied, regardless of the content of the law. The fundamental purpose of procedural due process is to guarantee a fair process that must be followed by the government when it takes action that deprives a person of life, liberty, or property. If a court analyzes a challenged law using *substantive* due process, it is reviewing not the procedures by which the right or law is applied but determining whether a substantive right (such as speech or press) should be applied to protect the individual from government restrictions.[104]

It is generally accepted that substantive due process has its origins in the "*Lochner* era," specifically in *Lochner v. New York*,[105] in 1905 in which the Court voided state economic regulations on the grounds that they violated an implied right of "liberty of contract" found in the due process clause of the Fourteenth Amendment. The term "liberty of contract," referring to the right of an employer and employee to establish the terms and conditions of their economic relationship free from governmental interference, is not enumerated in the Constitution but implied by the due process clause of the Fifth and Fourteenth Amendments. Liberty of contract fell out of favor with the Court, however, as the New Deal era of the 1930s came to a close. In cases such as *West Coast Hotel v. Parrish*,[106] the Court abandoned the use of substantive due process to review economic regulations but left open the possibility of applying the substantive due process doctrine to protect personal rights and liberties. This set the stage for the elevation of the concept of privacy as autonomy to a constitutional right.

Two early cases illustrate this point. In *Meyer v. Nebraska*[107] in 1925, the Court adopted an expansive definition of liberty to overturn the conviction of a public school teacher who taught the German language to students in violation of a state law. The Court held that the law interfered with the profession of language teachers, the educational opportunities of students, and the right of parents to educate of their children. The state's interest in promoting a common language and "American ideals" was not a justified restriction on those fundamental interests. Liberty is not limited to freedom from physical restraint but extends to the freedom to acquire new knowledge, to marry, to bring up children, to be employed, and to pursue happiness, the Court held.[108]

Skinner v. Oklahoma[109] in 1942 augmented this definition of liberty using a Fourteenth Amendment equal protection argument to recognize a much broader fundamental right. In doing so, the Court struck down an Oklahoma law requiring mandatory sterilization of criminal offenders after a third conviction for a felony involving moral turpitude.[110] Under the law, if a jury found that the defendant was a "habitual criminal," a court could order the sterilization of the defendant by vasectomy for a male and by salpingectomy for a female. The Court ruled that the law infringed on one of the most basic human rights—procreation. Justice Douglas reasoned that the law violated the due process guarantee of liberty: "We are dealing here with legislation which involves one of the basic civil rights of man. Marriage and procreation are fundamental to the very existence and survival of the race."[111]

Skinner sets the stage for the Warren Court's expansion of civil rights and liberties during the 1950s and 1960s. Not since the *Lochner* era's substantive due process arguments to protect fundamental economic liberty had the Court applied strict scrutiny to a challenged law in order to protect an unenumerated fundamental liberty, the right to procreate.

Reproductive Rights

The Court's recognition of the fundamental right to marriage, procreation, and parenting presages the elevation of privacy to a constitutionally protected right in the landmark case *Griswold v. Connecticut*[112] in 1965. By far the most well-known and influential privacy ruling, the case originated when Connecticut law criminalized the use of any drug or instrument for the purpose of preventing conception. The law imposed possible fines and or imprisonment for "[a]ny person who uses any drug, medicinal article or instrument for the purpose of preventing contraception."[113] Physicians who counseled woman in the use of contraceptives, with the diaphragm being the most widely used contraceptive device in Connecticut, could also be punished under the law. Further, an "accessory statute" punished anyone who assists, abets, counsels, or commands another person to violate the law.[114]

The Supreme Court overturned the Connecticut law for directly and adversely affecting the intimacy of the marital relationship and creating an unwarranted governmental intrusion into the sphere of private matters: sexual relations between a husband and wife. The law placed constraints on a woman's ability to decide whether to have children. In a broader sense, such constraints restricted her right to freely choose her own life plans and moral convictions regarding the fundamental issues of sexual relations and the control of her private life.

Plaintiffs challenging the constitutionality of the law had initially argued that the statute violated their freedom of association, an implied right in the First Amendment. However, this approach met with opposition from the justices. Justice Hugo Black was quick to oppose using this line of reasoning and quipped that "[t]he right of association is for me a right of assembly and the right of the husband and wife to assemble in bed is a new right of assembly for me."[115] Justice Douglas disagreed with Black, arguing that the First Amendment right of association did not merely protect the right of assembly, but extended to the intimacy of the marital relationship. Douglas convinced his colleagues that the law placed severe limitations on a woman's personal autonomy, or freedom to enter into the most fundamental personal and intimate relations. Citing a long line of the Court's rulings, Douglas constructed his argument for an implied right to privacy as follows: privacy can be implied from guarantees in the Bill of Rights that have "penumbras, formed by emanations from those guarantees of liberty that help give them life and substance. These various guarantees create zones of privacy." The right of association contained in the penumbra of the First Amendment is one. The Third Amendment in its prohibition against the quartering of soldiers "in any house" in time of peace without the consent of the owner reflects another dimension of privacy. The Fourth Amendment explicitly states the "right of the people to be secure in their persons, houses, papers, and effects, against unreasonable searches and seizures." The Fifth Amendment privilege against self-incrimination "enables the citizen to create a zone of privacy which government may not force him to surrender to his detriment." The Ninth Amendment provides: "The enumeration in the Constitution, of certain rights, shall not be construed to deny or disparage others retained by the people." The language and history of the Ninth Amendment reveal that the Framers of the Constitution believed that there are additional fundamental rights, protected from governmental infringement, which exist alongside those fundamental rights specifically mentioned in the first eight constitutional amendments.[116]

It is important to note that most discussions of *Griswold* focus on Justice Douglas's "penumbras and emanations" argument but neglect the long line of precedent cases that protect privacy interests cited in his opinion. To bolster his argument, Douglas cites *Pierce v. Society of Sisters*,[117] *Meyer v. Nebraska*,[118] *NAACP v. Alabama*,[119] *Poe v. Ullman*,[120] and *Boyd v. United States*.[121] This new understanding of privacy recognized in *Griswold*—"privacy inherent in a relationship" or "privacy as autonomy," as it is called—is broader than privacy interests found either in common law doctrines or Fourth Amendment caselaw.[122]

Cognizant that the Court had historically "steered clear" of the Ninth Amendment, Justice Goldberg, concurring, wrote that although marital privacy is not mentioned explicitly in the Constitution it is supported by the language and history of the Ninth Amendment. The Ninth Amendment states, "The enumeration in the Constitution, of certain rights, shall not be construed to deny or disparage others retained by the people." Goldberg reminds us that even though the Amendment has been (and still is) shunned by most courts in the country, it is a part of the Constitution and was adopted with the understanding that a bill of enumerated rights would not be sufficiently inclusive of all essential rights.[123]

Eisenstadt v. Baird[124] in 1972 extended the right to privacy to unmarried couples as well, striking down a Massachusetts law that made it a felony to give anyone other than a married couple or a married person contraceptive medicines or devices. Justice William Brennan argued that the intent of the Massachusetts law was overly vague. Was its purpose the regulation of contraceptive devices or was it enacted to regulate premarital sex? The Court believed it was the latter and struck down the law as unconstitutional, with Brennan citing a 1970 Massachusetts court decision as proof that the same statute was upheld on the basis of protecting morality through "regulating the private lives of single persons."[125] The Court ruled the goal of deterring premarital and extramarital sex is not a legitimate basis to ban contraceptives.[126] Further, the legal distinction between married and unmarried couples was ruled to be arbitrary: a married couple is not a single and independent corporate entity but "an association of two individuals each with a separate intellectual and emotional makeup."[127] By providing "dissimilar treatment for married and unmarried persons" the statute violates the Equal Protection Clause of the Fourteenth Amendment. Brennan wrote: "If the right to privacy means anything, it is the right of the *individual*, married or single, to be free from unwarranted intrusion into matters so fundamentally affecting a person as the decision whether to bear or beget a child."[128]

Abortion

One year after *Eisenstadt*, the Supreme Court extended the right of privacy to a woman's decision to terminate a pregnancy in *Roe v. Wade* in 1973.[129] Prior to *Roe*, abortion rights varied from state to state and abortion was, in many instances, regarded more of a matter of a woman's access to healthcare or medical services rather than a political matter. Abortion politics exceeds the scope of this book—although we will briefly return to the topic of the privacy implications of the overturning of *Roe* in chapter 4; its relevance here is how abortion decisions shaped the definition and scope of privacy rights.

In *Roe* the Court adopted the *Griswold-Eisenstadt* formulation of the right of privacy to strike down a Texas law making it a felony to abort a fetus except "upon medical advice for the purpose of saving the life of the mother." Justice Harry Blackmun, writing for the majority, examined the reasons criminal abortion laws had been enacted over the past hundred years. Laws were intended to discourage sexual promiscuity in women, while others aimed at protecting pregnant women from dangerous abortion practices. The third and most controversial rationale for criminalizing abortion reflected the state's interest in protecting prenatal life based on the belief that life begins at conception and that the fetus is a person in possession of fundamental rights. In *Roe*, the Court held that although the state does have an interest in protecting prenatal life; its interest must be balanced with a woman's right to privacy. To this end, Blackmun developed a trimester framework. Prior to the end of the first trimester, the abortion decision must be left up to the woman and her attending physician. During the second trimester, the state may regulate the abortion procedure in ways that are reasonably related to maternal health. At the stage subsequent to viability, however, the state may regulate or prohibit abortion on the grounds of its interest in the potential human life. Thus, it is only at the point of viability—when the fetus has the capability of "meaningful life" outside of the mother's womb—that the state's interest is compelling enough to ban all abortions if it so chooses. In a famous passage that expanded the right to privacy, Justice Blackmun writes:

> This right of privacy, whether it be founded in the Fourteenth Amendment's concept of personal liberty and restrictions upon state action, as we feel it is, or, as the District Court determined, in the Ninth Amendment's reservation of rights to the people, is broad enough to encompass a woman's decision whether or not to terminate her pregnancy.[130]

Blackmun continues:

> The Constitution does not explicitly mention any right of privacy. In a line of decisions, however, going back perhaps as far as *Union Pacific R. Co. v. Botsford*, 141 U. S. 250, 251 (1891), the Court has recognized that a right of personal privacy, or a guarantee of certain areas or zones of privacy, does exist under the Constitution.

The majority explicitly rejected the argument that the abortion right is absolute and as such a woman is entitled to terminate her pregnancy at any time and for any reason. A state may properly assert important interests in protecting health, maintaining medical standards, and in protecting potential life. The privacy right itself as applied to abortion is not absolute. No one "has an unlimited right to do with one's body as one pleases."[131]

In his concurring opinion, Justice Douglas articulated an even broader definition of privacy, writing that the right to privacy encompasses autonomous control over the development and expression of one's intellect, interests, tastes, and personality. It is the right to care for one's own health and to be free from bodily restraint or compulsion in the basic decisions of procreation and contraception. It is the "freedom to walk, stroll, or loaf."[132]

Dissenting, Justice William Rehnquist, who in 1973 had been on the Court for only two years, rejected the majority's holding that a state may impose virtually no restrictions on the performance of abortions during the first trimester of pregnancy[133] and refused to recognize that the right of "privacy" applies to abortion. Abortion as a medical procedure is not "private" in the ordinary usage of that word, he wrote, but a medical practice that can legitimately be regulated by the state.[134] Nor is the Court's definition of "privacy" "even a distant relative" of the freedoms from searches and seizures protected by the Fourth Amendment to the Constitution.[135] This argument was consistently applied by Rehnquist throughout his long tenure on the Court; it was also embraced by conservative justices on the Roberts Court at the time of *Dobbs* in 2022.

Contrary to the polemics of both sides of the abortion debate over fifty years, just as the Court never created an absolute privacy right in *Griswold* and its progeny, so too did the justices stop short of creating an absolute constitutional right to an abortion beyond the reach of the state. True, initially in *Roe*, the right was near absolute during the first three months of pregnancy, but as the fetus developed the state's interest in protecting prenatal became more compelling while the woman's privacy interest diminished. So too, in the decades post-*Roe*, did the Court uphold a large number of state restrictions on abortion rights, including bans on the use of public funds[136] or facilities, laws requiring parental or spousal notification and consent,[137] "gag-orders on abortion counseling,"[138] and requirements that abortion providers have hospital admitting privileges,[139] to name only a few.

Today, when referring to the right to an abortion, which was rescinded by *Dobbs v. Jackson Health*,[140] it is common to see references to "*Roe-Casey*" or "*Roe and Casey*." The reason for this appellation is that in 1992 a majority on the Court was prepared to overturn *Roe*. However, in *Planned Parenthood v. Casey*, by a five-to-four margin, *Roe* was upheld—although a central element of *Roe*, the trimester framework, was expunged and replaced by "undue burden" standard. The definition of "undue" was any "substantial obstacle in the path of a woman seeking an abortion before the fetus attains viability."[141] In a way, *Roe* was partly overruled in *Casey* by the replacement of the trimester framework with the undue burden rule. Nevertheless, *Casey* did preserve the right and served as a precedent along with *Roe* until *Dobbs*. *Casey* reaffirmed the essence of *Roe*: a woman has the right to choose to terminate her pregnancy before viability without undue interference from the state. As such, the state may not it impose a substantial obstacle to the right to elect the procedure.[142] *Casey* reflects O'Connor's pragmatic attempt to build a consensus on the Court in order to avoid the consequences of overturning *Roe*. Nullifying *Roe*, O'Connor reasoned, would represent a dramatic departure from *stare decisis* that would not only harm women but also undermine the legitimacy of the Court.[143] An entire generation of women had come of age under *Roe* with the understanding that the right to make private autonomous reproductive decisions was protected by the Constitution.[144]

As the nation moved closer to *Roe-Casey*'s ultimate reversal in *Dobbs v. Jackson Women's Health*,[145] it seemed unlikely that a majority of justices would vote for an outright reversal. More plausible was a ruling that would leave *Roe* intact but uphold the Mississippi law (the Gestational Age Act) that banned all abortions of an "unborn human being" after the fifteenth week of pregnancy.[146] The law made exceptions for medical emergencies and cases involving a "severe fetal abnormality" but did not make exceptions for cases involving rape or incest. Mississippi made the bold argument that the law was constitutional for the simple reason that *Roe* and *Casey* were constitutionally flawed decisions. Holding fast to *Roe* and *Casey*, the conservative Fifth Circuit Court of Appeals enjoined the enforcement of the law. However, the Supreme Court reversed the Court of Appeals and overturned *Roe*, thus erasing from American constitutional law a woman's right to an abortion. In doing so, the Court also narrowed the definition and scope of privacy as autonomy. Justice Samuel Alito—writing for the narrow five-to-four majority[147]—argued that although unenumerated rights are protected by the due process clause of the Fifth and Fourteenth Amendments, abortion is not one of them. Rights that are unenumerated or implied must be "deeply rooted in our Nation's history." Abortion is not; if anything, it is an aberration. *Roe* and *Casey* should be overruled, Alito continued, despite the principle of *stare decisis*, which does not impose a "straitjacket,"[148] especially when the decision underlying the precedent was "egregiously wrong and deeply damaging."[149] Alito concluded that the issue of abortion should "return . . . to the people's representatives."[150] Since abortion is no longer a constitutional right, the states have full discretion to regulate or ban abortion as they see fit based on the state's reserved powers or "police powers." As for the matter of privacy, Alito argued that none of the Court's privacy cases that were cited in *Roe* in 1973 "involved what is distinctive about abortion: its effect on what *Roe* termed 'potential life.'"[151] Alito assured Americans that *Dobbs* would not undermine other decisions by the Court involving fundamental rights that the Constitution does not expressly articulate, such as the right to contraception, sexual intimacy, and same-sex marriage. Unlike those rights, abortion terminates what *Roe* and *Casey* refer to as "potential life" and what the Mississippi law refers to as an "unborn human being." "Nothing in this opinion," Alito concluded, "should be understood to cast doubt on precedents [such as *Griswold* or *Obergfell*] that do not concern abortion."[152]

The dissenting justices[153] objected to the majority's opinion as not only a rejection of a women's privacy as autonomy, but a flagrant disregard for *stare decisis*, which is the cornerstone of our legal system. As Justice O'Connor reasoned in *Casey* in 1992 so too did the *Dobbs* dissenters warn that the nullification of a fifty-year-old precedent undermines the Court's legitimacy. The right to privacy at the core of *Roe* and *Casey*, the dissenters explained, is "part of the same constitutional fabric"[154] as the rights to contraception and same-sex intimacy and marriage. By declaring that the right to abortion does not exist, the Court is knowingly unraveling that fabric.

Sexual Orientation and Same-Sex Marriage

After *Griswold*, *Eisenstadt*, and *Roe* advocates for LGBT rights argued that substantive due process privacy should also encompass adult homosexual conduct and same-sex relationships and marriage; that the right of privacy extends beyond the sphere of reproductive freedom into the area of sexual privacy. However, in 1976, the Court rejected this argument in *Commonwealth's Attorney for the City of Richmond v. Doe*,[155] in which the Burger Court (1969–1986) denied the appeal of a man convicted under a Virginia sodomy law. Ten years later, the attempt to extend the right of privacy was again thwarted in *Bowers v. Hardwick*[156] in 1986, when the Court was asked to invalidate a Georgia sodomy law on the grounds it violated the most intimate personal association with another consenting adult. The Court refused, holding that privacy interests relating to marriage, contraception, and abortion set forth in *Griswold*, *Eisenstadt*, and *Roe* bore no resemblance whatsoever to a claimed constitutional right of persons to engage in homosexual conduct. While the earlier cases conferred a broad and fundamental individual right to decide whether to conceive or to have a child, the Court was not inclined to broaden privacy in order to overturn state sodomy laws. In fact, notwithstanding the court of appeals' privacy argument in *Bowers*, the majority of the justices refused even to mention the right of privacy as such. For the Burger Court, and later Rehnquist Court (1986–2005), the term "privacy" had become a forbidden word—conspicuously missing from the Court's majority opinions. If there were a "liberty interest" as conservatives on the Court framed it, found in the Fourteenth Amendment that protects intimate relationships, the majority of justices refused to extend it homosexual conduct. "[I]n constitutional terms there is no such thing as a fundamental right to commit homosexual sodomy," wrote Chief Justice Warren Burger.[157]

Seventeen years later in *Lawrence v. Texas*[158] in 2003 the Supreme Court voted six to three to overturn *Bowers*. Two Houston men were convicted in a state district court of deviate sexual intercourse in violation of a Texas law, which has never been repealed,[159] that made it a crime (misdemeanor) for two persons of the same sex to engage in intimate sexual conduct.[160] On appeal, a three-judge state appeals panel ruled two-to-one that their convictions "impermissibly discriminate on the basis of sex" under the Equal Rights Amendment of the Texas Constitution.[161] However, the full Texas Court of Appeals reversed, citing *Bowers*. The Texas Court of Criminal Appeals—the highest court for criminal appeals—refused to grant review. The case was also appealed to the Texas Supreme Court—the highest court for civil appeals—but the majority of justices refused to give the case a full review. Lawrence then appealed to the US Supreme Court.[162]

By a six-to-three vote, the US Supreme Court held that the Texas statute making it a crime for two persons of the same sex to engage in certain intimate sexual conduct violates the due process clause of the Fifth and Fourteenth Amendments of the US Constitution. Finding it "necessary to reconsider" *Bowers*, the Court ruled that as adults the two men were free to engage in private conduct in the exercise of their liberty. Writing for the majority, Justice Kennedy argued that this case, as well as *Bowers* before it, deals not merely with the right to engage in certain kinds of sexual conduct, but whether the State can regulate "the most private human conduct, sexual behavior, in the most private of places, the home." The sodomy law granted to the State of Texas control of a personal relationship—whether heterosexual or homosexual. The liberty protected by the Constitution allows all persons the right to choose to enter into intimate relationships in the privacy of their homes and to "retain their dignity as free persons."[163] Citing *Griswold*, *Eisenstadt*, and *Roe*, the Court's decision in *Lawrence* recognized the fundamental right to engage in consensual sexual activity free from government intrusion. In doing so, it broadened the scope of privacy as autonomy.

As we discuss in chapter 2, the Texas Supreme Court came within one vote of overturning the sodomy law on state privacy grounds in *Texas v. Morales*[164] in 1994, nine years prior to Lawrence.

Privacy as autonomy is also a cornerstone of *Obergefell v. Hodges*,[165] the 2015 decision in which the Court applied a substantive due process analysis to guarantee the right to marry as a fundamental liberty to same-sex couples. The reasoning in *Obergefell* consists of a sprawling exegesis of the history of institution of marriage and the purpose and scope of the Fourteenth Amendment, but for our purposes in this chapter, at the heart of the Court's decision are the privacy as autonomy rulings: *Griswold-Eisenstadt*, *Roe-Casey*, and *Lawrence*. These rulings, according to Justice Kennedy, who wrote for the slim five-to-four majority, suggest that the right to marry is a fundamental liberty "inherent to the concept of individual autonomy . . . protecting the most intimate association between two people." Kennedy wrote:

> A first premise of the Court's relevant precedents is that the right to personal choice regarding marriage is inherent in the concert of individual autonomy. This abiding connection between marriage and liberty is why *Loving* invalidated interracial marriage bans under the Due Process Clause. . . . Like choices concerning contraception, family relationships, procreation, and childrearing, all of which are protected by the Constitution, decisions concerning marriage are among the most intimate that an individual can make.[166]

It is important to understand—as we will discuss in chapter 2—that Texas state courts have never adopted the privacy as autonomy doctrine, and it has been adopted only in rare instances by courts in other states. The doctrine is relevant to Texans only insofar as it is applied in privacy disputes where plaintiffs seek relief in state courts based on federal precedent rather than state grounds. An example of a case of this nature might involve the state's attempt to regulate contraceptives (*Griswold*) or punish same-sex intimacy (*Lawrence*). Of course, residents of Texas can also file privacy suits in federal courts located in Texas. Since there is no longer a constitutional right to abortion after the *Dobbs v. Jackson Health* ruling and abortion is de facto banned in Texas, all future abortion litigation in state or federal courts originating from disputes in the state will necessarily focus on the interpretation of various state statutory restrictions on abortion, such as the extent to which physicians can perform abortions to save a woman's life without risking punishment. We will return to a brief account of how abortion laws affect privacy issues in Texas in the final chapter of the book.

Reasonable Expectation of Privacy Doctrine

The reasonable expectation of privacy doctrine has had an impact on criminal and civil privacy case law, as well as on statutory privacy protections, in Texas. As stated at the outset, the massive body of criminal search and seizure law that relies on this privacy doctrine—as articulated by federal precedent—is beyond the purpose and scope of this book; only a cursory examination of this doctrine is provided.

In general terms, under this doctrine the scope and limits of privacy protection are determined not objectively by where the person is located or by the nature of the type of search or surveillance technology used, but rather subjectively by the expectation of privacy that the individual has in a particular situation. The reasonable expectation of privacy doctrine has its origins in the Fourth Amendment which guarantees "[t]he right of the people to be secure in their persons, houses, papers, and effects, against unreasonable searches and seizures, shall not be violated, and no warrants shall issue, but upon probable cause." In 1886, in *Boyd v. United States*[167] the Court reasoned that both the Fourth and Fifth Amendments extend to "all invasions on the part of the government and its employees of the sanctity of a man's home and privacies of life . . . it is the invasion of his indefeasible right of personal security, personal liberty, and private property."[168]

Twenty-five years after Warren and Brandeis first published their call for a right to privacy in the *Harvard Law Review* in 1890, in which they predicted that "mechanical devices" would someday be used to intrude upon our private lives, Brandeis was nominated to the US Supreme Court by President Woodrow Wilson in 1916. It was during Brandeis's tenure (1916–1939) that the Supreme Court ruled on an electronic eavesdropping case for the first time. In *Olmstead v. United States*[169] in 1928 the Court held that wiretapping did not constitute a search or seizure in the traditional sense under the Fourth Amendment. The Fourth applied only to unreasonable physical intrusions, or trespasses, not to electronic eavesdropping because, according to Chief Justice Willam Taft, a person uses a telephone with wires connecting the device to the outside world does so with the intent to project their voice to the public. Thus, the message passing through these wires is not within the scope of protection of the Fourth Amendment.[170]

Dissenting, Justice Brandeis rejected this understanding of the Fourth, insisting that new inventions made it necessary to move beyond the Court's traditional interpretation of Fourth Amendment protection that extends to physical intrusions alone. "[I]nvasion of the privacy of the telephone is far greater than that involved in tampering with the mails. Whenever a telephone line is tapped, the privacy of the persons at both ends of the line is invaded and all conversations."[171]

The Fourth Amendment is broad enough to encompass a right to privacy and, thus, to protect the "most intimate occurrences of the home."[172] Once again, Brandeis was ahead of his time, but his ideas would not be adopted until 1967 in *Katz v. United States*.[173] Charles Katz, a bookie, was convicted in a federal district court—based on a warrantless Federal Bureau of Investigation (FBI) wiretap—for telephoning bets and wagers from a glass-enclosed public telephone. Citing *Olmstead*, the government argued that because the telephone booth from which Katz made his calls was constructed of glass—rendering him visible to the FBI agents—he had no Fourth Amendment protection in the booth. Katz responded that because the public telephone booth is "a constitutionally protected area," the evidence obtained without a warrant was obtained in violation of the Fourth Amendment. Contrary to the trespass doctrine espoused by Chief Justice Taft in *Olmstead*, the Court in *Katz* held that nonphysical penetration of a constitutionally protected area violates the Fourth Amendment.[174]

In *Katz*, Justice Potter Stewart penned the famous line that the Fourth Amendment "protects people, not places"[175] against unreasonable searches and seizures. Rather than creating a "constitutionally protected area" around the phone booth, the Fourth Amendment protects a person's "reasonable expectation of privacy." By entering the telephone booth and closing the door, Katz intended to keep what he said private. Thus, even though the area of surveillance was neither a private residence nor a hotel room but a glass booth, Katz had a reasonable expectation of privacy in his conversation.

In both state and federal privacy cases, judges and justices are quick to point out that a person's subjective expectation of privacy does not always square with objective reality or what society is prepared to accept as reasonable. For example, it might not be reasonable for a person to expect that the Fourth Amendment protects them from aerial observation by law enforcement. In *California v. Ciraolo*[176] the Court concluded that an individual's expectation of privacy in his backyard marijuana patch was not reasonable and was "not an expectation that society is prepared to honor."[177] While he might reasonably expect that his ten-foot fence would keep police or passersby at street level from peering into his backyard, the fence would not necessarily shield his activity from the eyes of a neighbor who lives in a two-story house or a police officer standing on top of a truck. It is not enough to assert that one's subjective expectation of privacy is reasonable; one must also prove that the government's intrusion infringes upon the personal and societal values protected by the Fourth. Such values include the fundamental privacy interests essential to the physical and psychological well-being of the person and the family. Illegal conduct in one's backyard falls outside the scope of those interests. While a person's backyard falls within the curtilage[178] of their home, it does not bar all observation.

Conversely, for example, a person has a reasonable expectation of privacy in activities taking place *inside* a home that may generate externally observable phenomena, such as heat signatures detectable by thermal imaging devices. In *Kyllo v. United States*[179] the Court reversed a conviction for illegal marijuana cultivation taking place inside a home. Without first obtaining a warrant, federal agents drove down the street with a thermal imaging device to scan for "hot spots" in a house, which are unusual amounts of emanating heat. The agents were not in possession of a warrant before conducting a physical search to scan Kyllo's home but after the scan they used inference from these hot spots to obtain a warrant pursuant to a physical search. However, the Court rejected the idea that Kyllo had forfeited his subjective expectation of privacy because he made no attempt to conceal or shield the heat emanating from his home. When a device (thermal imaging) "not in general public use" is employed to examine the contents of a private home that would otherwise have been unknowable without actual physical entry, the initial surveillance prior to the issuance of the warrant constitutes an unreasonable search.[180] Even in light of modern technology that can, in some sense, see through walls, a person still retains an expectation of privacy in their home. Obtaining information regarding the home's interior by thermal scanning, which could not otherwise have been obtained without physical intrusion into a constitutionally protected area, constitutes a Fourth Amendment search.[181] The Court also disagreed with the government's reasoning that Kyllo's privacy was not violated because the device did not detect "intimate details" in the home, such as Kyllo showering or locked in a loving embrace with his partner, both of which would produce higher heat signatures relative to the ambient temperature in the house.[182]

The concept of a reasonable expectation of privacy reaches far beyond search and seizure cases. It has influenced how state judges, legal practitioners, and legislators analyze a range of civil as well as criminal privacy issues. For instance, the Texas wiretapping law—discussed along with other statutory privacy protections in chapter 4—provides civil and criminal remedies for private parties using electronic means to violate privacy. State courts adjudicating disputes dealing with the interpretation of the wiretapping law rely heavily on the reasonable expectation doctrine. The massive corpus of criminal search and seizure decisions in Texas exceeds the scope and coverage of this book, since most of these cases relied on federal Fourth Amendment precedent. Article I, Section 9 of the Texas Constitution,[183] which mirrors the language of the Fourth Amendment of the US Constitution, also protects privacy interests. To assert a privacy interest under the reasonable expectation doctrine, a person must demonstrate a subjective expectation of privacy that society recognizes as reasonable. The extent to which the reasonable expectation doctrine intersects the common law doctrine of invasion as well as statutory privacy interests of Texans warrants examination. The right to privacy in Texas owes much to *Katz v. United States*.[184] As a point of comparison, since *Billings* was decided in 1973 the number of civil cases dealing with common law privacy doctrines heard by Texas appellate courts is 1,506.[185] However, the number of criminal search and seizure cases before all courts of appeal and the Texas Court of Criminal Appeals since 1973 is 7,733—of those cases 1,859 applied the reasonable expectation of privacy doctrine[186], 176 of which cited *Katz*.[187]

NOTES

1. Samuel D. Warren (1852–1910) was a prominent Boston lawyer and businessman who practiced law with Brandeis.

2. Louis D. Brandeis (1856–1941) practiced law in St. Louis and Boston. He is the author of the famous "Brandeis Brief" and served as a justice on the US Supreme Court from 1916 to 1939.

3. The article can be found by searching most law content or social science databases; or see Samuel D. Warren, and Louis D. Brandeis, *The Right to Privacy*, with an insightful forward by Steven Alan Childress (New Orleans: Quid Pro Books), *Legal Legends Series* (2010).

4. If we stick with the apocryphal origin story "it" all begins when an obnoxious photographer invades Warren's daughter's wedding and prints pictures of private moments. Warren, a prominent lawyer and member of Boston's elite, was accustomed to newspaper coverage, but for some reason was incensed by this particular paparazzi incident. However, the real story may have been unearthed by Professor Amy Gajda. Combing through old newspapers she found that at the time of the alleged incident Warren's daughter was only seven years old so it was not at her wedding that the injury to Warren occurred. Warren's injury may actually have occurred at his own wedding to a US Senator's daughter, who was twenty years younger than Warren. For a fascinating account of this possibility, see Amy Gajda, "'What if Samuel D. Warren hadn't married a Senator's daughter': Uncovering the press coverage that led to 'The Right to Privacy,'" *Michigan Law Review* 35 (2008).

5. Ibid.

6. *Anderson v. Romero*, 72 F.3d 518, 521 (7th Cir. 1995).

7. Ibid, 521.

8. Ibid.

9. James Gray Denton (May 27, 1917–June 10, 1982) was a Justice of the Supreme Court of Texas from January 1, 1971, to June 10, 1982.

10. *Billings v. Atkinson*, 489 S.W. 2d 858, 859 (Tex. 1973).

11. *Nader v. General Motors Corp.*, 31 A.D. 2d 392, 397 (1969) (Steuer, J., dissenting).

12. Elbridge L. Adams, "The right of privacy, and its relation to the law of libel," American Law Review, 39 (1), 37–58.

13. Ibid, 38.

14. Ibid.

15. Samuel D. Warren and Louis D. Brandeis, "The Right to Privacy," *Harvard Law Review*, 4, no. 5 (Dec. 15, 1890).

16. Ibid, 196.

17. Ibid, 214.

18. Ibid, 220.

19. Ibid, 196.

20. David Flaherty, *Privacy in Colonial New England* (Charlottesville: University of Virginia Press, 1972), 248.

21. *Semayne's case*, 5 C. Rep. 91a, 91b, 77 Eng. Rep. 194, 195 (1605).

22. *Entick v. Carrington*, 19 How. St. Tr. 1029 (C.P. 1765).
23. *Boyd v. United States*, 116 U.S. 616 (1886).
24. Ibid, 630.
25. *Christian v. State*, 96 Ala 89, 91, 11 So. 338, 338–39 (1892).
26. *Mitchell v. Commonwealth*, 88 Ky. 349, 353, 11 S.W. 209, 210 (1889).
27. *State v. Armfield*, 9 N.C. (2 Hawks) 246, 247 (1822).
28. *Wien v. Simpson*, 2 Phila. 1548, 158–159 (Pa. Dist. Ct. 1857).
29. *Ilsley v. Nicholas*, 29 Mass (12 Pick.) 270, 277 (1832).
30. *Ives v. Humphrey*, 1 E.D. Smith 1996, 201–02 (N.Y. Ct. C. P. 1851).
31. Ibid.
32. 4 W. Blackstone Commentaries on the Laws of England *223.
33. *Commonwealth v. Lovett*, 6 Pa. L.J.R. 226, 227 (1831).
34. *Moore v. New York Elevated R.R.*, 130 130 N.Y. 523, 527–28 (1892).
35. Congressional Act of March 3, 1825, chapter 64, §22, 4 Stat. 102.
36. *Hoyt v. Mackenzie*, # Barb. Ch. 320, 324–25 (N.Y. Ch. 1848).
37. See *Rice v. Williams*, 32 F. 437, 439 (C.C.E.D. Wis. 1887).
38. "A man's house his castle," 9 Public Opinion 342 (1980) (reprinted from Chicago Mail).
39. *Henisler v. Freedman*, 2 Pars. Eq. Cas. 274 (Pa. Ct. C.P. 1851).
40. See, for example, Western Union Telegraph Company, Rules, Regulations, and Instructions (Cleveland 1866).
41. See *Johnson v. State*, 63 Miss. 313, 317 (1885); *Collins v. Mack*, 31 Ark. 684, 689 (1877); *Sanford v. Murphy*, 63 Ga. 410, 416 (1879).
42. See, for example, E. L. Godkin, "Libel and its legal remedy," *Journal of Social Science*, 69 (1880): 729–38; The Kodak Fiend, *Boston Evening*, June 2, 1890, at 6, column 4; John Gilmer Speed, "The right to privacy," *North American Review*, 64, no. 73 (1896); Alan Westin, *Privacy and Freedom* (1967), 172, 338; Harvard Law Review Association, "The right to privacy in nineteenth century America," *Harvard Law Review*, 94, no. 8 (June 1981): 1892–910.
43. See William L. Prosser's classic "Privacy," *California Law Review*, 48 (1960). Also see William L. Prosser, "Privacy," *California Law Review*, 48, no. 338 (1960). The development of privacy in the United States owes much to Prosser, whose name and work is cited in nearly every privacy case. Yet some scholars are critical of Prosser as well for stunting the development of privacy. See Neil M. Richards and Daniel J. Solove, "Prosser's privacy law: A mixed legacy," 98 Cal. L. Rev. 1887 (2010).
44. William L. Prosser, "Selected topics on the law of torts: Five lectures," delivered at the University of Michigan February 2–6, 1953; William L. Prosser, "Selected topics on the law of torts" (1954).
45. See William L. Prosser's classic "Privacy," *California Law Review*, 48 (1960).
46. William L Prosser, *Handbook of the Law or Torts*, second edition (1955).
47. *De May v. Roberts*, 46 Mich. 1960 (1881), at 161. The headnotes of this case refer to it as "intrusion upon case of confinement."
48. Ibid.
49. Ibid.

50. Ibid, 165–66.
51. *Pritchett v. Board of Commissioners*, 42 Ind. App. 3 (1908).
52. See *McDaniel v. Atlanta Coca-Cola Bottling Co.*, 60 Ga App. 92 (1939).
53. See *Walker v. Whittle*, 83 Ga. App. 445 (1951).
54. See *McDaniel v. Atlanta Coca-Cola Bottling Co.*, 60 Ga App. 92 (1939).
55. *LeCrone v. Ohio Bell Tel. Co.*, 120 Ohio App. 129 (1963); and *McCormick v. Haley*, 37 Ohio App. 2d 73, 307 N.E. 2d 34, 38 (1973).
56. *House v. Peth*, 165 Ohio St. 35 (1956).
57. *Lecrone v. Ohio Bell Telephone Co.*, 120 Ohio App. 129, 131 (1963).
58. See the Ohio case of *McCormick v. Haley*, 307 N.E.2d 34 (1973) which references early intrusion cases.
59. *Brents v. Morgan*, 229 S.W. 967 (1927).
60. *Melvin v. Reid*, 112 Cal. App. 285, 297 (1931).
61. Ibid, 291.
62. *Sidis v. F-R Publishing Corporation*, 113 F.2d 806 (2d Cir. 1940).
63. Ibid.
64. *Daily Times Democrat v. Graham*, 102, 2d 474 (1964).
65. Restatement (Second) of Torts sec. 652E.
66. Restatement (Second) of Torts sec. 652A; and see generally Robin Baker Perkins, "The truth behind false light—A recommendation for Texas's re-adoption of false light invasion of privacy," *Texas Tech Law Review*, 1199 (2003).
67. Prosser, "Privacy," 338, 339.
68. See *Leverton v. Curtiss Publishing Co.*, 78 F. Supp. 305 (D.D.C. 1948).
69. 239 P.2d 630 (Cal. 1952).
70. *Norris v. Moskin Stores, Inc.*, 132 So.2d 321 (1961).
71. Ibid.
72. Prosser, "Privacy," 406.
73. *Pavesich v. New England Life Insurance Company*, 122 Ga. 190 (Ga. 1905).
74. Ibid, 220.
75. See *Fairfield v. American Photocopy Equip. Co.*, 138 Cal. App. 2d 82 (1955).
76. *Schuyler v. Curtis*, (Sup. 1892) 15 N.Y. Supp. 787.
77. Ibid.
78. *Atkinson v. Doherty*, 121 Mich. 372 (1899).
79. Ibid.
80. *Roberson v. Rochester Folding Box Co.*, 64 N.E. 442 (1902).
81. Ibid.
82. See Elbridge L. Adams, "The right of privacy, and its relation to the law of libel," *American Law Review*, 39 (1905): 37–58.
83. N.Y Session Laws 1903, chapter 132, §§ 1–2.
84. *Pavesich v. New England Life Insurance Company*, 50 S.E. 68, 122 Ga. 190 (Ga. 1905).
85. Ibid, 69–70.
86. Ibid.
87. Ibid, 72.
88. Ibid, 72.

89. Ibid, 74.
90. Ibid, 80.
91. See discussion of Pavesich in Judith Wagner DeCew, (1997). *In Pursuit of Privacy: Law, Ethics, and the Rise of Technology* (Ithaca, NY: Cornell University Press, 1997), 23. The case is cited in over two hundred cases.
92. *Munden v. Harris*, 134 S.W. 1076 (1911).
93. *Roberson v. Rochester Folding Box Co.*, 64 N.E. 442 (1902).
94. *Munden v. Harris*, 134 S.W. 1076 (1911).
95. Ibid, 665–66.
96. *Fitzsimmons v. Olinger Mortuary Association*, 1 Colo. 544, 17 P.2d 535 (1932).
97. Ibid.
98. Ibid.
99. *Flake v. Greensboro News Co.*, 195 S.E. 55 (1938).
100. *Hinish v. Meier Frank Company*, 113 P.2d 438 (1941).
101. Ibid.
102. *Spahn v. Julian Messner, Inc.*, 18 N.Y.2d 324 (N.Y. 1966).
103. Ibid, 328.
104. See Edward Keynes, *Liberty, Property, and Privacy: Toward a Jurisprudence of Substantive Due Process* (University Park: Pennsylvania State University Press, 1996).
105. *Lochner v. New York*, 198 U.S. 45 (1905).
106. *West Coast Hotel. v Parrish*, 300 U.S. 379 (1937).
107. *Meyer v. Nebraska*, 262 U.S. 390 (1925).
108. Ibid.
109. *Skinner v. Oklahoma*, 316 U.S. 535 (1942).
110. Compare this to the infamous *Buck v. Bell*, 274 U.S. 200 (1927) which upheld a state law permitting the sterilization of persons with intellectual disabilities.
111. Ibid.
112. *Griswold v. Connecticut*, 381 U.S. 479 (1965).
113. Ibid, 480.
114. Ibid.
115. See Bernard Schwartz, *Super Chief: Earl Warren and His Supreme Court—A Judicial Biography* (New York: New York University Press, 1983), 577.
116. *Griswold v. Connecticut*, 381 U.S. 479, 480–486 (1965).
117. *Pierce v. Society of Sisters*, 268 U.S. 510 (1925).
118. *Meyer v. Nebraska*, 262 U.S. 390 (1925).
119. *NAACP v. Alabama*, 357 U.S. 449 (1958).
120. *Poe v. Ullman*, 367 U.S. 497 (1961).
121. *Boyd v. United States*, 116 U.S. 616 (1886).
122. There is a voluminous body of literature on this subject; for a good overview, see several classic works: Gerald Gunther, *Constitutional Law* (New York: Foundation Press, 1985), 448–585; Robert McCloskey, "Economic due process and the Supreme Court," *Supreme Court Review: 1962*, edited by Phillip Kurland (Chicago: University of Chicago Press, 1962), 34–62; and Bernard Seigan, *Economic Liberties and the Constitution* (Chicago: University of Chicago Press, 1980).

123. *Griswold v. Connecticut*, 381 U.S. 486–495 (1965).
124. *Eisenstadt v. Baird*, 405 U.S. 438 (1972).
125. Ibid, 442.
126. Ibid, 452.
127. Ibid, 453.
128. Ibid.
129. *Roe v. Wade*, 410 U.S. 113 (1973).
130. Ibid, 153.
131. Ibid, 154.
132. Ibid, 486.
133. Ibid, 171.
134. Ibid, 172.
135. Ibid.
136. See *Beal v. Doe*, 432 U.S. 438 (1977).
137. *Planned Parenthood of Central Missouri v. Danforth*, 428 U.S. 552 (1976).
138. *Rust v. Sullivan*, 500 U.S. 173 (1991).
139. *Whole Woman's Health v. Hellerstedt*, 579 U.S. 582 (2016).
140. *Dobbs v. Jackson Women's Health Organization*, 597 U.S. 215 (2022).
141. *Planned Parenthood v. Casey*, 505 U.S. 833 (1992).
142. Ibid.
143. Ibid, 867.
144. Ibid, 912.
145. *Dobbs v. Jackson Women's Health Organization*, 597 U.S. 215 (2022).
146. Ibid, 221.
147. Ibid, 294. Justices Clarence Thomas, Neil Gorsuch, Brett Kavanaugh, and Amy Coney Barrett joined Samuel Alito's opinion. Chief Justice John Roberts did not join the majority opinion: although he agreed that the Mississippi abortion law at issue in the case should be upheld, he did not believe that the Court should overturn *Roe*.
148. Ibid, 285.
149. Ibid.
150. Ibid, 223.
151. Ibid, 264.
152. Ibid, 281.
153. Justices Stephen Breyer, Sonia Sotomayor, and Elena Kagan.
154. *Dobbs v. Jackson Women's Health Organization*, 597 U.S. 215 (2022).
155. *Commonwealth's Attorney for the City of Richmond v. Doe*, 425 U.S. 901 (1976).
156. *Bowers v. Hardwick*, 478 U. S. 186 (1986).
157. Ibid, 190–91.
158. *Lawrence v. Texas*, 539 U.S. 558 (2003).
159. Alex Nguyen and William Melhado, "Bill striking unconstitutional state law that criminalized homosexuality fails to meet critical deadline in the Texas House," *Texas Tribune*, May 11, 2023, https://www.texastribune.org/2023/05/11/texas-sodomy-ban-repeal-bill/.
160. Ibid, 563–64.

161. Texas Constitution, Article 1, Section 3a. Bill of Rights.
162. *Lawrence v. Texas*, 539 U.S. 563.
163. Ibid, 564–67.
164. *Texas v. Morales*, 869 S.W. 2d 941 (1994).
165. *Obergefell v. Hodges*, 576 U.S. 644 (2015).
166. Ibid, 647–68.
167. *Boyd v. United States*, 116 U.S. 616 (1886).
168. Ibid.
169. *Olmstead v. United States*, 277 U.S. 438 (1928).
170. Ibid.
171. Ibid, 475.
172. Ibid.
173. *Katz v. United States*, 389 U.S. 347 (1967).
174. Ibid.
175. Ibid, 353.
176. *California v. Ciraolo*, 476 U.S. 207 (1986).
177. Ibid.
178. The common law notion of curtilage is worth noting as it is the area in which the intimate activity associated with the privacy of one's home takes place: the expectation of privacy is most heightened in an area intimately linked to the home.
179. *Kyllo v. United States*, 533 U.S. 27 (2001).
180. Ibid.
181. Ibid.
182. Ibid, 33–35.
183. Texas Constitution, Article I, section 9, https://statutes.capitol.texas.gov/Docs/CN/htm/CN.1.htm
184. *Katz v. United States*, 389 U.S. 347 (1967).
185. Westlaw search conducted September 2023 of cases heard by the Courts of Appeals and Texas Supreme Court.
186. Westlaw search conducted November 2023 of criminal cases heard by the Court of Criminal Appeals and Courts of Appeals.
187. Ibid.

Chapter 2

The Common Law Right to Privacy in Texas

Privacy did not become an actionable legal claim in Texas until the 1973 landmark case of *Billings v. Atkinson*.[1] Early privacy cases reveal that many Texas judges were cognizant of other states' adoption of privacy doctrines, and cited many of these cases in their opinions, but they refused to recognize that it should be an actionable legal claim in the state.

This chapter examines the privacy decisions of Texas courts based on common law doctrines and state constitutional provisions. Here we focus on the judicial explication of the four privacy doctrines defined in the previous chapter: (1) intrusion, also referred to as invasion; (2) public disclosure of private information; (3) false light; and (4) appropriation of name or likeness for commercial gain. These cases were decided by the Texas courts on independent state grounds, *not* on federal privacy precedent such as *Griswold v. Connecticut*. *Griswold* and other US Supreme Court decisions are sometimes referenced—typically in footnotes—in many of these opinions but play no decisive role since these disputes are addressed through the application of state tort law privacy doctrines or, in some instances, state privacy statutes.

EARLY PRIVACY CLAIMS IN TEXAS

Many or all of the four tort privacy doctrines that constitute the right to privacy were adopted in other states decades before privacy became an actionable legal claim in Texas in *Billings*. None of the four doctrines were adopted in Texas until 1973; however, privacy claims were frequently heard in Texas courts decades earlier. In one prominent pre-*Billings* case—*U.S. Life Insurance Co. v. Hamilton*[2] in 1951—a court refused to recognize the right to privacy as a cause of action in a case alleging that a plaintiff's name and signature were appropriated by the defendant in the promotion of his business.

As part of an advertising campaign, an insurance company drafted a form letter promoting a health insurance plan that bore a facsimile of the signature of a former employee, E. B. Hamilton. While he was employed by the company, similar letters bearing his signature were routinely mailed to prospective customers, but the mailings continued after he had been fired from the company. Hamilton claimed that he suffered emotional distress because the letters bearing his signature were still being mailed after it was common knowledge that he had been wrongfully terminated from his position at U.S. Life. The Texas Court of Civil Appeals (Waco) clearly acknowledged that in *other* states invasion of privacy for the appropriation of one's signature was a cause of action but ruled that in Texas the unauthorized use of a signature was a violation of a property right, not an intrusion upon one's privacy. Justice Hale wrote:

> The right to privacy as an independent and distinctive legal concept stems from the publication of a law review article written by Warren and Brandeis (later Justice Brandeis). . . . Its development affords a striking illustration of the healthy manner in which the great body of American law grows in meeting the demands of new conditions as they arise in the expanding social order. While we know of no case in which any court has directly passed upon the question as to whether or not an action for damages on account of injury resulting from a wrongful invasion of the right to privacy is cognizable in the courts of Texas, we are inclined to view that the courts of this State should and would, under appropriate circumstances, recognize damages as a proper remedy for the wrongful invasion of that right.[3]

Notwithstanding Justice Hale's foray into the realm of sociological jurisprudence or legal realism, he concluded that although the courts of the state "should and would," under the right circumstances, recognize the right to privacy, the injury sustained by Hamilton was not an invasion of privacy as this concept was then understood in other states (as the right to be let alone). Although the court stated that the appropriation of Hamilton's signature was a privacy action recognized in other states, in Texas the unauthorized appropriation of a person's signature is a violation of a property right—one's ownership of an expression of identity which is recognized as distinct to each person. Whether a person makes a simple "X" or pens an artistic flourish, a signature is proof of one's identity or agreement or intent. The ruling in *Hamilton* may have been a setback for the right to privacy in the state, but it was significant for laying the foundation for the modern right of privacy in Texas. Hamilton has been cited and discussed in many subsequent opinions as well as in scholarly writing.

In 1952, just one year after *Hamilton* in *Milner v. Red River Valley Publishing Co.*,[4] the Texas Court of Civil Appeals (Waco) refused to adopt the right to privacy in a case involving a newspaper's publication of a story about the death of a Sherman, Texas man.[5] In reporting the death of Ben Milner in a traffic accident, the *Sherman Daily Democrat* decided to add context to the story by explaining that Milner had been indicted in a grain theft case the year before. Milner's family argued that even though the story was true and in the public record, the disclosure of Milner's criminal indictment was an invasion of their right to privacy in the form of an intrusion into their right to mourn their beloved husband, father, and son "unmolested by such inexcusable and offensive publicity . . . while they were in the depths of their great mourning and profound grief."[6] In sum, they argued that the publication was an actionable invasion of the right to be let alone. In its defense, the newspaper countered that the news article referring to Milner's indictment was public record and a common practice by newspapers was to identify the deceased by reference to his past history. The newspaper further argued Milner was a "figure of public interest" both because of the indictment as well as his untimely death. The court agreed with the newspaper and ruled that Milner's family could not recover damages on a theory of a right of privacy.[7]

Writing for the majority, Justice Cramer acknowledged that since the publication of Warren and Brandeis article the right of privacy had been "recognized by a few of the States but denied by many other States."[8] However, demonstrating judicial restraint, Cramer crafted a creative argument to forestall the adoption of privacy in Texas. He refused to adopt any common law doctrines protecting privacy because "Texas courts are limited to the enforcement of rights under the common law as it existed on January 20, 1840."[9] The right to privacy was not a common law right, Cramer explained, and since Texas's common law is a fixed body of law that can only be changed by the legislature, no recovery for invasion of privacy is possible in Texas.[10] The court noted that the Milners could have brought a libel action for the publication of statements made about them but the fact that Milner's history was of public record would likely preclude recovery for damages. In short, *Milner* reaffirmed the Texas judiciary's refusal to adopt invasion of privacy as a common law doctrine.

That same year, citing *Milner*, the Court of Civil Appeals (Austin) rejected the asserted privacy rights of a man whose photographs were displayed in law enforcement "rogue's gallery."[11] Arrested on the misdemeanor offense of "accosting females," which in today's terms constitutes stalking,[12] he was booked and his mugshot taken. Later acquitted of all charges, he argued that the retention and circulation of the mugshot was a violation of his right to privacy. The trial court agreed that the "circulation of the photos and accompanying records would expose him to ridicule, obloquy and disgrace" but that the right to privacy as such is not recognized under the common law in Texas.[13] The court concluded that the taking of photographs and fingerprints cannot be regarded as a violation of privacy or as a punishment but merely an administrative police procedure.[14]

Pre-*Billings* privacy cases reveal that Texas judges were cognizant of the adoption of privacy doctrines in other states—as well as the interstate diffusion or cross-pollination of the doctrines that occurred over time and even cited many of these cases in their opinions. Some Texas judges agonized over whether to recognize privacy as distinctive in itself—not incidental to some other right or tort—and whether it is an actionable legal claim in the state. Some Texas judges dismissed plaintiffs' assertions of a generalized "right to privacy" in cases heard as early as the 1940s, as in *Meadows v. First National Bank of Harlingen*, in which the Court of Civil Appeals (San Antonio) found that an aggressive and "oppressive" method of collecting a debt that had already been paid did not constitute a violation of the plaintiff's right to privacy.[15]

RECOGNITION OF THE RIGHT TO PRIVACY IN TEXAS

Invasion of Privacy Doctrine

Billings v. Atkinson,[16] the first Texas case to adopt the right to privacy as a distinct tort that constitutes a legal injury, originated when Lloyd Billings heard "popping noises" for several days on his phone. Billings soon discovered that a telephone repairman for Southwestern Bell Telephone Company named Norman Atkinson climbed a telephone pole near Billings's house and attached a wiretap device to his home phone line. The device transmitted private and intimate conversations taking place in Billings's home over a standard FM radio transmitter. Mr. Atkinson was fired after Billings reported him to the telephone company. A trial court jury found that Atkinson intentionally violated Billings's right to privacy, causing mental anguish. The Court of Civil Appeals[17] (Dallas) reversed the jury verdict citing *Milner v. Red River Publishing Company*, holding that according to precedent no common law right to privacy existed under Texas law.[18] Notwithstanding the lack of precedent, however, the Texas Supreme Court reversed the appeals court and ruled that a right to privacy is an independent right, distinctive in itself, and not incidental to some other right or tort or doctrine that extends to wiretapping.[19] The violation of the right to privacy is a tort, Justice James Gray Denton pointed out. While no Texas court expressly granted relief for an injury resulting directly from the "invasion of privacy," he wrote, the right to be let alone could be found emanating from three sources: the tort of defamation, an invasion of a property right, and a person's breach of another's confidence.[20] The term right of privacy, Justice Denton continued, was not introduced into the legal lexicon until the 1890 publication of Warren and Brandeis's *Harvard Law Review* article.[21] It was there that the authors concluded that a distinct common law right to privacy exists independently of the common law rights of property, contracts, protection of one's reputation, and physical integrity.[22] Although Denton argued that the state did not recognize invasion of privacy cause of action in *Milner*, it did recognize that many of the protections or interests contained in the right to privacy have been expressed under the doctrines of libel and slander, wrongful search and seizure, eavesdropping and wiretapping, as well as other intrusions into the private business and personal affairs of a person.[23] Justice Denton further opined that eavesdropping was an offense at common law in the nineteenth century, defined as those persons who "listen under walls or windows or eaves of houses to harken after the disclosure and thereupon proclaim slanderous and mischievous tales."[24] The argument in *Milner* that no right to privacy exists because it was not found in the common law of 1840 failed to recognize not only just how much society has changed but how because of technology our private lives and affairs have been threatened and exploited. By eavesdropping on Billings's conversation, the telephone company invaded the right to privacy; henceforth, "an unwarranted invasion of the right to privacy constitutes a legal injury for which a remedy will be granted."[25] Denton's adoption and definition of privacy is the not only the first but the most expansive in Texas jurisprudence up to this day. He wrote:

> [T]he right to be free from the unwarranted appropriation or exploitation of one's personality, the publicizing of one's private affairs with which the public has no legitimate concern, or the wrongful intrusion into one's private activities in such manner as to outrage or cause mental suffering, shame or humiliation to a person of ordinary sensibilities.[26]

The definition of privacy adopted in *Billings* is exceptionally capacious, encompassing three tort doctrines: (1) intrusion in the form of eavesdropping on Billings conversation, (2) public disclosure of personal information or private affairs, and (3) what Denton calls the "unwarranted appropriation or exploitation of one's personality." Another perspective on the ruling is that Denton is interpreting the intrusion doctrine in a manner that includes (to borrow a phrase from *Griswold v. Connecticut*) penumbral privacy interests. No Texas court would again define privacy as broadly as Denton did in *Billings*. In fact, post-*Billings*, many conservative Texas judges and justices seemed to go out of their way to reign in Denton's privacy definition as if the ruling had left them with a bitter taste of judicial activism, believing that Denton had gone too far.

From a state constitutional law standpoint, the most the most influential invasion of privacy case is *Texas State Employees Union (TSEU) v. Texas Department of Mental Health & Mental Retardation*[27] in 1987 in which the Texas Supreme Court ruled that the right to privacy contained in the Texas Constitution offered broader protections than the right to privacy under the US Constitution and federal caselaw. The Employee's Union challenged the department's polygraph policy that required employees to submit to a polygraph test during any investigation of suspected patient abuse, theft, or other criminal activity that posed a threat to the health or safety of patients or employees.[28] The Texas Supreme Court held that although the Texas Constitution does not contain an express guarantee of a right to privacy, the state's constitution *does* contain the following five provisions from which the right to privacy is derived:

1. Section 19 of the Texas Bill of Rights protects against arbitrary deprivation of life and liberty.[29]
2. Section 8 provides the freedom to speak, write, or publish.[30]
3. Section 10 protects a person's privilege against self-incrimination.[31]
4. Sections 9 and 25 guarantee the right to be free from intrusions into the sanctity of the home and person.[32]
5. Section 6 protects an individual's right to freedom of conscience and religion.[33]

Chief Justice John Hill wrote: "This right to privacy should yield only when the government can demonstrate that an intrusion is reasonably warranted for the achievement of a compelling government objective that can be achieved by no less intrusive, more reasonable means."[34] Did the polygraph testing policy achieve a compelling governmental objective? Hill concluded that although the department is entitled to require employees to answer questions that are related to their job duties, the use of lie detectors constitutes an unnecessary intrusion that violates the employee's right to privacy.[35] When the state acts as an employer it may not without compelling justification condition a person's employment on the waiver of their constitutional rights.

Following *TSEU*, protection against invasion of privacy would rest upon two pillars: the common law and the Texas Constitution. *Billings v. Atkinson* in 1973[36] adopted the right to privacy as a distinct tort that constitutes a legal injury, and TSEU recognizes an implied state constitutional right. In many subsequent privacy cases, courts rely on either or both.

An unusual case that had the potential to greatly expand privacy protection was *Colquette v. Forbes*[37] in 1984. The question at bar was: can the terms of an allegedly unfair consensual agreement made between two adults implicate or violate the right to privacy? If so, which privacy doctrine or analysis might apply? In 1984, the Court of Appeals (Austin) addressed these questions. The case originated when Nancy Colquette claimed that the terms of the property settlement of her divorce decree violated her constitutional right to privacy.[38] As part of a divorce property settlement, Thomas Forbes agreed to convey his interest in the marital home to Nancy Colquette if she signed a promissory note that would come due in five years, "with immediate acceleration of maturity upon Colquette's remarriage or . . . cohabitation with an unrelated adult male" at the home.[39] Ms. Colquette was faced with a decision: if she remarried or entered into a relationship that involved any form of "cohabitation," the balance of the note would be due immediately. If she did not have the money to pay the note in full, she would need to stay single or not cohabitate with a man in the home.

Mr. Forbes brought suit to collect on the note, claiming that the note had matured early since Colquette had been cohabitating with an adult male for weeks.[40] The trial court held that the note was due, agreed that Forbes could place a lien on the house, and ordered foreclosure if the note was not paid in full.[41] Ms. Colquette appealed and argued that the acceleration of the note and the placing of the lien, merely because of her personal decision to cohabitate with an adult male, violated her right to privacy as autonomy as defined in *Griswold v. Connecticut*[42] and her rights under the common law of Texas.

Ms. Colquette's lawyers argued that any contract or policy supporting the terms of such a contract is void if it intrudes upon one's right to enter into a relationship with another person.[43] The court of appeals dismissed the application of *Griswold* to a private contractual agreement and ruled for Forbes.[44] Writing for the majority of the court, Justice Bob Gammage,[45] who forged a strong record on the right to privacy while on the court of appeals and later on the Texas Supreme Court, argued that Colquette had willingly agreed to the terms of the contract so that she could keep her house.[46] However, would a contract be void if it violated the privacy interest in living with one's lover or partner? Can it be assumed that merely because Colquette was cohabitating with a boyfriend or new husband, that she now had the ability to pay the note in full? The so-called acceleration clause was an intrusion upon Colquette's personal and intimate decisions. Yet Gammage reasoned that the acceleration clause was a part of a mutual agreement between two individuals; it was *not* public policy promulgated by the government.[47] If it had been public policy then Colquette could assert her privacy rights against the intrusion of the state, but the only involvement of the state in this case was the "judicial enforcement of private contractual obligations."[48] Though she may not have known it when she signed the divorce decree, Colquette consented to the intrusion into her privacy and relationship choices when she signed the promissory note.[49]

But doesn't "judicial enforcement" constitute state action? As an aside, this is the main question surrounding Texas's highly restrictive abortion bill Senate Bill 8 passed in 2021.[50] That law leaves its enforcement in the hands of private citizens who are empowered to bring suits in civil courts against abortion providers. We will return to the issues arising from Senate Bill 8 in chapter 4. Without state action or state enforcement of a law, does a law become immunized against judicial review? In *Colquette*, the majority rejected the contention that the judicial enforcement of the cohabitation clause of the promissory note was contrary to public policy and in violation of *Shelley v. Kramer*.[51] In *Shelley*, the US Supreme Court struck down judicially enforced, racially restrictive covenants.[52] If the state by law had *required* the cohabitation clause, then it might have been possible to challenge the law under *Shelley*—asserting that a state action had violated the Constitution.[53] Justice Gammage concluded:

> It is apparent to us that the justifications for the *Shelley* rule are not present in this case. Here, the affected parties consented to the intrusion (of privacy)—if acceleration of maturity of the debt and the particular conditions giving rise thereto can be construed as such—by their mutual acceptance of the terms of the note. . . . We hold that, under the facts of this case, judicial approval of the property settlement agreement and subsequent enforcement of the obligations created therein are, in nature and degree, not the type of government involvement restrained by a constitutional right of privacy.[54]

Colquette v. Forbes brings up an intriguing privacy claim. Family and real estate law in Texas provides the legal language but in no way requires such a property settlement agreement between private parties. Forbes was no doubt anxious to receive payment for his interest in the house but agreed, per the promissory note, to wait a period of five years to be paid by Colquette.[55] Colquette agreed to these conditions to give her time to save money.[56] The likely presumption made was that if Colquette remarried or cohabitated with an unrelated adult male at the home, money would be available to help the ex-wife pay the note in full. Could Forbes have insisted to conditions that the note be accelerated if she merely dated a man who regularly spent the night? What if she had a female lover as opposed to male as stipulated in the agreement? Suppose further that a tenant agrees not to have premarital sex as a mutually agreed upon condition of a lease agreement. Then, based on information that the tenant was engaging in premarital sex, the landlord evicts the tenant. Can the tenant bring a cause of action for a tort invasion of privacy if the landlord has valid grounds for terminating the lease?[57] Such agreements seem very intrusive into a person's private intimate affairs, but it is all academic since the obligations created by the note were consensual and did not constitute the type of government involvement that would infringe on a constitutional right to privacy. Thus, Colquette's privacy argument was summarily rejected by the court; the case exists today only in a scattering of footnotes and citations in four cases. Yet even though the privacy claim was rejected, the decision is one of a number of cases in which the Texas courts stated that although the Texas Constitution does not contain an express guarantee of a right to privacy,[58] it does contain provisions and protections that parallel those provisions in the US Constitution that have taken together imply protected zones of privacy.

The problem of competing rights in Texas privacy jurisprudence—pitting the invasion of privacy against freedom of expression—has often been at its most intractable when a tension exists between a woman's right to have an abortion and the anti-abortion activist's freedom of expression to protest the exercise of that right. Anti-abortion activists have long exercised their First Amendment rights in locations far removed from the traditional public forums of courthouses and state capitol buildings. Groups have demonstrated near medical facilities where abortions are performed, in front of the private residences of the physicians who perform abortions, and even in front of schools attended by the children of those physicians.[59] The courts find themselves not only in the middle of two competing rights, when protestors from across the political spectrum push the limits of freedom of expression and in doing so violate the privacy rights of individuals. It is in this context that, in 1993, the Texas Supreme Court heard the case of *Valenzuela v. Aquino* in 1990.[60]

The case originated when a physician, Dr. Eduardo Aquino, sued Eliseo Valenzuela, Jr., and other anti-abortion protestors for negligent infliction of emotional distress and breach of privacy caused by incessant protesting outside of his home.[61] Aquino had an obstetrics and gynecological practice, a small part of which provided abortions. In 1982, a group called South Texans for Life began picketing at Aquino's offices. Even after the group threatened his personal safety, Aquino never attempted to stop them.[62] However, in 1988, the demonstrators began picketing the Aquinos' family home, often beginning their protest activities shortly after the Aquino children returned from school but before Dr. Aquino came home from work.[63] The group held signs bearing messages such as "Nice House Dr. Eduardo, How Many Babies Paid the Price," "Beware Abortionist in Your Block," and "God Gives Life, Aquino Takes Away."[64] Police cars were regularly parked on the street, and Aquino's neighbors lined the streets to watch the demonstrations.[65] Protestors photographed the Aquino home, and on one occasion, a protestor followed Ms. Aquino as she attempted to leave for the grocery store.[66] There was little doubt that this "circus-like" environment traumatized the family. Ultimately, Ms. Aquino was diagnosed with post-traumatic stress disorder and prescribed antidepressants.[67] The children were traumatized and suffered signs of emotional distress, and the oldest son was placed in a psychiatric hospital.[68]

At last, a temporary injunction was granted by the trial court prohibiting the protestors from conducting a wide range of activities, "including all residential picketing within one-half mile of the Aquinos' home."[69] After the jury found for the Aquinos, the trial court awarded the Aquino family actual and punitive damages for infliction of emotional distress resulting from the breach of privacy caused by the demonstrators.[70] The district judge wrote:

> I believe Texas recognizes a right to privacy. This right, I believe, includes the right to be free from willful intrusions into one's personal life at home and at work—this right to be left alone from unwanted attention that may be caused by picketing or other unwanted demonstrations . . . is protected by injunctive relief.[71]

The court of appeals (Corpus Christi), in affirming the trial court's permanent injunction, found that there was a "significant governmental interest in protecting the privacy and domestic tranquility of the home," and the injunction was "narrowly tailored to serve [that] interest."[72] The court of appeals did, however, reverse the jury's award of damages for the Aquinos' emotional distress resulting from an invasion of privacy because the court believed the monetary award constituted an infringement or "chill" on the protestors' freedom of speech.[73]

On appeal, the Texas Supreme Court focused on a number of questions. First, should the justices analyze the dispute under the state or federal constitution? The US Supreme Court made clear in *Frisby v. Schultz* that a "focused" and extended demonstration by anti-abortion protestors in front of a physicians' residence can be prohibited in the interest of the homeowner's right to privacy.[74]

The Texas Supreme Court reversed the permanent injunction and remanded the case back to the trial court.[75] Writing for the majority, Justice Nathan Hecht refused to address what he believed to be the "hypothetical" constitutional question of competing rights. Aquino theoretically *could* have recovered damages for invasion of privacy, but the trial court would have needed to determine whether the picketing "would be highly offensive to a reasonable person."[76] Dr. Aquino could have claimed that the protestors' acts resulted in an *intentional* intrusion on his privacy that was highly offensive to the average person, but the majority wrote that the testimony among the protestors and witnesses, relating to the presences of an intent to intimidate, was ambiguous and contradictory to establish the second element of invasion of privacy.[77] The majority reasoned that, as horrible as the effect of the intense protesting might have been on the family, it could be argued that the demonstrators were not trying to intimidate Aquino but merely trying to express their heartfelt belief that abortion was morally wrong.[78]

Reading the opinion, it is at first unclear why the majority split hairs by focusing solely on the question of intentional versus negligent infliction of emotional distress when the basis for Aquino's original petition was an invasion of privacy based on the US Supreme Court's ruling in *Frisby v. Schultz*.[79] Was the majority simply avoiding a thorny political issue in conservative Texas or was it an understandable and legitimate reluctance to expand the number of privacy suits by allowing for negligent acts? Notwithstanding a half-decade of protesting, Aquino's lawyers could not convince the majority that the breach of privacy was intentional and offensive.

In a dissenting opinion, Justice Gammage agreed that under the Texas Constitution's Bill of Rights—Article I, section 8—a person cannot win damages from a group engaged in protected speech; however, the targeted individual may be allowed to recover damages that arise from conduct (namely intrusion into one's privacy) unrelated to protected expression.[80] He argued that the picketing of the doctor's home was an invasion of privacy in the form of an assault on his family domain. Citing the Texas Supreme Court's ruling in *Casso v. Brand* in 1989, Gammage argued that under article I, section 8, of the Bill of Rights of the Texas Constitution, speech loses protection and may give rise to liability for damages where the conduct associated with the speech is "so excessive and intrusive" that it does not deserve protection.[81] Also relying on another Texas case, *James v. Brown*, Gammage added that liability for one's speech may arise only when "unprotected conduct is intertwined with protected expression," and the award for damages is based on that unprotected conduct involving the invasion of privacy.[82]

Dissenting Justice Rose Spector wrote a lengthy instructive analysis of the privacy interests at stake in this case.[83] Spector argues that the case originated as what she called a "breach-of-privacy claim."[84] By remanding the case back to the trial court, "the majority needlessly prolongs this litigation and effectively endangers a family's most basic rights."[85] When a violation of the right to privacy exists, injunctive relief is necessary, especially when legal remedies are inadequate, there are inadequacies with damages, or there is evidence of future violations.[86] Here, the evidence and the jury's finding that the picketing was "focused and directed" at the Aquino residence met the *Frisby* standard discussed earlier, which protects the right to residential privacy.[87] The dissenters relied on *Billings v. Atkinson*, which defines the right to privacy under Texas law as "the right of an individual to be left alone, to live a life of seclusion,"[88] to be free "from unreasonable intrusion,"[89] and "to preserve the sanctity of the home."[90] The conduct also threatened other privacy rights. By targeting and harassing doctors as the "weak link," anti-abortion rights groups know that they could make *Roe v. Wade* "an empty promise."[91] In the end, the dissenters agreed with the court of appeals that the award of damages in this case *would* inhibit debate on public issues, but that an injunction is a reasonable restriction on expressive conduct.[92] The dissenting justices appeared puzzled by the absolute refusal of the majority to discuss the constitutional tension between Aquino's right to privacy and the expressive conduct rights of South Texans for Life, even though this issue was brought up during oral argument and is mirrored by *Frisby*. The Aquino family suffered one of the most intrusive and punishing campaigns undertaken by an anti-abortion group. In a competing rights claim, the Texas courts have generally favored expression over privacy,[93] but one cannot help but wondering after reading the Aquino opinion whether in this instance the right to privacy was trumped by politics.

Does privacy in Texas extend beyond the common law right to be let alone into the realm of privacy as autonomy as articulated in *Griswold v. Connecticut*? The Texas Supreme Court had the opportunity to address this question nearly a decade after *TSEU* when the justices unanimously ruled that the right to privacy does not confer a right to commit adultery, something that the *Austin American-Statesman* pointed out in a news article following the ruling.[94] *City of Sherman v. Henry* originated when Otis Henry, a Sherman, Texas, police officer, was denied a promotion because he was sexually involved with another officer's wife.[95] Before he was denied the promotion, the police chief authorized an extensive investigation to determine if the rumors of the affair were true. Colleagues were interviewed and love letters discovered. A district court ruled in favor of Henry, and a court of appeals agreed that the investigation and denial of promotion because of this admittedly morally wrong but distinctly private and intimate matter violated his right to privacy. The district court found that the city violated Sherman's right to privacy under the Texas and US Constitution. Applying *TSEU*, the Court of Appeals (Dallas) found that Henry's private, legal sexual conduct is protected under the Texas Constitution.[96] However, the Texas Supreme Court reversed in a seven-to-two vote.

Writing for the majority, Justice Greg Abbott wrote a strong reaffirmation of the right to privacy established in the *TSEU* decision but did not apply the principles contained in *TSEU* to the facts of *Henry*, that is, to the question of whether Henry's right to privacy was violated by the city. Instead, Abbott reasoned that that the right to privacy under the Texas Constitution or US Constitution does not include a right to maintain a sexual relationship with the spouse of another person. Abbott stated that the decision "does not mean . . . that the government is free to engage in intrusive investigation methods to determine the sexual practices of individuals," but what was at issue in *Henry* was not intrusion into his private life, but more a matter of the "autonomy aspect of privacy—the right to make certain fundamental decisions and engage in certain conduct without state interference."[97] This definition of privacy as autonomy, while recognized by *Griswold* and *Roe*, is definitely not a recognized doctrine in Texas, Abbott concluded.

In a concurring opinion, Justices Rose Spector and Priscilla Owen conceded the point made by the majority that the denial of the officer's promotion was not a violation of a constitutional right, but argued that in deciding Henry the majority "shriveled" the right to privacy "to the point that the most personal aspects of our lives are the government's business." Of course, this decision was handed down prior to the US Supreme Court ruling on sexual privacy in *Lawrence v. Texas* so the majority's decision relied in part on *Bowers v. Hardwick*.[98] Laws criminalizing adultery in Texas were repealed in 1973,[99] but the court ruled that adultery is not protected by the concept of privacy as autonomy which extends to such activities as marriage, procreation, contraception, and parenting.[100] Privacy as autonomy as an independent doctrine or right has never been recognized by the Texas Supreme Court.

Recall that in *TSEU*, Chief Justice John Hill wrote that *a right of individual privacy in Texas parallels those found in the US Constitution* and protects personal privacy from unreasonable intrusion.[101] Sections 9 and 25 of the Texas Constitution guarantee the right to be free from intrusions into the sanctity of the home and person.[102] The majority in *Henry* did not apply *TSEU* in this case. Nor does it apply two important court of appeals privacy rulings regarding the Texas sodomy law: *City of Dallas v. England* and *State v. Morales*. In 1993, the Court of Appeals (Austin) set an important precedent in *England* by ruling that the City of Dallas had discriminated against a lesbian who applied for a position as a police officer.[103] Police departments across the state had routinely invoked the state's anti-sodomy law to deny employment to openly gay and lesbian job applicants on the grounds that they *might* potentially be engaged in criminal behavior.[104] The trial court struck down the law as an unconstitutional violation of the right to privacy under the Texas Constitution[105] and enjoined the city from enforcing the statute in a discriminatory manner. The Court of Appeals upheld the trial court's decision, but the Texas Supreme Court did not rule on the merits of the case because the city never filed a motion for rehearing within the required deadline.[106] In *Morales*, the Court of Appeals at Austin relied on *TSEU* to conclude that the sodomy law violated the fundamental right of two consenting adults to engage in private sexual behavior.[107] In *Morales*, three lesbian women and two gay men[108] challenged the law on the grounds that it violated the Texas Constitution.[109] The case took five years to work its way through the Texas court system, although similar laws had been challenged in a number of states for two decades.[110] At the time of the *Morales* decision in 1994, sodomy was a criminal offense in over twenty states and the District of Columbia.[111] The US Supreme Court 1986 ruling *Bowers v. Hardwick*,[112] which upheld the Georgia's sodomy law, was still the law of the land, but the *Morales* plaintiffs challenged the sodomy statute in state court under the constitutional right to privacy, due course of law,[113] and equal protection[114] provisions of Texas constitution.[115] According to the record, the sodomy law was rarely if ever enforced, and it was unlikely that the state would enforce it in the near future.[116] Nevertheless, the law was used to stigmatize and discriminate against homosexuals in areas such as housing, family law, and employment.[117]

The fact that the criminal law was not currently being enforced made it more difficult to challenge its constitutionality. Unless a person was prosecuted for an act of sodomy, the case would not go to Texas's highest criminal court, the Texas Court of Criminal Appeals. Texas has a bifurcated court system with distinct civil and criminal courts. The Supreme Court hears appeals in civil matters, while the Court of Criminal Appeals hears appeals in criminal matters. In a criminal court, a constitutional challenge to the sodomy law could be used as a defense, so that an affirmative or negative vote on its constitutionality would take place.[118] Since there were no pending prosecutions under the law, the only feasible strategy for the *Morales* plaintiffs was to challenge the law in a civil court. At the time of *Morales*, Texas civil courts had only twice reviewed the constitutionality of unenforced criminal statutes.[119] The *Morales* case could have been brought in one of four federal districts in Texas rather than a state court. Then, conceivably, on appeal either the US Court of Appeals for the Fifth Circuit or the US Supreme Court could overturn the sodomy law.[120]

In a surprise ruling, the Texas trial court declared the sodomy statute[121] unconstitutional and enjoined the enforcement of the law.[122] The state countered with a procedural argument that the civil court was precluded from deciding the case, because the court's equity jurisdiction did not extend to questions regarding the constitutionality of criminal statutes.[123] As aforementioned, the Court of Appeals (Austin) rejected the state's procedural argument and affirmed the trial court's ruling,[124] relying on the key 1987 Texas Supreme Court privacy ruling, *TSEU v. Texas Department of Mental Health & Mental Retardation*, in which the justices ruled that the policy of requiring certain employees to take mandatory polygraph tests impermissible violated the right to privacy found in the Texas Bill of Rights. Recognizing that right to privacy contained in the Texas Constitution offered broader protections than the right to privacy under the US Constitution, the court of appeals held that the sodomy law violated the fundamental right of two consenting adults to engage in private sexual behavior.[125] The court of appeals added in *Morales* that since the sodomy law did not advance any compelling governmental interest, section 21.06 of the Texas Penal Code was therefore unconstitutional.[126]

In the end, the Texas Supreme Court had the opportunity to make history by striking down the invidious law but in a narrowly decided (five-to-four) decision it rejected the appellate court's holding on procedural grounds and remanded the case back to the trial court with orders to dismiss.[127] The narrow majority argued that when no actual or threatened enforcement of a criminal statute occurs, a civil court cannot enjoin the enforcement of the statute.[128]

The majority also rejected the appellate court's interpretation of *Passel v. Fort Worth Independent School District*, which held that equity power *did* extend to the protection of personal privacy rights violated by a criminal statute. *Passel* involved a lawsuit brought against an unenforced criminal statute prohibiting fraternities, sororities, and secret societies in public schools below college level. Because the law itself was never enforced, nor was anyone punished by it, the lawsuit challenged Fort Worth Independent School District's administrative policy based on the statute on the grounds that it deprived students of their personal privacy rights.[129] Citing the Attorney General's position, the majority concluded:

> [T]here is no record of even a single instance in which the sodomy statute has been prosecuted against conduct that the plaintiffs claim is constitutionally protected; none of the plaintiffs claims a specific instance of career or employment opportunities having been restricted by the existence of the statute; none of the plaintiffs alleges having been the victim of a hate crime, or a fear of becoming the victim of any specific threatened future event.[130]

Dissenting, Justice Bob Gammage[131] responded:

> This court also offers a confusing discussion of lack of jurisdiction because reaching the merits would be an advisory opinion, which is somehow linked to this absence of harm. . . . The State *stipulated* that plaintiffs' job choices are limited, that they face discrimination in housing, family, and criminal justice matters, and that *they suffer psychological harm to their relationships because they are labeled criminals by the very existence of the statute*.[132]

Justice Gammage reasoned that the majority "confuses harm with prosecution" by its insistence that the sodomy statute causes no harm, merely because there is no actual or imminent prosecution.[133] The question of whether the prosecution of gays and lesbians is imminent, rather than a possibility, is relevant only if the allegations made are based on anticipated or hypothetical harm rather than an injury that has already occurred. As the appellate court acknowledged, the *Morales* plaintiffs suffered actual harm under the statute independent of the threat of criminal prosecution. The dissent criticized what they saw as the majority's procedural maneuvering to prevent the court from ruling directly on the constitutionality of the sodomy law. The Court *does* have the power to address Morales' challenge to the sodomy law, Gammage concluded.[134]

Gammage concluded that the majority abdicated its duty to apply judicial scrutiny to laws that infringe upon the rights of citizens. He wrote:

> [T]he court allows the State to insulate its laws from judicial scrutiny. Under the court's analysis, the State may adopt all manner of criminal laws affecting the civil or personal rights of any number of citizens, and by declining to prosecute . . . them, ensure that no court ever reviews them.[135]

The *Morales* decision was one vote short of striking down the sodomy law by overcoming a procedural wall intentionally erected to avoid ruling on the constitutionality of a highly controversial law. Research shows that the sodomy law was not and is not just languishing, ignored, and dusty in the penal code, but has been modified and preserved by social conservatives. As of now, the law is still on the books despite *Lawrence v. Texas*.

In a rare 2002 privacy as autonomy/abortion rights case, *Bell v. Low Income Women of Texas*,[136] the Texas Supreme Court ruled that the state constitution's implied guarantee of the right to privacy is not violated by the Texas Medical Assistance Program funding scheme, which prohibits funding for abortions unless pregnancy results from rape or incest or places the woman in danger of death. Notwithstanding the Court's ruling, the justices, citing *Henry* and *TSEU*, posited a very broad definition of privacy by stating that the Texas Constitution "protects personal privacy from unreasonable governmental intrusions and unwarranted interference with personal autonomy."[137] Although the Court discussed federal abortion rulings, particularly the matter of whether a right to an abortion requires state assistance in obtaining one—and now made moot by the US Supreme Court's ruling in *Dobbs v. Jackson Health Services*—the justices declined to discuss whether the Texas Constitution "creates privacy rights coextensive with those recognized under the United States Constitution."[138]

Do the rights of married individuals include the common law right to privacy, or do spouses relinquish a degree of their right to privacy when living in the same house and sharing a bedroom? Would the act of placing a camera in a spouse's bedroom be an invasion of privacy? In 1999, Marie Clayton, the estranged wife of Gary Clayton, hired private investigator James Richards to install a video camera in her husband's bedroom just prior to Mrs. Clayton departing for Virginia to visit her family. Mrs. Clayton had visited her psychic recently, who informed her that her husband, with whom she was in divorce proceedings, might be committing adultery. While in Virginia, Mrs. Clayton contacted Richards by phone to arrange for him to reenter the house and change the tape in the recorder, obtaining entry into the home from a neighbor with a spare key. Upon discovering this invasion after the fact, Mr. Clayton sued the investigator, claiming that his intrusion into personal seclusion was a tortious invasion of privacy. *Clayton v. Richards*[139] in 2001 addressed the question was whether the act of one placing a camera in a spouse's bedroom was an invasion of privacy. Richards was acting on the orders of Mrs. Clayton in this scenario, having only entered the house at her request. As such, was he merely being used as an agent of Mrs. Clayton's capacity as a spouse? The Court of Appeals (Texarkana) concluded that this was indeed the case. To determine whether his actions were an invasion of privacy, they would instead need to view the case as if Mrs. Clayton were the one who installed the camera. However, citing Professor Prosser, the court produced one caveat, that the investigator Richards was still a party in this case. Prosser states:

> All those who, in pursuance of a common plan or design to commit a tortious act, actively take part in it, or further it by cooperation or request, or who lend aid or encouragement to the wrongdoer, or ratify and adopt his acts done for their benefit, are equally liable with him.[140]

While Justice Grant acknowledged that a person willingly loses a degree of their right to privacy upon entering a marriage, this in no way meant that their bedroom was no longer a private subspace. Citing *Collins v. Collins*,[141] a 1995 Texas spousal wiretapping case, he concluded that the rights of married individuals still include the common law right to privacy. Justice Grant also attempted to reason by analogy in order to determine where the line is drawn. If a spouse looked through a bedroom door to view their partner, would they still be violating that spouse's expectation of privacy just as if they placed a hidden camera? Grant wrote a comprehensive account of marital privacy in Texas:

> A spouse shares equal rights in the privacy of the bedroom, and the other spouse relinquishes some of his or her rights to seclusion, solitude, and privacy by entering into marriage, by sharing a bedroom with a spouse, and by entering into ownership of the home with a spouse. However, nothing in the Texas Constitution or our common law suggests that the right of privacy is limited to unmarried individuals.[142]

When a person, married or not, enters their bedroom they have the expectation of privacy in their seclusion. An audio or video recording made when the person believes that a condition of complete privacy exists is offensive to any reasonable person.[143]

The video recording of the husband without his consent in the privacy of the bedroom even if it is carried out by his wife violates his right to privacy. Although there was disclosure of embarrassing facts, the actions taken by the wife and the private investigator were a violation of privacy interests even without public disclosure. The court did not analyze the case from the standpoint of the public disclosure doctrine, but rather the doctrine of intrusion or invasion into personal solitude. This doctrine does not consider whether the disclosure or potential for disclosure of information to the public to constitute a tortious act. Instead, it focuses on the physical intrusion to be the actionable invasion of privacy.

Public Disclosure Privacy Doctrine

The doctrine of public disclosure of private information can best be understood as a right to exert control over one's personal information. The issues and questions that fall under its rubric are diverse, ranging from the release of candid photos or videos of celebrities to the unauthorized release of medical records. According to Prosser, the general intent of the doctrine is to protect a person's self-image and reputation.[144] Three years after the landmark *Billings* decision, in *Industrial Foundation of the South v. Texas Industrial Accident Board* in 1976 the Texas Supreme Court expressly adopted the public disclosure doctrine, recognized as the right to be free from the public disclosure of embarrassing private facts. Industrial Foundation of the South, a private non-profit organization, requested that the State of Texas's Industrial Accident Board furnish personal information of all persons who filed claims for workers' compensation.[145] The state board refused to turn over records, arguing that such information is protected by the right to privacy.[146] As it turned out, several claimants for employment compensation had arrest records, and the foundation sued to release these records.[147] The Texas Supreme Court ruled that the board could not withhold information: "[T]he State's right to make available for public inspection information pertaining to an individual does not conflict with the individual's constitutional right of privacy unless the State's (Board) action restricts his freedom in a sphere recognized to be within a zone of privacy protected by the Constitution."[148] The Court found that no privacy interests were violated because the records dealt with public arrests and not personal information protected by the constitutional right to privacy, such as the nature of injuries or matters of marriage, procreation, or association. Nevertheless, in *Industrial Foundation*, the Court did expressly recognize the right to be free from public disclosure of embarrassing private facts.[149] Justice Ross E. Doughty wrote:

> We must decide. Therefore, whether any of the information requested by the Foundation is "private" within the meaning of the tort law, and whether the Board's action in making the information available to the public would

constitute a wrongful "publicizing" of such information and thus an invasion of a claimant's right to privacy.[150]

According to *Industrial Foundation*, in order to recover under public disclosure doctrine of privacy, a person must prove that the information contains intimate and embarrassing facts about a person's private affairs and that its publication to the public at large would be objectionable to a person or ordinary sensibilities. The privacy interest protected by the public disclosure doctrine also requires the injured party to show that publicity is given to the individual's private affairs. The definition of publicity requires the communication of private information to more than a small group of persons—that is, to the public at large and, lastly, the information that is publicized is not of legitimate concern to the public. Thus, the Court expressly adopted the public disclosure privacy doctrine—the right to be free from public disclosure of embarrassing private facts. The Court's decision in *Industrial Foundation* relied on both the constitutional right to privacy and a tort doctrine, in this instance public disclosure.

An appellate court rejected a public disclosure claim against a newspaper citing press freedom in the 1992 case of *McNamara v. Freedom Newspapers, Inc.* The *Brownsville Herald* published a story about a high school soccer match. Accompanying the story was a photo of a McNamara, a student soccer player, with his genitals exposed as he ran full stride after the ball.[151] The court noted that the exposure was caused by McNamara's failure to wear an athletic supporter. McNamara sued the newspaper for invasion of privacy for intentional infliction of emotional distress because of the public disclosure of private facts, citing *Industrial Foundation*. The newspaper argued that the publication of the photo was protected by the First Amendment of the US Constitution and Article I, Section 8, of the Texas Constitution because it was taken at a public event.[152] The trial court ruled for the newspaper, and the court of appeals affirmed. McNamara appealed, arguing further that in addition to invading his privacy the newspaper violated laws promoting public decency. Writing for the majority, Justice Benavides reasoned that even though the news coverage may have been offensive to ordinary sensibilities, because it was a factually accurate depiction of a spectator sport in a public place and that the persons involved with the publication noticed that McNamara's genitals were exposed, he was precluded from recovering for damages for public disclosure of private facts. "[T]he First Amendment sometimes protects what would otherwise be an actionable invasion of privacy when a publication of the media in involved."[153]

The Texas Supreme Court again addressed the public disclosure privacy doctrine 1995 in *Star-Telegram, Inc. v. Doe*.[154] *Star-Telegram* weighed the freedom of the press against the individual's right to privacy, and, more specifically, whether a newspaper may be held liable for invasion of privacy after disclosing private facts about a victim of sexual assault.[155] The case originated when *The Fort Worth Star-Telegram* published a news article based on a police report for the crime.[156] The attack occurred in the victim's home in the darkness of the early morning. Doe was bound with strips of her bed sheets, but she freed herself and called the police. Police apprehended her assailant two days after the crime, driving the woman's car in Oklahoma. The news article did not name the victim, but it provided so much detail about her that it was almost impossible for acquaintances and neighbors not to know her identity.[157] The news report disclosed Doe's age, her neighborhood, the fact that she drove a Jaguar, and even the medication she took.[158] A second published story gave an account of her sexual assault and added that she owned a travel agency.[159] The "police beat" reporter for the newspaper obtained information about the crime from an unredacted police report at the Fort Worth Police Department.[160] Jane Doe sued the newspaper and Betsy Tong, the "police beat" reporter, for invasion of privacy and intentional and/or negligent infliction of emotional distress.[161] The newspaper responded that the information published was of legitimate public concern, citing the federal constitutional standard adopted by the US Supreme Court in *Florida Star v. B.J.F.*, which provides that "[i]f a newspaper lawfully obtains truthful information about a matter of public significance, then state officials may not constitutionally punish publication of the information absent a need to further a state interest of the highest order."[162] The *Florida Star* newspaper ran a similar story about a sexual assault victim based on an official police press report. However, the report identified B.J.F. by her full name, and made it available to reporters in the sheriff's department's press room. A reporter-trainee copied the police report verbatim, including B.J.F.'s full name, and ran the story in the paper contrary to state law which made it unlawful to publish the names of sexual assault victims. B.J.F. then won civil damages against the newspaper. The trial court denied the *Florida Star*'s claim that civil sanctions against the newspaper violated the First Amendment. The verdict was upheld on appeal. The US Supreme Court reversed, holding that imposing damages on the *Star* for publishing B.J.F.'s name violates the First Amendment.[163]

Returning to *Star-Telegram*, the trial court granted summary judgment in favor of the newspaper and reporter without specifying the grounds upon which judgment was based.[164] The Texas court of appeals reversed and remanded the case for the trial court to answer the question of whether the information had been lawfully obtained by the newspaper.[165] Even if the news articles contained information of legitimate public concern, the appeals court reasoned, the publications were not protected by the First Amendment because the information was unlawfully obtained. Oral argument before the Texas Supreme Court illustrated the fact that the justices all seemed reluctant to challenge the newspaper's assertion of press freedom. The Court then unanimously reversed the court of appeals and held that no privacy violation had occurred, since the public disclosure of private facts disclosed about Doe, a crime victim, were of legitimate public concern.[166]

Writing the opinion for the unanimous court, Justice Gammage began his analysis of the competing privacy rights versus freedom of expression claim by arguing that the right to be let alone "is as much a part of personal liberty as the right to be free from physical restraint and the right to possess property."[167] The concept has since been incorporated into a common law tort in Texas and serves to protect individuals from invasion of privacy.[168] However, Gammage concluded that *Star-Telegram*'s detailed account of Jane Doe did not violate her right to privacy. Newspapers should take precautions to avoid the public disclosure of private facts, and under Texas law the public has no legitimate interest in embarrassing facts about private citizens. A chilling effect on the freedom of press would occur if newspapers were required by law to take measures to avoid the publication of facts that may or may not subject innocent persons to unwanted or unpleasant notoriety.[169] Doe was correct in her argument that more personal information was published than was necessary in the name of a legitimate public interest in newsworthy information; however, the media should *not* be expected to comb through all of the facts and "catalogue each of them according to their individual and cumulative impact."[170]

Several of the justices in the *Star* decision were concerned that ruling for the newspaper might leave private citizens naked to media scrutiny simply because they are involved in a newsworthy event of legitimate public concern. If death penalty protesters incite a small riot in front of a courthouse and a well-known attorney is inadvertently assaulted on the way to their car, does the media have the right to publish personal information about the lawyer? Gammage suggested that this question must be answered on a case-by-case basis. The determination of whether privacy can be sacrificed in the name of newsworthiness must be made "in the context of each particular case, considering the nature of the information and the public's legitimate interest in its disclosure."[171]

Can an injured party recover for negligent invasion of privacy, or must the breach be intentional act? The caselaw shows that negligent invasion of privacy is not a settled matter. The authoritative Texas precedent rejecting negligence as a cause of action for privacy torts remains *Billings v. Atkinson*, with its firm declaration that negligence does not apply to privacy. A 2001 public disclosure case, *Doe v. Mobile Video Tapes*,[172] revisited the question of whether a person can recover for negligent invasion of privacy for public disclosure. The case originated when an anonymous person delivered several video tapes found in a dumpster to a local television station. These tapes contained recordings made by a local high school band director using a video camera hidden in the girls' locker room. The band director had placed the camera there ostensibly for security reasons, as someone was stealing belongings from the locker room. After discovering that the thief was actually the assistant band director, he presumably discarded the tapes in the dumpster, leaving them to be found soon thereafter. The television station aired distorted parts of this footage the next day, reusing it in subsequent broadcasts after the band officials were fired and under investigation by the district attorney. The parents of the students on the videotape sued the station, claiming that the station negligently invaded their privacy by publicly disclosing private facts and causing intentional infliction of emotional distress. A trial court ruled in favor of the television station, but a portion of the original group of plaintiffs chose to appeal. One of their claims detailed an error made by the trial court, in refusing to submit a jury question on the subject of negligent invasion of privacy. They argued that if libel actions can be based on negligent conduct by the tortfeasor[173] so too should invasion of privacy tort actions.[174]

The Court of Appeals (Corpus Christi) rejected the concept of negligent invasion of privacy, deciding to adhere to *Billings v. Atkinson* by stating, "Invasion of privacy is an intentional tort."[175] Writing for the majority, Justice Hinojosa rejected appellants' claims that if libel can be negligent[176] so too should invasion of privacy tort actions. The appellants argued that Texas courts had recognized a negligent standard of invasion of privacy,[177] but Justice Hinojosa responded to their argument by citing caselaw from the previous decade rejecting negligent invasion of privacy, including *Dallas County v. Harper*,[178] *Fulmer v. Rider*,[179] and *Childers v. A.S.*[180] Hinojosa used the principle that negligent standards of recovery should not be applicable to scenarios of intentional action. He wrote:

> Although some courts in Texas recognize negligent invasion of privacy, we decline to adopt a negligent invasion of privacy cause of action. We agree with the Fort Worth Court of Appeals that invasion of privacy has been recognized as an intentional tort and "appellant should not be able to recover for intentional conduct under a negligence theory."[181]

In *Comptroller v. Attorney General*[182] in 2010 the Supreme Court of Texas again attempted to clarify boundaries between the media's freedom of the press and the privacy of persons. The Texas Comptroller of Public Accounts, Susan Combs, was approached by the *Dallas Morning News* requesting that highly personal information about public officials be made available to the newspaper under the Texas Public Information Act (PIA).[183] The newspaper sought access to this information in the claimed interest of detecting potential corruption in state government. The decision used a balancing test, with the public interest in the information pitted against the officials' right to privacy.

The PIA is intended to shed light on the inner workings of government, while ensuring that doing so is within the bounds of protection by state privacy doctrines, in particular the doctrine of public disclosure of private facts. Under the PIA, any citizen may request that information created or assembled by a government agency be made available to them. The law ensures that confidential information and information in a personnel file that would, upon disclosure, be a "clearly unwarranted" invasion of privacy and are therefore exempt from disclosure. If the governmental body believes the requested information to be excepted from disclosure, they may seek a ruling from the Office of the Attorney General. In this case, the information requested included the dates of birth of governmental employees, which then-Comptroller Susan Combs believed to be exempt from disclosure.[184] After the Office of the Attorney General issued a decision favoring the news outlet, Combs sued for declaratory relief against then-Attorney General Greg Abbott. The district court held for the newspaper that disclosure of date of birth information was not an invasion of privacy, which was affirmed by the appellate court. The Texas Supreme Court also used the findings of the appellate court to assert that the tests to determine confidential information and information whose disclosure would invade an individual's right to privacy were fundamentally equivalent to the test for invasion defined by *Industrial Foundation.* Applying this test would allow the court to analyze the issue under Texas's common law privacy doctrines, as opposed to the shallower statutory protections. As such, the case evolved from a statutory interpretation case into one involving the issue of competing rights: those of the privacy of individuals whose information would be disclosed against the public's right to view government information.

Writing for the Court, Chief Justice Wallace Jefferson analyzed the competing rights claim by arguing that the public interest (and therefore the media's right to access the information) in the birth dates was minimal in this case, as the newspaper admitted it would not disclose this information to the public and would only use it behind the scenes to look into the state's hiring practices and other statistics. However, after information is disclosed once under the PIA, it must be disclosed at any time to any member of the public who requests it, including anyone who could potentially use this information to harm the individuals to whom the information belongs. According to Chief Justice Jefferson, the disclosure of birth dates was inconsistent with the intentions of the PIA:

> Employee birth dates shed little light on government actions. The *News* points out that the public has an interest in monitoring the government, and birth dates

> could be used to determine whether governmental entities like school districts and hospitals have hired convicted felons or sex offenders. But when a protected privacy interest is at stake, the requestor must identify a sufficient reason for the disclosure; mere allegations of the possibility of wrongdoing are not enough.[185]

In other words, the Court believed that the newspaper's justification did not warrant the release of data. Potentially, if the newspaper were conducting a specific investigation of a matter of significant public interest and requested the birth dates of certain officials, this may have played out differently. The most important caveat of this decision is the Chief Justice's assertion that "[a]n individual's interest in controlling the dissemination of information regarding personal matters does not dissolve simply because that information may be available to the public in some form."[186] The government employee's right to privacy is not voided simply because their birth date can be found from other public sources. As such, the information is indeed exempt from disclosure under PIA.

In 2011 the Texas Supreme Court declined to expand common law and constitutional exceptions to mandatory disclosure under the PIA. *Industrial Foundation* held that information is protected from disclosure under the PIA if (1) the information contains highly intimate or embarrassing facts the publication of which would be highly objectionable to a reasonable person, and (2) the information is not of legitimate concern to the public. The *Austin American-Stateman* and other newspapers filed suit against the Department of Public Safety seeking access to information relating to travel outside of the state by Governor Rick Perry. The Department of Public Safety argued that the information was confidential due to the common law right to privacy. If such information were to be released to the newspapers, the Department of Public Safety argued, there would be a possibility of an imminent threat to the governor. Since the information did not contain highly intimate or embarrassing facts, the common law right to privacy does not apply to the governor's travel information.[187] The Texas Supreme Court has ruled that in some instances there is a common law right to privacy that protects against PIA disclosure, as in the case of withholding the identity of a pharmacy that supplied lethal injection drugs used for an execution.[188] Citing *Cox* and *Industrial Foundation*, the Court argued that disclosing the pharmacy's identity would create a substantial threat of physical harm to the source's employees and others. The Court argued:

> Relevant to our discussion here is the common law interest in freedom from physical harm, which extends to every person. ("Freedom from physical harm is . . . a hallmark of our common law.") This common law exception to the PIA's

disclosure requirements as recognized in *Cox* makes information confidential when disclosure would create a substantial threat of physical harm.[189]

Appropriation Privacy Doctrine

Appropriation of name or likeness applies to the unauthorized use of a person's name, image, notoriety, or prestige for commercial gain. As discussed in chapter 1, the doctrine of appropriation was adopted as early as the late nineteenth century in cases involving the unauthorized use of names for the purpose of commercial gain. The doctrine of appropriation differs from the other three privacy doctrines in that it deals with the proprietary nature of the tortious action.[190] In other words, one has a privacy interest in one's name or likeness and invasion of that privacy occurs when that name or likeness and is used without consent for commercial or pecuniary gain. Early cases involve an unauthorized use of the plaintiff's name and photograph for the purpose of selling a product or service,[191] the publication of an image without consent in an advertisement,[192] and use of a person's notoriety or prestige without permission. It is not merely the plaintiff's name that is at issue here, but a symbol of a person's identity.[193]

Texas recognizes the appropriation dimension of privacy through the adoption of the Restatement (Second) of Torts,[194] which states that "One who appropriates to his own use or benefit the name or likeness of another is subject to liability for invasion of privacy." To recovery for "misappropriation" a plaintiff must prove the existence of three elements: (1) unauthorized appropriation of the plaintiffs' name or likeness occurred because of the value association with it, (2) the plaintiff can be clearly identified from the publication, and (3) the defendant received some pecuniary advantage or benefit from the misappropriation. In many appropriation cases, a plaintiff's identity is used for some form of commercial gain, whether to obtain credit, promote or publicize a product, or secure personal information. It is not merely one's name that is at issue here, but also control of one's name as a symbol of identity.[195]

Recall that in a prominent pre-*Billings* Texas court of appeals ruling—*U.S. Life Insurance Co. v. Hamilton*[196]—the court refused to recognize the right to privacy as a cause of action in a case alleging that a plaintiff's signature was appropriated by the defendant in the promotion of his business. Justice Hale writing for the majority in *Hamilton* clearly acknowledged that invasion of privacy for the commercial appropriation of Hamilton's signature was a cause of action recognized in other states, but instead ruled that in Texas the unauthorized use of a signature of a well-respected person such as Hamilton was a violation of the property or ownership right in his signature and reputation, not an intrusion upon his privacy. Hale's characterization of Hamilton's signature and reputation as a property right is arguably an implicit recognition of a right of publicity—the right to one's identity free from unauthorized commercial exploitation. Also, as we discussed in *Billings*, the court adopted a broad definition of privacy, encompassing intrusion (the eavesdropping on Mr. Billings), public disclosure of personal information, and what Justice Denton called the "unwarranted appropriation or exploitation of one's personality."

The appropriation doctrine was adopted for the first time by a Texas court in *Kimbrough v. Coca-Cola/USA*,[197] two years after the recognition of the right to privacy in *Billings*. A former Texas A&M University football legend named Kimbrough learned from his daughter who attended a football game that the Coca-Cola company had used his name and likeness in an advertisement that appeared in a college football programs. Coca-Cola made requests of various colleges in the Southwest Conference to name outstanding former football players. Paintings or illustrations depicting each player would be sent to players, schools, and to a Texas Sports Hall of Fame. They would also be used in advertisements in football game programs. Kimbrough sought recovery from Coca-Cola for invasion of privacy, violation of proprietary right, fraud, and misrepresentation, among other theories. Coca-Cola denied Kimbrough's charges, arguing that he had consented to the use of his image, that nothing in the publication was offensive or defamatory, and that the football star was a public figure, citing *O'Brien v. Pabst Sales Co.*, a case the denied relief to a famous "public person" whose name was used with a beer advertisement.[198] The question in *Kimbrough* was whether a public figure in Texas can bring a legal action for the unauthorized use of his name or likeness for commercial gain. The Court of Civil Appeals (Eastland) found that while no Texas case directly provides relief in Kimbrough's case, the court, relying on what it believed to be a broad right to privacy found in *Billings*, argued that unauthorized use of his name or likeness for commercial gain is justiciable in Texas. Writing for the court, Justice Brown stated first that that courts in other states had adopted the appropriation doctrine as a privacy doctrine[199] and second that although a public person like Mr. Kimbrough may be considered newsworthy there is no automatic right to commercialize his likeness or personality in a way that is distinct from regular news coverage or the dissemination of information to the public.[200] Further, the court cited the *Billings* precedent, pointing out that in recognizing the right to privacy for the first time the Texas high court had cited a New Jersey Supreme Court's decision in an action involving the appropriation doctrine as one part of a broad definition of privacy in a case involving famous professional golfers, including Arnold Palmer, Jack Nicklaus, and Gary Player.[201]

Although Kimbrough was a legendary public figure and was aware of Coca-Cola's paintings and advertisements, Coca-Cola did not meet the burden of proving that it had Kimbrough's explicit consent to publish the photographs for the purpose of an advertising campaign. In the end, although the court of appeals did not reach a conclusion as to whether the right articulated in *Billings* recognized the doctrine of appropriation specifically, it held that the definition of privacy in *Billings* was broad enough to support a cause of action for appropriation of name or likeness under Texas common law. Brown argued that "the invasion of that right [privacy] gives rise to a cause of action"[202] and that:

> We hold that Kimbrough has pleaded a cause of action for the unauthorized appropriation or exploitation of his name and likeness by the defendants and such cause is justiciable in Texas.[203]

Even the most famous people in society have a privacy right against the unauthorized commercial appropriation of their names and images. However, it is important to note that in order to pursue a successful misappropriation claim a person need not be a celebrity or even known to the public at large or some segment of the public as long as it is proved that the wrongly appropriated likeness was of value or benefited the person who appropriated it. *Topheavy Studios, Inc. v. Doe*[204] is an oft-cited 2005 case involving the unauthorized use of a photo of an anonymous woman (Doe) in a computer trivia game. The object of the "Guy Game" was to "win" glimpses of women in various stages of undress by answering a series of trivia questions. To that end, Doe was recruited by the video game company for the purpose of photographing her with her consent during spring break reveries at South Padre Island. After learning from her brother that she appeared topless in the game, several months after its release, Doe sued Topheavy for invasion of privacy based on the appropriation doctrine. Topheavy's defense was that because Doe completed a release form before photos were taken and that the photos were taken in public place[205] she could not recover for an invasion of privacy. The trial court issued an injunction against Topheavy and the Court of Appeals (Austin) ruled in her favor, stating that the defendant's actions constituted an invasion of privacy by misappropriation of her likeness to use in the game and the advertisement of the game. The court upheld the trial court's injunction against the video game company,[206] arguing that Doe provided sufficient evidence regarding the recognized elements of invasion of privacy by misappropriation in Texas precedent.[207] The court wrote that "[l]iability for such an invasion of privacy will arise if the defendant appropriates, for their own benefit, the commercial standing, reputation, or other values associated with the plaintiff's likeness."[208]

The significance of the *Topheavy* ruling, beyond the fact that the court did not question or disturb existing privacy precedent, was that the appropriation doctrine was extended to an average person whose name and likeness, in any other context, had no commercial value to the person or persons misappropriating the name or likeness. Doe was not famous or well-known by any means, just a face in the crowd, if you will. Topheavy did not recruit her to pose for the photo because she was a well-known person or a sports figure or a prominent businessperson. Her name, likeness, or reputation had no known commercial value—she was merely an anonymous person whose image appeared in a video game marketed toward a male audience. Unlike most appropriation cases, the challenge was to ascertain why Doe's image had value other than the fact that she was deemed attractive and was naked from the waist up. The case is atypical in this regard. Doe was able to prevail because her misappropriated image had value associated with it, although, oddly, the court did not explain what that value was.[209]

Although this book focuses on cases decided by state courts in Texas, many appropriation opinions cite or rely on rulings from the federal Fifth Circuit Court of Appeals, particularly those rulings that speak to the question of what the guiding precedent is in Texas. For example, an oft-cited case is *Meadows v. Hartford Life Ins. Co.* (2007) which held that Texas courts rely on the Restatement of Torts as the "definitive source of guidance in cases involving invasion of the right of privacy."[210] According to the Restatement, "One who appropriates to his own use or benefit the name or likeness of another is subject to liability for invasion of his privacy."[211] However, in *Meadows* the court ruled against the plaintiff's right of publicity claim because the use of Meadows's name was of "incidental" commercial benefit to the insurance company.[212] Meadows, a former employee of the Camelot Music company, learned that without his authorization Camelot had purchased a life insurance policy for him (as well as for over a thousand employees) naming Camelot as beneficiary. To purchase the policy Camelot used Meadows's personal information, such as name, date of birth, and social security number. Since Camelot would have benefited financially in the event of Meadows's death, he claimed that both his employer and the insurance company misappropriated his name and identity for commercial gain. The Fifth Circuit rejected his claim, arguing that to recover under the tort of misappropriation Meadows would need to show "excessive exploitation" of this information that results in a diminution of the value of his identity.[213] Thus, in order to recover a plaintiff would need to show that the defendant appropriated the name or likeness for its commercial value and not for "incidental use."[214]

As appropriation caselaw evolved over time, some Texas courts began to adopt the term misappropriation,[215] which is the act of wrongly appropriating, rather than appropriation. To establish liability under this tort, a plaintiff must show that (1) their name is clearly identifiable; (2) was appropriated to benefit the reputation, prestige, social or commercial standing of the defendant; and (3) was not in an incidental manner or for a newsworthy purpose.[216] Texas courts recognize name misappropriation as a "species of invasion of privacy" but interpret the tort narrowly.[217] Protection is not extended to a name by itself but "the value associated with it."[218] To establish liability for misappropriation of name, a plaintiff bears the burden of showing that the defendant benefits from the reputation, prestige, or social or commercial interest associated with the plaintiff's name.[219] The courts have consistently reaffirmed precedent holding that name misappropriation is a species of invasion of privacy in Texas.[220]

A decade would pass before a Texas appellate court handed down a full opinion in another major appropriation case. In *Watson v. Talia Heights*[221] in 2018 the Court of Appeals (Houston) found that a real estate development company's use of a well-known investor's name without his knowledge or consent did not amount to an invasion of privacy under the appropriation doctrine. Watson, the investor, claimed that the developer used his name as a prominent buyer of the properties in order to secure a higher price in the transaction. Citing the elements for a misappropriation claim in *Express One Int'l, Inc. v. Steinbeck*[222] and reiterating the established fact that in that case Texas law applies a very restrictive interpretation of the appropriation tort and that, according to the court, Watson did not provide sufficient proof that his name was misappropriated for the value associated with it, or to exploit his reputation, prestige, or other value associated with his name. The caselaw does not protect a name per se but the value associated with it. His name was merely placed on a list of investors; its inclusion on a list of buyers had nothing to do with his unique skills or reputation. Other investors placed on the list had almost identical qualifications. Watson asserted that Talia's profits resulted from the misappropriation of his name.

Another 2018 appropriation case, *Doggett v. Travis Law Firm*,[223] originated when two lawyers, Travis and Hammond, agreed to form a working relationship and change the name of Travis's firm to Travis & Hammond, PC. The nature of the relationship was unclear and subject to dispute. Hammond claimed that he was a partner, but Travis maintained that Hammond was only a contract employee. A third lawyer, Doggett, claimed that he was hired in an "of counsel" capacity, although Travis denied Doggett's status as such. When a client that Doggett was representing while working for the firm sued Doggett and the Travis Law Firm for legal malpractice, the Travis Law Firm then sued Doggett, alleging invasion of privacy by appropriation of name or likeness because Doggett, in seeking and representing clients, used Travis Law Firm's name or likeness for the value associated with it. The jury agreed that Travis Law Firm suffered an injury as a result of Doggett's misappropriation and awarded the firm damages. The Court of Appeals (Houston) reversed, arguing that the Travis Law Firm could not recover damages for invasion of privacy by appropriation because corporations are not protected by the right to privacy.[224]

The tort doctrine of appropriation provides the means by which an injured party to recover damages for invasion of privacy if their name or likeness is misappropriated. Arising from this body of law is the right to publicity, adopted in federal suits brought in Texas. How is this right related to appropriation? A discussion of the right to publicity goes beyond the scope of this book—and enters the realm of federal case law and state statutory protections—but it is useful to offer a few thoughts on the subject. A 1953 federal appeals court case, *Haelan Laboratories v. Topps Chewing Gum*, adopted the term "right to publicity" to define as the right of persons to control the use of their name or likenesses from misappropriation for commercial gain or other value. Federal claims have from time to time used this term in appropriation/misappropriation cases. How appropriation differs from the right of publicity is opaque. A review of the caselaw found that in some instances the right of publicity exists as an offshoot of the doctrine of appropriation; in other instances, the terms are used synonymously or interchangeably.[225] To appropriate a person's name or likeness for commercial gain robs a person of their right to publicity, which is defined as a loss of control over one's name or reputation. Right to publicity cases involve persons whose identity is of greater commercial value because of their fame or celebrity. The cause of action in right of publicity cases is similar to appropriation. For example, if a business decides to use the image or identity of a famous person, either living or deceased, said business must first obtain permission from the current owner of that person's right of publicity. A defense against misappropriation or the right to publicly claim might be that the reporting on a person or event involving that person that is considered to be newsworthy, protected by the First Amendment. Courts have been reluctant to find defendants liable in right of publicity lawsuits if the noteworthy person's identity is appropriated for use in newspapers, magazines, articles, and online forums and blogs.

In contrast to a common law right of publicity, the statutory right of publicity in Texas extends beyond the grave through a postmortem state statutory right.[226] The postmortem right of publicity protects a property right in a deceased person's name, voice, signature, photograph, or likeness for fifty years after that person has died.[227] The right is transferable under the property code before or after death by a will, trust, testamentary document, or contract.[228] Known as the "Buddy Holly Bill," this statute protects a person's name, voice, signature, photograph, or likeness. As with the common law right of publicity, the statute allows for a "newsworthiness" defense against misappropriation if that person that is considered to be newsworthy or appears in an original work of art or music.[229]

False Light Privacy Doctrine

The "false light" invasion of privacy doctrine involves communicating information that portrays an individual to the public in a false and offensive manner. It unreasonably places a person in a false light before the public. To be subject to liability for invasion of privacy under this doctrine, the plaintiff must show that the false information is highly offensive to a reasonable person and that the defendant acted recklessly.[230] False light doctrine is different from the tort of public disclosure because it requires some element of untruth, whereas the public disclosure doctrine is applicable regardless of whether the information is true or false. *Gill v. Snow* in 1982 was the first false light invasion of privacy case heard by a Texas appellate court.[231] H. D. Snow and H. C. Gill owned adjoining ranch property along Fossil Creek in Haltom City, Texas. After Snow made modifications to his property, the creek flooded Gill's land. Snow attempted to address the flooding problem, but not to Gill's satisfaction. Gill then took out a full-page advertisement in the local newspaper that included a copy of a letter that was sent to Snow by the Texas Water Development Board and language in the advertisement that suggested Snow was complicit with the mayor, city council, and other "privileged" people in town. Snow then sued Gill and the owners of the newspaper for invasion of privacy based on the four invasion of privacy doctrines: intrusion, appropriation, public disclosure, and false light.[232] On appeal, addressing Snow's allegation that Gill placed Snow in a false light, the Court of Appeals (Fort Worth) considered Snow's false light claim as legitimate but reversed the trial court's finding for Snow on the grounds that in this instance no false statements were ever publicized; the information contained in the advertisement was obtained from the public record and there was no evidence of false statements proved at trial. The court of appeals considered Snow's claim to be legitimate, but at the same time recognized that there were no prior false light cases in Texas.

The Texas Supreme Court heard an appeal involving a false light claim for the first time in *Diamond Shamrock Refining v. Mendez* in 1992. A fired refinery employee brought an action against his former employer alleging, among his numerous injuries, false light invasion of privacy caused by the circulation of information regarding his termination for theft of a five dollar box of nails from a refinery construction site.[233] Recall that the false light doctrine involves the communication of information that portrays individual to the public in a false and offensive manner.[234] Information that distorts, exaggerates, or fictionalizes one or more facets of a person's life can be humiliating, disturbing, or harmful to one's reputation. Although Mendez was guilty of taking a box of nails off company property in his lunch box, exaggerated accounts of the nature of the theft and gossip about his termination spread like wildfire. Before long, his reputation was that of a dishonest man. Even several potential employers learned about his termination from the refinery. Mendez argued that the refinery publicized a private matter which placed him in a false light before the public in a manner that would be highly offensive to the reasonable person. The trial court ruled in his favor on the basis of both false light and intentional infliction of emotional distress and awarded damages. The court of appeals affirmed, holding that all one needed to prevail in a false light case was to show negligence rather than actual malice as in defamation cases. However, a divided Texas Supreme Court reversed both the trial court and appeals court decisions, arguing that although false light is one of the four categories of tort action for invasion of privacy, the high court has never ruled that the tort exists in Texas. The aggrieved employee's case was then remanded for a new trial without the Supreme Court deciding whether the tort exists and whether it should be applied in the new trial.[235]

Writing for the majority, Chief Justice Thomas Phillips stated that while false light had been recognized by a number of courts of appeal in the state, the majority of justices in *Diamond Shamrock* were simply not inclined to do so. The court clearly affirmed its support for the right to privacy established in *Billings* (invasion) and in *Industrial Foundation* (public disclosure) but clearly stated that it had never adopted, *nor would it adopt*, the false light doctrine.[236] Phillips wrote:

> This court has never expressly held that a tort for false light invasion of privacy exists in Texas, although we recognized that it is one of the four usual categories of private actions for invasion of privacy. . . . Even assuming the availability of this cause of action, however, Mendez would not be entitled to recover on the record before us, as he did not submit all the essential elements of false light.[237]

Hypothetically, following the Court's logic, if the false light privacy tort did exist in Texas, it would require the plaintiff to show actual malice to recover damages. Mendez was not given an opportunity to show actual malice during his first trial.

Justice Hightower concurred but wrote separately to "express [his] continuing support for the right to privacy under the Texas Constitution."[238] Justice Gonzales wrote separately to reject the false light invasion of privacy outright because it duplicates the tort of defamation.[239] In an angry dissent, Justice Doggett believed that the court's ruling was an assault not only on the false light doctrine—which he believed to be well-established law in the state and now subject to reversal by the majority—but on the right to privacy itself. He wrote that "[n]umerous Texas courts of appeals, following our decisions in *Billings* and *Industrial Foundation*, have applied or recognized the false light cause of action."[240]

A question related to false light is whether recovery for damages requires the injured party to show actual malice, or merely negligence. In practical terms, the adoption of the doctrine suggests that the Court would allow for a range of lawsuits by injured persons by providing them with a new legal remedy. An amicus brief submitted jointly in this case by "Reporters Committee for Freedom of the Press," the A.H. Belo Corporation, the National Association of Broadcasters, the Houston Chronicle Publishing Company, and others, categorically stated that the media, both print and electronic, oppose the adoption of the false light doctrine for fear of its impact on press freedom or profit or some combination of the two.[241]

In 1994 the Texas Supreme Court sealed the fate of false light invasion in Texas by again expressly rejecting the doctrine as an independent privacy tort. In *Cain v. Hearst Corporation*, the justices stressed that false light is unnecessary and dangerous because it "substantially duplicates the tort of defamation."[242] In *Cain*, a prison inmate sued the Hearst Corporation, claiming that the *Houston Chronicle* invaded his privacy by placing him in a false light.[243] The newspaper article stated that he had killed as many as eight people, but Cain complained only about his depiction as a member of the "Dixie Mafia."[244] In rejecting Cain's claim, the five-to-four narrow majority produced an impressive exegesis of the right to privacy, detailing the four privacy torts. The majority explained that even in light of several federal court rulings that permitted causes of action for false light invasion to be brought in Texas law, the Texas Supreme Court was unwilling to adopt the "least-recognized and most controversial aspect of invasion of privacy." Justice Raul Gonzales wrote:

> We reject the false light invasion of privacy tort for two reasons: 1) it largely duplicates other rights of recovery, particularly defamation; and 2) it lacks many of the procedural limitation that accompany actions for defamation, thus unacceptably increasing the tension that already exists between free speech guarantees and tort law.[245]

In his dissenting opinion,[246] Justice Hightower disputed the majority's argument that "false light unduly increases the tensions between tort law and free speech law."[247] The two torts are intended to protect different interests, Hightower argued: "Defamation preserves individuals' reputational interests, but false light invasion of privacy extends to what people know and believe about them."[248]

When the news media obtains information about a crime or other event that is in the public's interest, freedom of the press must be weighed against the privacy of the individual such as crime victims or anyone who might be harmed by the disclosure of private facts. Privacy actions are often brought against the media for invasion of privacy, but they rarely prevail. If a news organization is held liable and punished for publishing the name or other personal information of a victim, then a chill on speech would occur giving pause to other news outlets for fear of litigation. Self-censorship would occur, leaving the news media unable or unwilling to play its pivotal role in a democratic society.

False light requires widespread publicity of false information. For example, a newspaper article that maliciously and falsely reports that a person suffers from a deadly contagious disease would not be defamatory but could depict that person in a false light so that their friends and co-workers would avoid her like the plague. She might lose her job or clients based on this false information. However, arguably, the fact that some overlap of false light and defamation occurs does not mean that the court should not recognize both torts.[249] The nature of the false light doctrine has the potential to address harms caused by irresponsible or reckless posts on social media platforms. On the matter of self-censorship on the part of the media because of the possibility of a successful false light claim, the requirement that the injured party show actual malice safeguards press freedoms.

This chapter examined select cases from a large corpus of privacy caselaw in Texas that spanned a period of more than five decades (1973–2023). The intent was to understand the origins and development of the right to privacy from at a time when the state's courts had not yet recognized either common law tort doctrines or constitutional provisions that allow recovery for intrusion into the private affairs of individuals and culminating with the adoption of a robust right to privacy in groundbreaking cases. The foundational discussion of the common law origins of the major doctrines in chapter 1 illustrates that many states adopted the right to privacy as early as 1900, over seventy years before Texas recognized privacy as an independent right. Texas did not create the right to privacy from whole cloth—the judicial decisions of other states, as well as the writings of Warren and Brandeis and William Prosser, influenced the development of privacy law in Texas. In early cases, judicial opinions in Texas acknowledged the importance of privacy doctrines but were highly resistant to the idea of a right to privacy or any form of innovation in a traditionalist legal culture. It was the consensus of judges at the time that because common law in the state is a fixed body of law that can only be changed by the legislature, no recovery for invasion of privacy is possible.[250] However, in 1973 in *Billings v. Atkinson* and *TSEU* in 1987, the Texas Supreme Court recognized a right to privacy distinctive in itself and not merely incidental to some other right or doctrine. Lastly, it is important to note that Texas state privacy caselaw developed independently of the privacy decisions of the US Supreme Court.

NOTES

1. *Billings v. Atkinson*, 489 S.W. 2d 858 (Tex. 1973).
2. *U.S. Life Insurance Co. v. Hamilton*, 238 S.W. 2d 289 (Tex. Civ. App. – Waco 1951, writ ref'd n.r.e.).
3. Ibid.
4. 249 S.W. 2d 277 (Tex. Civ. App. – Dallas 1952, no writ).
5. *Milner v. Red River Publishing*, 249 S.W.2d 227,229 (Tex. Civ. App. 1952).
6. Ibid.
7. Ibid, 228.
8. Ibid, 229.
9. Ibid.
10. Ibid.
11. *Hansson v. Harris*, 252 S.W.2d 600 (1952).
12. Ibid, 601.
13. Ibid.
14. Ibid, 603.
15. See generally *Meadows v. First National Bank of Harlingen*, 149 S.W. 2d 591 (1941).
16. *Billings v. Atkinson*, 489 S.W. 2d 858, 861 (Tex. 1973).
17. At the time of Billings, the Court of Appeals was then known as the Court of Civil Appeals.
18. Ibid (citing *Milner v. Red River Publishing Company*, 249 S.W. 2d 227 (Tex. Civ. App. – Dallas 1952, no writ)).
19. Ibid, 860–61.
20. Ibid, 859–60.
21. Samuel D. Warren and Louis D. Brandeis, "The right to privacy," *Harvard Law Review*, 4 (1890): 193. Warren and Brandeis's article is the most well-known and oft-cited law review article in American legal history. The article can be found by searching most law content or social science databases; or see Samuel D. Warren and Louis D. Brandeis, *The Right to Privacy*, with a forward by Steven Alan Childress (New Orleans: Quid Pro Articles), *Legal Legends Series* (2010).
22. *Billings*, 489 S.W.2d at 860.
23. Ibid, 860.
24. Ibid.
25. Ibid.
26. Ibid, 859.
27. 746 S.W.2d 203 (1987).
28. Ibid, 204.
29. Texas Constitution, article 1, section 19.
30. Texas Constitution, article 1, section 8.
31. Texas Constitution, article 1, section 10.
32. Texas Constitution, article 1, sections 9 and 25.
33. Texas Constitution, article 6.
34. *Industrial Foundation*, 540 S.W.2d at 205.

35. Ibid, 206.
36. *Billings v. Atkinson*, 489 S.W. 2d 858, 861 (Tex. 1973).
37. *Colquette v. Forbes*, 680 S.W.2d. 536 (Tex. App.—Austin 1984, no writ).
38. Ibid, 537–38.
39. Ibid, 537.
40. Ibid, 537–38.
41. Ibid, 538.
42. Id Ibid, 538–39 (citing *Griswold v. Connecticut*, 381 U.S. 479 (1965)).
43. Ibid, 539.
44. Ibid,
45. See John C. Domino, *Texas Supreme Court Justice Bob Gammage: A Jurisprudence of Rights and Liberties* (Lexington Press 2019).
46. Ibid.
47. Ibid.
48. Ibid.
49. Ibid.
50. https://capitol.texas.gov/tlodocs/87R/billtext/html/SB00008F.HTM.
51. Ibid (discussing *Shelley v. Kraemer*, 334 U.S. 1 (1948)).
52. *Shelley*, 334 U.S. at 23.
53. See generally *Colquette*, 680 S.W.2d at 539.
54. Ibid.
55. Ibid, 537.
56. Ibid, 539.
57. See generally *Billings v. Atkinson*, 489 S.W. 2d 858, 859 (Tex. 1973) (recognizing that an invasion of privacy is a legal injury).
58. *City of Sherman v. Henry*, 928 S.W.2d 464 (Tex. 1996); *Texas State Employees Union v. Texas Dept. of Mental Health and Mental Retardation*, 746 S.W.2d 203 (Tex. 1987); In re H.E.B. Grocery Co., L.P., 2014 WL 700749 (Tex. App. Corpus Christi 2014).
59. See Elizabeth J. Hall, "Protecting California's abortion clinic workers from harassment and violence," *McGeorge Law Review*, 36 (2005): 797, 797, 800, 802; see also *Valenzuela*, 853 S.W.2d at 521.
60. *Valenzuela*, 853 S.W.2d at 512.
61. Ibid, 513.
62. Ibid,520–21.
63. Ibid,521.
64. Ibid, n.2.
65. Ibid, 521.
66. Ibid.
67. Ibid.
68. Ibid.
69. Ibid, n.3. The temporary injunction was subsequently dissolved for being overly broad; see *Valenzuela v. Aquino*, 763 S.W.2d 43, 45–46 (Tex. App.—Corpus Christi 1988, no writ).
70. *Valenzuela*, 853 S.W.2d at 521 (Spector, J., dissenting).

71. Ibid, 522.

72. *Valenzuela v. Aquino*, 800 S.W.2d 301, 305 (Tex. App.—Corpus Christi 1990) *aff'd in part, rev'd in part*, 853 S.W.2d 512 (Tex. 1993).

73. Ibid, 309. Justice Gonzalez, in agreeing with the court of appeals' reversal, stated that "[t]he uncertainty of not knowing where one might be penalized for expressive speech would have an unacceptable *chilling effect* on the right of free speech." *Valenzuela*, 853 S.W.2d at 519 (Gonzalez, J., dissenting) (emphasis added).

74. *Valenzuela*, 853 S.W.2d at 517 (Gonzalez, J., dissenting) (discussing *Frisby*, 487 U.S. at 486).

75. See *Valenzuela*, 853 S.W.2d at 514 (majority opinion) (affirming the court of appeals' judgment "insofar as it sets aside the trial court's award of damages, and revers[ing] in all other respects").

76. See Ibid, 513 (quoting Restatement (second) of Torts § 652B (1977)). In discussing the two elements for an invasion of privacy cause of action, the Texas Supreme Court noted that Aquino failed to request that *either* element be submitted to the jury; furthermore, the evidence presented failed to conclusively establish either element.

77. Ibid, n.1.

78. Ibid.

79. *Frisby v. Schultz*, 487 U.S. 474 (1987).

80. Ibid, 519–20 (Gammage, J., dissenting) ("[e]very person shall be at liberty to speak, write or publish his opinions on any subject, *being responsible for the abuse of that privilege*" (emphasis in original) (quoting Texas Constitution, article I, section 8)) (citing *Hustler Magazine, Inc. v. Falwell*, 485 U.S. 46, 56–57 (1988); United States v. O'Brien, 391 U.S. 367, 382 (1968)).

81. *Valenzuela*, 853 S.W.2d at 520 (Gammage, J., dissenting) (citing *Casso v. Brand*, 776 S.W.2d 551, 556 (Tex. 1989)).

82. Ibid (citing *James v. Brown*, 637 S.W.2d 914, 917 (Tex. 1982)).

83. Ibid, 519.

84. Ibid, 522 (Spector, J., dissenting).

85. Ibid, 520.

86. Ibid, 522 (citations omitted).

87. Ibid, 523 (citing *Frisby v. Schultz*, 487 U.S. 474, 486–87 (1987)).

88. Ibid, (quoting *Billings v. Atkinson*, 489 S.W.2d 858, 859 (Tex. 1973)).

89. Ibid (citing *Texas State Employees Union v. Tex. Department of Mental Health & Mental Retardation*, 746 S.W.2d 203, 205 (Tex. 1987)).

90. Ibid (citing *Iken v. Olenick*, 42 Tex. 195, 198 (1874)).

91. Ibid, 524–25 (quoting David A. Grimes, "Clinicians who provide abortions: The thinning ranks," *Obstetrics & Gynecology*, 80 (1992): 719, 721–22); see *also* Angela Christina Couch, "Wanted: Privacy protection for doctors who perform abortions," *American University Journal of Gender and Law*, 4 (1996): 361, 361–62, for a scholarly account written at the time of the case.

92. *Valenzuela*, 853 S.W.2d at 525 (Spector, J., dissenting).

93. See *Operation Rescue-National v. Planned Parenthood of Houston and Southeast Texas, Inc.*, 975 S.W. 2d 546 (1998) and Ex parte Tucci, 859 S.W. 2d 1 (1993).

94. See Peggy Fikac, "Privacy rights don't protect adultery, court rules," *Austin American-Statesman*, July 9, 1996.

95. *City of Sherman v. Henry*, 928 S.W.2d 464 (1996).

96. Ibid.

97. Ibid, 468–69.

98. For a scholarly commentary of the case shortly after it was handed down, see Shelly L. Skeen, "*City of Sherman v. Henry*: Is the Texas constitutional right of privacy still a source of protection for Texas citizens?" *Texas Wesleyan Law Review*, 4 (Fall 1999): 99.

99. Act of June 14, 1963, 63rd Legislature, R.S. chapter 399, 3, 1973 Texas General Laws 883, 992 repealing Texas penal Code article 499 (1925).

100. See *Henry*, 928 S.W.2d at 470–71.

101. 746 S.W. 2d 203,(1987) 206.

102. Texas Constitution, article 1, sections 9 and 25.

103. *England* and *Morales* were decided at roughly the same time in the Texas court system. In *Morales*, the supreme court stated that it was not addressing the merits of *England*. See *Texas v. Morales*, 869 S.W. 2d 941 (1994).

104. *See City of Dallas v. England*, 846 S.W.2d 957, 958 (Tex. App.—Austin 1993, writ dism'd w.o.j.).

105. In *Texas v. Morales*, 826 S.W. 2d 201, 205 (Tex. App. – Austin 1992), the Third Court of Appeals in Austin ruled that although the right to privacy is not expressly contained in the Texas Constitution, it is created or implied by sections 6, 8, 9, 10, 19, and 25 of the Texas Bill of Rights.

106. *State v. Morales*, 869 S.W.2d 941, 942, n. 5.

107. See *Texas State Employees Union v. Texas Department of Mental Health & Mental Retardation*, 746 S.W.2d 203, 204 (Tex. 1987), in which the Texas Supreme Court ruled that the policy of requiring certain employees to take mandatory polygraph tests impermissible violated the right to privacy found in the Texas Bill of Rights.

108. Linda Morales, Tom Doyal, Patricia Cramer, Charlotte Taft, and John Thomas.

109. *See Morales*, 869 S.W.2d at 942 n.4 (citing Tex. Const. art. I, §§ 3(a), 13, 19).

110. Michael H. Garbarino, "Homosexuality and Texas law: An analysis of *Texas v. Morales* and its implications," *Texas Journal on Civil Rights and Civil Liberties*, 1 (Spring 1994): 50.

111. See *Lawrence*, 539 U.S. at 572 (explaining that at the time of the *Bowers v. Hardwick* decision, over twenty states and the District of Columbia had sodomy laws).

112. *Bowers v. Hardwick*, 478 U.S. 186 (1986), *overruled by Lawrence v. Texas*, 539 U.S. 558 (2003).

113. Texas Constitution, article I, sections 13, 19.

114. Texas Constitution, article I, sections 3, 3A.

115. See *State v. Morales*, 826 S.W.2d 201, 202 (Tex. App.—Austin 1992), *rev'd*, 869 S.W.2d 941 (Tex. 1994).

116. Ibid, 203, 205.

117. Ibid, 203.

118. See *Morales*, 869 S.W.2d at 953.

119. See *City of Austin v. Austin City Cemetery Association*, 28 S.W. 528, 528–29 (Tex. 1894) (discussing whether it was constitutional for a city to enforce an ordinance regulating the burial of the dead by prohibiting funerals on specific property); see also *Passel v. Fort Worth Independent Sch. Dist.*, 440 S.W.2d 61, 62 (Tex. 1969) (questioning whether a statute prohibiting school-age children from joining clubs constituted an unwarranted interference with their constitutional rights to free speech and private association).

120. See generally Christopher R. Leslie, "Procedural rules or procedural pretexts? A case study of procedural hurdles in constitutional challenges to the Texas sodomy law," *Kentucky Law Journal*, 89 (2001): 1109, 1115 (discussing in detail the history of challenges to the Texas sodomy law and the procedural hurdles faced).

121. Section 21.06 of the Texas Penal Code.

122. *Morales*, 826 S.W.2d at 202.

123. Ibid.

124. Ibid, 202–03.

125. See *Texas State Employees Union v. Texas Department of Mental Health & Mental Retardation*, 746 S.W.2d 203, 204 (Tex. 1987), in which the Texas Supreme Court ruled that the policy of requiring certain employees to take mandatory polygraph tests impermissible violated the right to privacy found in the Texas Bill of Rights.

126. Ibid, 205.

127. *State v. Morales*, 869 S.W.2d 941, 942 (Tex. 1994).

128. See Ibid.

129. Ibid, 946–47 (citing *Passel v. Fort Worth Independent School District*, 440 S.W.2d 61, 63–64 (Tex. 1969)). Ibid, 62–63.

130. *State v. Morales*, 869 S.W.2d 941, 942.

131. Joined by Chief Justice Phillips, Justice Doggett, and Justice Spector. Ibid, 941.

132. Ibid, 953–54 (Gammage, J., dissenting) (emphasis added) (footnote omitted).

133. Ibid, 953.

134. Ibid.

135. Ibid, 954.

136. 95 S.W.3d 253 (Tex. 2002).

137. Ibid, 265.

138. Ibid, 265.

139. *Clayton v. Richards*, 47 S.W.3d 149 (2001).

140. W. Prosser, *Handbook of The Law of Torts* § 46 at 292 (fourth edition, 1971).

141. *Collins v. Collins*, 904 S.W.2d 792 (1995).

142. *Clayton v. Richards*, 47 S.W.3d 149, 155 (2001).

143. Ibid.

144. Prosser, supra note 10.

145. *Industrial Foundation of the South v. Texas Industrial Accident Board*, 540 S.W.2d at 672. (1976)

146. Ibid, 678.

147. Ibid.

148. Ibid, 680–81.

149. Ibid, 682.

150. *Industrial Foundation of the South v. Texas Industrial Accident Board*, 540 S.W.2d. at 672. (1976)

151. *McNamara v. Freedom Newspapers, Inc.*, 802 S.W.2d 901 (Tex. App.—Corpus Christi 1991, writ denied).

152. Ibid, 903.

153. Ibid, 904.

154. 915 S.W.2d 471 (Tex. 1995)

155. *Star-Telegram, Inc. v. Doe*, 915 S.W.2d. 471, 472 (Tex. 1995).

156. Ibid, 472–73.

157. Ibid, 473.

158. Ibid, 472.

159. Ibid, 472–73.

160. Ibid, 472.

161. Ibid, 473.

162. Ibid (alteration in original) (quoting *Fla. Star v. B.J.F.*, 491 U.S. 524, 533 (1989)).

163. Ibid.

164. Ibid.

165. Ibid.

166. Ibid, 474–75. The Texas Supreme Court did not address the question of whether the information was legally obtained.

167. Ibid, 473 (citing Samuel D. Warren & Louis D. Brandeis, "The right to privacy," *Harvard Law Review*, 4 (1890): 193, 193.

168. *Star-Telegram, Inc.*, 915 S.W.2d. at 473.

169. *See Star-Telegram, Inc.*, 915 S.W.2d at 474–75.

170. Ibid, 475.

171. *Indus. Found.*, 540 S.W.2d at 685.

172. *Doe v. Mobile Video Tapes, Inc.*, 43 S.W.3d 40 (2001).

173. Citing *Foster v. Laredo Newspapers, Inc.*, 541 S.W.3d 809 (1976).

174. Such as *Boyles v. Kerr*, 806 S.W.2d 255 (1991), overturned by the Texas Supreme Court in 2001; and *C.T.W. v. B.C.G,* 809 S.W.2d 788 (1991).

175. Ibid, 32.

176. Citing *Foster v. Laredo Newspapers, Inc.*, 541 S.W.3d 809 (1976).

177. Such as *Boyles v. Kerr*, 806 S.W.2d 255 (1991), overturned by the Texas Supreme Court in 2001; and *C.T.W. v. B.C.G*, 809 S.W.2d 788 (1991).

178. *Dallas County v. Harper*, 913 S.W.2d 207 (1995).

179. *Fulmer v. Rider*, 635 S.W.2d 875, 881 (1982).

180. *Childers v. A.S.*, 909 S.W.2d 282, 291 (1995).

181. Citing Childers, 909 S.W.2d at 291 (citing *Fulmer v. Rider*, 635 S.W.2d 875, 881 (Tex.App.—Tyler 1982, writ ref'd n.r.e.) and *National Union Fire Ins. Co. v. Bourn*, 441 S.W.2d 592, 596 (Tex.Civ.App.—Fort Worth 1969, writ ref'd n.r.e.

182. *Texas Comptroller of Public Accounts vs. Attorney General of Texas*, 354 S.W.3d 336 (2010).

183. See Texas Government Code, section 552.101 and 102.

184. Ibid.

185. Jefferson cited *National Archives and Records v. Favish*, 541 U.S. 157 (2004) at 172, noting that, when protected privacy interests are at stake, the requestor must "establish a sufficient reason for the disclosure."

186. Ibid (quoting *U.S. Department of Defense v. Federal Labor Relations Authority*, 510 U.S. 487, 500, 114 S.Ct. 1006, 127 L.Ed.2d 325 (1994)).

187. *Texas Dept. of Public Safety v. Cox Texas Newspapers*, L.P, 343 S. W. 3d 112 (2011).

188. *Texas Department of Criminal Justice v. Levin*, 2019 WL 1575407.

189. *Texas Department of Criminal Justice v. Levin*, 572 S.W. 3d 671 (2019), 675.

190. Prosser, supra note 10, at 406.

191. *Pavesich v. New England Life Insurance Company*, 122 Ga. 190 (Ga. 1905).

192. Ibid, 220.

193. See *Fairfield v. American Photocopy Equip. Co.*, 138 Cal. App. 2d 82 (1955).

194. See Restatement (second) of Tort, sections 652A–652I. Section 652C (1977) states "One who appropriates to his own use or benefit the name or likeness of another is subject to liability for invasion of privacy."

195. See *Fairfield v. American Photocopy Equip. Co*., 138 Cal. App. 2d 82 (1955).

196. 238 S.W. 2d 289 (Tex. Civ. App. – Waco 1951, writ ref'd n.r.e.).

197. *Kimbrough v. Coca-Cola/USA*, 521 S.W. 2d 719 (Tex. Civ. App. – Eastland 1975, writ ref'd n.r.e).

198. *O'Brien v. Pabst Sales Co*., 124 F.2d 167 (5th Cir. 1941).

199. See *Birmingham Broadcasting v. Bell*, 259 Ala. 656 (1953), *Arnold Palmer, Gary Player, Doug Sanders, and Jack Nicklaus v. Schonhorn Enterprises, Inc*, 96 N.J Super. 72 (1967),

200. *Gautier v. Pro-Football, Inc.*, 304 N.Y. 354 (1952).

201. *Arnold Palmer, Gary Player, Doug Sanders, and Jack Nicklaus v. Schonhorn Enterprises, Inc*, 96 N.J Super. 72 (1967).

202. 521 S.W. 2d 719, 722 (Tex. Civ. App. – Eastland 1975, writ ref'd n.r.e).

203. Ibid.

204. *Topheavy Studios, Inc. v. Doe*, No. 03-05-00022-CV (Tex. App.—Austin Aug. 11, 2005, no pet.). (mem. op.)

205. Doe admitted that she misrepresented her age (she was a minor) and address. Much of the opinion dealt with whether the release for signed by Doe was valid because she was a minor.

206. Ibid, 1, 8.

207. Citing *Express One Int'l, Inc. v. Steinbeck*, 53 S.W.3d 895, 900 (Tex. App.—Dallas 2001, no pet.).

208. *Topheavy Studios, Inc. v. Doe*, at *3.

209. Ibid.

210. See *Meadows v. Hartford Life Ins. Co*, 492 F.3d 634, 638 (quoting *Moore v. Big Picture Co*., 828 F.2d 270 (5th Cir. 1987)). 5th Cir. 2007).

211. Restatement (Second) of Torts, Section 652C (1977).

212. The Fifth Circuit came to similar conclusions in *Benavidez v. Anheuser-Busch, Inc.*, 873 F.2d. 102, 104 (5th Cir. 1989).

213. *Meadows v. Hartford Life Ins. Co.*, 492 f. 3d 634, 638–39 (5th Cir. 2007).

214. *Henley v. Dillard Department Stores*, 46 F. Supp. 2d 587, 596 (N.D. Tex. 1999) (citing Restatement (second) of Torts section 652C (1977)).

215. *Watson v. Talia Heights*, 566 S.W. 3d 326, 329–330 (2018).

216. Citing *Express One Int'l, Inc. v. Steinbeck*, 53 S.W.3d 895, 900 (Tex. App.—Dallas 2001, no pet.).

217. See *Cardiovascular Provider Res. Inc. v. Gottlich*, No. 05-13-01763-CV (Tex. App. –Dallas 2015, pet. Denied (mem. op.)

218. *Express One Int'l, Inc. v. Steinbeck*, 53 S.W.3d 895, 900 (Tex. App.—Dallas 2001, no pet.).

219. *Moore v. Big Picture Co.*, 828 F.2d 270, 275 (5th Cir. 1987).

220. See *Watson v. Talia Heights*, 566 S.W. 3d 326 (2018) citing *Cardiovascular Provider Res. Inc. v. Gottlich*, No 05-13-01763-CV (Tex. App. – Dallas Aug. 18, 2015, pet. Denied) (mem. Op.).

221. *Watson v. Talia Heights*, 566 S.W. 3d 326, 329–330 (2018).

222. Ibid, *4. *Citing Express One Int'l, Inc. v. Steinbeck*, 53 S.W.3d 895 (Tex. App.—Dallas 2001, no pet.).

223. *Doggett v. Travis Law Firm*, 555 S.W. 3d 127 (2018)

224. Ibid, and see also *United Locating Services, LLC v. Fobbs*, 619 S.W. 3d 863 (2021).

225. 202 F.2d 866 (1953); and see *Henley v. Dillard Department Stores*, 46 F. Supp.2d 587 (N.D. Tex. 1999).

226. Title 4, Chapter 26 of the Property Code.

227. Texas Property Code Ann. section 26.003(2).

228. Texas Property Code Ann., section 26.004.

229. Texas Property Code Ann. section 26.012; see also *Whitehurst v. Showtime Networks, Inc.*

230. Restatement (Second) of Torts sec. 652A; and see generally Robin Baker Perkins, "The truth behind false light—A recommendation for Texas's re-adoption of false light invasion of privacy," *Texas Tech Law Review*, 34 (2003): 1199.

231. *Gill v. Snow*, 644 S.W. 2d 222 (Tex. App. – Fort Worth 1982, no writ.).

232. Ibid, 223, citing the Restatement (Second) of Torts, sec. 652A (1977).

233. *Diamond Shamrock Refining and Marketing Company v. Roque Mendez*, 844 S. W.2d 198 (1992).

234. Restatement (Second) of Torts sec. 652E.

235. Ibid.

236. *Diamond Shamrock Refining*, 844 S. W.2d 198, at 199, 200.

237. Ibid.

238. Ibid, 203.

239. Ibid.

240. Ibid, 215, 216.

241. Ibid.

242. *Cain v. Hearst Corporation*, 878 S.W.2d at 577 (Tex. 1994).

243. Ibid.

244. Ibid.

245. *Cain*, 878 S.W.2d at 580 (Tex. 1994).

246. Ibid, 584 (Hightower, J., dissenting).

247. Ibid, 586.

248. Ibid (citing *Godbehere v. Phoenix Newspapers, Inc.*, 783 P.2d 781, 787 (Ariz. 1989)).

249. See Gary T. Schwartz, "Explaining and justifying a limited tort of false light invasion of privacy," *Case Western Reserve Law Journal*, 885 (1991): 885.

250. Supra note 51. *Milner v. Red River Publishing*, 249 S.W.2d 227,229 (Tex. Civ. App. 1952).

Chapter 3

Statutory Protection of Privacy in Texas

The right to privacy in Texas also receives protection from state statutory law that codifies many of common law and constitutional remedies discussed in previous chapters. In instances where older doctrines did not meet the need of modern technological society, lawmakers enacted legislative solutions to deal with emerging technologies and matters such as cybercrime and online impersonation. Most statutory privacy protections are embedded in sections and chapters of civil and criminal codes that cover areas such as business and commerce, education, health and safety, governmental administration, and criminal justice policy. It is there that the criminal penalties and civil remedies are found, addressing matters such as unlawful wiretapping, interception of confidential information or images, the use of spyware and tracking devices, identity theft, health privacy, consumer privacy, the use of drones, cybercrime, and student records and data.

This chapter provides an overview of the privacy interests protected by Texas statutes, referencing select court decisions dealings with appeals from adverse rulings under the statutes. As in the earlier chapters of this book, here we deal mainly with civil law—privacy invasions caused by private individuals and corporations, not the actions of law enforcement or the state—although many statutes call for both civil and criminal penalties.

THE TEXAS WIRETAP LAW: UNLAWFUL INTERCEPTION OF PRIVATE ELECTRONIC COMMUNICATIONS

Invasion of privacy as a result of unlawful interception of private electronic communications (or wiretapping) is regulated by the Texas wiretap law.[1] This statute codifies one dimension of the invasion of privacy common law doctrine as it relates to electronic eavesdropping by a private individual, not by law enforcement. Under this law, a person can bring a civil lawsuit against another person for violating the law. The term wiretapping brings to mind detectives in trench coats "bugging" or placing a listening device in a light fixture or behind a picture frame, but in contemporary society, since nearly everyone is carrying a sophisticated audio and video recording device called a smartphone, wiretapping—the unlawful interception of private communications—has taken on a myriad of new forms and occurs with greater frequency. We should proceed with the assumption that we are at risk of being recorded by someone at any time.

The rules and conditions that apply to the wiretapping law are complex and can be a challenge to understand.[2] The following is general summary of the rules created by the law:[3]

1. A person can record a conversation without a second person's consent in a one-party state (Texas). All that is needed is that the person recording the conversation consents, unless the person who is recording is doing so for the purpose of committing a criminal or tortious act.
2. A person can record a conversation to which they are not a party if one of the participants in that conversation gives them permission. You must be an adult and competent to give consent.
3. A person can record a conversation in a public setting to which they are not a party, where no consent is granted, when the participants in the conversation do *not* have a reasonable expectation of privacy. For example, a person could legally record an in-person conversation with another person in a coffee shop without their consent. However, if they were to record the same conversation in the privacy of their home, where a reasonable expectation of privacy exists, then the person recording would need to secure consent before recording to avoid possible criminal or civil liability.
4. It is illegal to "tap," or record, a telephone conversation to which one is not a party and does not have consent from one of the parties, and where one could *not* naturally overhear the conversation. This action falls under the traditional definition of wiretapping. The legal burden would fall on the person recording to show that informed consent was obtained prior to recording. That consent could be given either orally or in writing.
5. It is illegal to record a private in-person conversation to which one is not a party and does not have consent from one of the parties, and where one could *not* naturally overhear the conversation.[4]

Since Texas is a one-party state, individuals are generally unfettered to record anyone they wish with their smartphone or other device, but the disclosure of the recording is altogether a different matter. The disclosure of the recording to third parties—individuals or social media sites—could be punishable civilly and criminally under a number of privacy laws and legal doctrines, such as public disclosure. Further, even if the recording was made with the consent of one or more parties, it is illegal to secretly plant a "wire" (a recording device) or illegally enter a house or building for the purpose of making a covert electronic communication or intentionally using a recording device to obtain any oral communication when the device has the capacity to transmit or broadcast a signal electronically. Disclosing the contents of a wire, oral, or electronic communication obtained through illegal recording is a felony.[5]

The penalty for wiretapping in Texas consists of two parts: civil liability and criminal penalties. Civil liability for wiretapping can result in the recorded person seeking a court injunction, a ten-thousand-dollar civil penalty for each recorded event, actual damages sustained as a result of the injury, punitive damages determined by a jury, and attorney's fees. Under the criminal section of the law, it is a crime to intentionally intercept or attempt to intercept or procure another person to intercept an electronic communication.[6] The law also makes it a crime when a person intentionally discloses to another person the contents of the electronic communication, or recording.[7] The penalty for unlawful interception of communications is a second-degree felony which could result in a sentence of two to twenty years in prison.[8] Determining whether the person injured has a reasonable expectation of privacy is often dispositive of the outcome in a dispute under the wiretapping law.

Long v. State[9] in 2017 is an important and instructive ruling regarding the wiretap law. It also proceeds from a set of facts straight from a made-for-television movie. *Long* originated when a middle school principal encouraged, or "procured," her daughter and daughter's friend to surreptitiously record a speech that a "mean" coach delivered to the girls' basketball team in a locker room at an away game. The game that night was between two basketball rivals, Argyle High School and Sanger High School, and played at Sanger High School. Wendee Long, the principal of a Wayside Middle School in Saginaw, Texas, and a member of the Argyle Independent School District school board schemed with her daughter and daughter's friend to sneak the friend into the opposing team's (Sanger) empty locker room and tape an iPhone inside a locker for the purpose of making a video and audio recording of Coach "Skip" Townsend's half-time and post-game speech to the team. Long's daughter, C.L., who attended Argyle High School, was assisted by a student who attended Sanger, P.S., who gained access to the locker room by claiming that she was a team manager for Sanger. It was clear that Long and her daughter disliked the coach, who had a reputation as a tough disciplinarian and often berated and scolded players.[10]

After the game, her daughter retrieved the phone and Principal Long downloaded the recording to her work computer. She then played the recording for her assistant principal at Wayside and emailed copies of the recording to other members of the Argyle Independent School District school board during a meeting at which the fate of the coach's contract renewal was being considered. The superintendent of the Argyle Independent School District then made the decision to turn over the recordings to the Sanger Police Department, concerned that Long had violated the Texas wiretap law. After a detective at the Sanger Police Department traced the recordings to Wendee Long and her daughter, Long was then charged in a two-count indictment for violating two sections of the Texas wiretap law: intercepting and disclosing the contents of an electronic communication. The state alleged that Long violated the law by procuring her daughter to record the coach's speech and by playing the recording to the assistant principal. The jury concluded that because Long wanted to discourage the school board from renewing the coach's contract, she conspired with her daughter to sneak into the locker room and record the coach's speech. A guilty verdict was rendered, and Long was sentenced to five years in prison, probation for three years, and a one-thousand-dollar fine.[11] Under the Texas wiretap law, an oral communication is that which is "uttered by a person exhibiting an expectation that the communication is not subject to interception under circumstances justifying that expectation."[12]

On appeal, the Court of Appeals (El Paso) reversed Long's conviction, reasoning that because the coach did not have a reasonable expectation that only his students would hear the contents of his communication, the recording of his speeches were not "oral communications" that fell under the wiretap statute. As such, Wendee Long could not be guilty of violating the law. Long's actions may have been unprofessional, but they were not criminal. The appeals court argued that it is long recognized that public school teachers, including coaches, do not have a reasonable expectation of privacy in classrooms, sports facilities, and locker rooms that are used for coaching or instruction.[13] The court pointed out that the coach even admitted in court that he assumed players would go home and tell their parents what he said about their performance on the basketball court, although he did not assume he was being recorded. The court did acknowledge that teachers and coaches do have a legitimate expectation of privacy outside of a shared instructional area, such as in a teacher's personal office space, including their desk, lockers, or file cabinets that may be reserved for the teacher's exclusive use. In these circumstances the teachers or coaches would have an expectation of privacy that society is willing to recognize as reasonable.[14]

The Texas Court of Criminal Appeals, however, reversed the Court of Appeals decision, thus affirming Long's conviction for her role in the interception and disclosure of Coach Townsend's locker room speech. The court found that Townsend had a reasonable expectation that his communication—his locker room talk to his athletes—would not be subject to recording or interception, much less disclosure. He legitimately believed that the locker room was private and that no one was allowed to access the locker room except the Argyle team and coaches. He could not have expected that after school hours an iPhone would be taped inside a locker. The appeal turned on two questions: (1) whether oral communication incorporates the reasonable expectation of privacy doctrine[15] and (2) whether the coach's speech was "oral communication."[16] The Texas Court of Criminal Appeals answered yes to both questions. Writing for the majority, Justice David Newell held that the coach's speech qualifies as oral communication under the Texas wiretap law and, most importantly, that the law incorporates the reasonable expectation of privacy standard found in state and federal judicial precedent. The state argued that when the legislature drafted the wiretap law, it did not incorporate the Fourth Amendment's reasonable expectation of privacy doctrine; instead, it adopted something called an "expectation-of-non-interception" doctrine. The court disagreed with this argument, citing a 2002 Texas Court of Criminal Appeals decision in *State v. Scheineman* and the US Supreme Court's ruling in *Katz v U.S.*[17] Under the state's wiretap law, Coach Townsend had a "subjective expectation of privacy . . . that society is prepared to regard as objectively reasonable." Further, contrary to the court of appeals holding, a locker room is not considered a school classroom, where there is little or no room for privacy.[18] A coach or teacher should expect that athletes or students will inform their parents what they say in the course of their duties, but this fact should not be interpreted to mean that students are free to place coaches and teachers under surveillance. Nor should the opinion be construed to mean that a school district lacks the authority to intercept communications between school employees and students.[19] Note that the one-party rule discussed here did not apply in this case because the coach had a reasonable expectation of privacy in the locker room *and* because the person(s) who recorded the coach was not a party to a conversation.

Taylor v. Tolbert[20] in 2022 raised the unusual question of whether an attorney can be sued under the Texas wiretap law for sharing electronic communications related to the parties in a lawsuit. The Texas Supreme Court held that the Texas wiretap statute did not prevent an attorney from asserting a common law attorney immunity defense where it was alleged that she violated the state law; however, that immunity did not protect her from liability under federal wiretap law. The issue arose from a child custody case, during which the mother sued the father's attorney for violating state and federal wiretap laws following an egregious use of the mother's text messages, emails, and even nude photos from an iPad belonging to the father's sister-in-law. The attorney claimed that the use of the messages fell within the scope of representing her client in an acrimonious custody battle and were necessary in the carrying out of her duties to the client in conducting discovery, in pleadings, and in obtaining a court order. The trial court dismissed the case against the attorney, but the court of appeals reversed and remanded, arguing that existing precedent did not explicitly extend attorney immunity to alleged criminal conduct. On appeal, the Texas Supreme Court held that the Texas wiretap law did not prevent the attorney from asserting a state common law attorney immunity defense against the mother's claims that she violated the statute; however, this common law immunity does not apply to the federal law.[21]

Graham v. Miller[22] in 2023 addressed the question of when a person is liable for allowing others who are not involved in a conversation to listen to or view a recording without consent. The case originated when in the midst of a pending petition to modify a parent-child relationship, a trial court appointed a psychologist, Dr. Graham, to serve as the children's counselor. During a counseling session a child informed the therapist that while staying with her father she had secretly recorded acrimonious and disturbing interactions between her father and stepmother. The therapist then shared the recordings with the child's mother, her husband, and her attorneys. Potentially, these recordings could be used as evidence in the decision to modify child custody in favor of the mother. The father then filed a petition against the psychologist for violating the Texas wiretap law on the grounds that she "divulged an illegally obtained recording to another individual."[23] He argued that the children made the recording without his consent and that the state's one-party rule would did not apply because the child was too young to consent to the recording. To avoid liability, Dr. Graham filed a motion to dismiss the complaint on the basis of the Texas Citizens Participation Act that permitted her to listen to the recordings as communication pertaining to a judicial (governmental) proceeding. The Texas Citizens Participation Act permits a person who is being sued to dismiss a legal action that is based on or in response to that person's right to freedom of speech, right to petition, and freedom of association.[24] The father argued that his suit was brought not because Dr. Graham discussed the recordings with the mother and others, but that she *replayed* the recordings for others. The trial court rejected Dr. Graham's motion to dismiss under the Texas Citizens Participation Act. On appeal, the Texas Court of Appeal (Dallas) affirmed the trial court's decision stating that although the children were still under her care, the judicial proceedings regarding the custody arrangement were long over—the matter was no longer under judicial review. The court was also critical of the therapist for not contacting the police or Child Protective Services after she heard the disturbing recordings.[25]

A large number of wiretap cases involve spouses recording spouses. In most instances, spouses share not only their homes but often computers and other electronic devices, raising the question of interspousal immunity: whether spouses can wiretap or video record each other with impunity because they do not have the same reasonable expectation of privacy as unmarried people. In *Miller v. Talley Dunn Gallery*[26] in 2016 a husband (Miller) placed a device in his wife's (Dunn) car to record phone conversations. He also recorded their conversations in their home without his wife being aware of this activity. A trial court issued an injunction against the husband, and a state appellate court held that the wife had a right to probable right to recovery under the federal Interception of Communication Act (ICA)[27] based on her claims that Miller violated ICA by intercepting communications without the consent of any party to the communication. The court also held that Dunn had a right to recover under the common law doctrine of invasion of privacy.[28] Miller admitted that he made the recordings in the privacy of their home and that Ms. Dunn was not aware that their conversations were being recorded, but Miller argued that his activities were legal under the Texas wiretap statute which requires the consent of only one party (himself) to the conversation. However, the court disagreed and held:

> The ICA creates a statutory cause of action for an individual whose communications are intercepted. . . . However, there is nothing in the ICA that precludes a common law claim for invasion of privacy for communication not covered by the ICA. The right to privacy is a right distinctive in itself and not incidental to some other recognized right for breach of which action for damages will lie. A violation of the right is a tort.[29]

Dunn could also recover under the Harmful Access by Computer Act which establishes a civil cause of action for a person who has been injured as a result of someone knowingly and intentionally accessing a computer without the consent of the owner. Computers, cell phones, and internet or cellphone service plans are often community property, but there is no interspousal exception to unauthorized wiretapping or recording in Texas.[30] It is illegal to "knowingly access a computer, computer network, or computer system without the effective consent of the owner."[31] A person who accesses their spouse's personal computer without consent can be subject to civil and criminal liability. However, the outcome of each case will differ depending on whether the spouses are joint owners of the electronic devices or regularly share the devices.

In *Collins v. Collins*, the Texas Court of Appeals (Houston) ruled that "spouses, as any other persons, have rights of privacy under both [state and federal] wiretap statutes."[32] The Court stated further that "[n]othing in the

Texas Constitution or common law suggests that the right to privacy is limited to unmarried individuals."[33] In *Clayton v. Richards* the Court of Appeals (Texarkana) ruled that there is not an exception for invasion of privacy between spouses for unauthorized video recording.[34] It would not be a violation of privacy under statute or common law doctrine for a spouse to open a bedroom door and watch the other spouse in bed. However, the videotaping of anyone without their consent or awareness when there is an expectation of privacy is unlawful, particularly when the recording of private matters may later be exposed to the public eye.[35] It is also a crime under both federal[36] and state[37] law to knowingly access a computer, computer network, or computer system without the effective consent of the owner.[38] When violations of privacy law are alleged, the responding party will often argue that the devices are routinely shared or owned as community property. This is what Miller unsuccessfully alleged. The court rejected his community property argument against his wife's privacy claim. Even if her cell phone was paid for out of a joint bank account or credit card and held as community property, Ms. Dunn had a "greater right to possession" of the cell phone, which under law is considered a computer.[39] Computer privacy is protected by statute as well as invasion of privacy doctrine in Texas, so even marriage or other forms of intimate relationship does not give license to access the other person's devices.

INVASIVE VISUAL RECORDINGS, REVENGE PORN, AND VOYEURISM

It is not illegal to use a visual recording device in areas to which the public has access or where there is no reasonable expectation of privacy, such as on a public street or in a coffee shop. However, it is an unlawful violation of privacy to photograph or record a person in a bathroom or private dressing room without that person's consent "with the intent to invade the privacy of the person or arouse or gratify the sexual desire of any person," or with the intent to publicly disclose any of the images.[40] Recording devices include security cameras and cell phones or similar devices. In addition, if a third person were to receive a sexually explicit image or recording—even unsolicited—and then forwarded it to another person, there could be criminal liability if there was knowledge that the person depicted in the explicit photo or video did not give their consent to being photographed or videotaped. Further, what is commonly known as the "revenge porn" law covers the intentional public disclosure of intimate visual material by a third party who obtains the images under circumstances in which the depicted person has a reasonable expectation of privacy *and* the public disclosure is carried out with the intent to do harm or exact revenge.[41]

The objective of laws punishing invasive video recording and revenge porn seems straightforward, but these laws have been subject to First Amendment challenges. For example, in *Ex parte Nyabwa*[42] in 2012, the Texas Court of Criminal Appeals held that the statutory prohibition on photographing or videotaping a person in public without that person's consent with the intent to arouse or gratify a sexual desire does not violate a defendant's free speech rights because the statute is not a regulation of speech or the contents of a visual image but rather a regulation of the photographer's or videographer's intent in creating the image or recording. A person commits a criminal offense if, without the consent of the depicted person, there is (1) intentional disclosure of visual material depicting another person with that person's intimate parts exposed or engaged in sexual conduct, and (2) the visual material was obtained by the person or created under circumstances in which the depicted person had a reasonable expectation that the visual material would remain private.[43] However, in *Ex parte Thompson*[44] in 2014 the Texas Court of Criminal Appeals struck down the invasive photography law as overbroad, arguing that photos, much like paintings and films, are "inherently expressive" and therefore protected by the First Amendment. The court reasoned that banning otherwise protected expression because it produces sexual arousal or gratification in the mind of the photographer amounts to the regulation of protected thoughts, and "such a regulation is outside the government's power." A law intended to protect someone who appears in public from being the object of sexual thought is "the sort of paternalistic interest in regulating the defendant's mind that the First Amendment was designed to guard against,"[45] Justice Keller argued. The law was impermissibly broad because it applied to *any* nonconsensual photograph, captured *anywhere* if it could be shown that the defendant had an intent to arouse or gratify sexual desire. The court pointed out that the law could be applied to an entertainment or paparazzi reporter who takes a photo of a film star or attractive celebrity on a public street. Keller wrote that "[a] person who walks down a public street cannot prevent others from looking at him or her with sexual thoughts in their heads,"[46] the opinion said. However, the court in Thompson left standing the section of the improper photography law that prohibited photos taken without consent in a bathroom or private dressing room. Justice Keller stated "that substantial privacy interests are invaded in an intolerable manner when a person is photographed without consent in a private place, such as the home, or with respect to an area of the person that is not exposed to the general public, such as up a skirt."[47]

The legislature subsequently modified the section of the law that the court found unconstitutional. The revised 2015 version of the law[48] stipulates that the invasive visual photographs and recordings extend to recordings, broadcasts, or transmissions of images of "intimate area[s]" of the body taken without consent in bathrooms and changing rooms or areas not subject to public view with the intent to invade a person's privacy. The constitutionality of the revised law was upheld in in 2020 in *Ex parte Metzger* as a narrowly tailored means to serve the state's compelling interest in protecting its citizens from "intrusive and offensive invasions of their substantial privacy rights."[49]

In *Ex parte Fairchild-Porche*[50] in 2021 the Court of Appeals (Houston) upheld the constitutionality of a similar invasive visual recording law—the revenge porn statute. The court found that although the statute was a content-based restriction of speech—that is, it punished the capture and disclosure of only those images that were sexually explicit as opposed to image that were not—the law was "narrowly tailored to serve a compelling governmental interest, namely protecting sexual privacy."[51] To prove that the statute is violated it is not enough that the image is sexually explicit, which may be protected speech. The state must show that the defendant (1) intentionally disclosed a sexually explicit image of a person who had a reasonable expectation of privacy, (2) knew that they did not have the consent of the person whose image was taken, and (3) knowingly and recklessly identified the depicted person and caused that person harm by the disclosure.[52] The compelling government interest that the revenge porn law has in protecting sexual privacy outweighs the defendant's First Amendment rights. Justice Wilson argued:

> Violations of sexual privacy are intrinsically harmful because sex is inherently private. The consequences of violations of sexual privacy can be serious and include harassment, job loss, and suicide. Victims of revenge porn cannot counterspeak their way out of a violation of their most private affairs and bodily autonomy or the serious harms that may accompany that violation. . . . The Legislature recognized the severity of these harms and passed this law to protect against them.[53]

Texas has a Peeping Tom, or voyeurism, law that protects privacy. Simply glancing in someone's window may not necessarily reach the level of behavior defined as voyeurism because the law states that an offense has been committed if a person observes another person, with the intent to arouse or gratify their sexual desire, without the other person's consent in circumstances in which person being viewed is in a dwelling or structure in which the person has a reasonable expectation of privacy.[54] The question before a court would boil down to the Peeping Tom's intent, whether the person's expectation of privacy is reasonable, and the duration of the observation. But even if the alleged victim is in a public pool, skinny-dipping in a creek, or kissing someone in an open window, if the alleged voyeur peered at them for a significant duration of time a jury might reasonably infer sexual motives. It would also depend on whether the alleged voyeur captured intimate images or video for the purpose of sexual gratification, in which case a person could also be charged with violating the Invasive Visual Recording Law.[55] This modern statute encompasses the old common law protection against Peeping Toms, a crime documented in Blackstone's *Commentaries* and prosecuted in America in the 1800s. It is based on the maxim that no one has a right to "pry into the secrecy of your own house."[56]

BIOMETRIC PRIVACY

Each day Texans leave residual digital "fingerprints" when using electronic devices such as smartphones, making online purchases, or walking through public spaces that are electronically monitored. Many devices allow fingerprints, voices, and face compositions as means of identifying their users. Financial institutions and vendors also use this data to verify and authenticate the person who is trying to access a bank account. Most if not all of these biometric interfaces are recorded and stored. Facial recognition maps face geometry detected in a photo, video, or real-time video surveillance by analyzing facial details such as the spacing of the eyes, bridge of the nose, contours of the lips, and other features. Each face in the database is assigned a code based on the facial measurements. This digital code of the person's face is known as a faceprint, or facial signature, which can be used for identification purposes like a fingerprint. These digital images are lifted like fingerprints every time we open our smartphones, shop at the local mall, or are stopped by law enforcement for a routine traffic violation.[57]

The Capture and Use of Biometric Identifier Act (CUBI),[58] enacted in 2009 by the Texas legislature, focuses on the unauthorized capture or use of a biometric identifier defined as a "retina or iris scan, fingerprint, voiceprint, or record of hand or face geometry."[59] If misused, biometric data can lead to a range of problems including targeted surveillance in public places, identity theft (discussed later in this chapter), and the collection and storage of personal information. There is also the possibility of misidentification leading to civil or criminal liability and false arrests. Even more insidious would be the use of biometric data to monitor a person who has a predisposition to commit a criminal act or participate in political protests.

CUBI applies to the unauthorized appropriation of such data for commercial purposes and includes the long-term storage and sale of data.[60] The law prohibits the capture of a biometric identifier of an individual for a commercial purpose unless the person from whom biometric data is being collected is informed prior to the capture of the biometric identifier and gives consent to its capture. Further, a person who possesses a biometric identifier of an individual that is captured for a commercial purpose may not sell, lease, or otherwise disclose the biometric identifier to another person unless (1) the individual consents to the disclosure for identification or (2) the disclosure is related to a financial transaction that the individual requested or authorized, the disclosure is required or permitted by a federal statute or by a state statute, or the disclosure is made by or to a law enforcement agency for a law enforcement purpose in response to a warrant.[61] Collected data must be stored, transmitted, and protected from disclosure using reasonable care, and all biometric identifiers must be destroyed within a reasonable time. If biometric data is collected by an employer, this information is to be destroyed by the date of employee's separation or termination.[62] A breach of this statute incurs a penalty of up to twenty-five thousand dollars for each violation. The Texas Attorney General is responsible for enforcing the law; private individuals are precluded from bringing lawsuits.[63]

In 2016 Amazon introduced facial recognition software bearing the Orwellian name "Rekognition" which was intended as a user-friendly tool that provided accurate facial analysis through photos and videos. After Amazon began selling the software to governments for surveillance and law enforcement purposes, the American Civil Liberties Union (ACLU) discovered that law enforcement was using the tool to scan faces during political protests. The ACLU and a coalition of civil rights and liberties groups eventually pressured Amazon, as well as IBM and Microsoft, to scale back the availability of facial recognition technology to governments.[64] The technology raises disturbing constitutional and legal issues, among them are restrictions on freedom of expression for fear of being identified at a political protest, violations of the reasonable expectation of privacy in public places, and deprivation of due process as a result of wrongful arrest or profiling.

In Texas, CUBI does not prevent recording of "face geometry"[65] but only the unauthorized capturing of such data for commercial purposes and the storage of data for extended periods of time. It does not ban its use or address any of the possible abuses with the exception of misappropriating one's likeness for the purpose of commercial gain, reflecting the appropriation tort doctrine discussed in chapters 1 and 2. CUBI provides a law enforcement exception to the appropriation and storage, so the data can be transferred to law enforcement without the consent of the individual but only upon issuance of a warrant.[66]

In October 2022, the Texas Attorney General sued Google for violating the state's Biometric Privacy Act[67] on multiple counts, including but not limited to the use of unlawfully obtaining millions of Texans' biometric identifiers without their consent. This was the first time an action was brought under the law since its passage in 2009. The alleged claim is that Google collected biometric identifiers, including face geometry, from photos, videos, and voiceprints, and maintained records of millions of consumers' voices and face geometries since 2015 through several of its apps like Google Photos and the Nest camera.[68] Under this law, Google's failure to destroy collected data in a timely manner may have violated the law. The courts have yet to rule, but the lawsuit seeks to make Google adhere to all sections of the law, most specifically sections on consent and the destruction of data records in a reasonable timely manner.[69] The Texas Attorney General also filed a petition against Facebook for violations, alleging that Facebook's photo "Tag Suggestions" function captures biometric identifiers without consent or notice.[70] The lawsuit seeks damages for "billions" of violations of the law that date back to 2010 and seeks an injunction to stop Meta from collecting biometric data in Texas and to delete the data already amassed.[71] In 2021 Facebook announced plans to discontinued biometric data collection,[72] but the Texas Attorney General alleges Meta's decision was not extended beyond Facebook to other Meta affiliates. The Attorney General's actions mirrored an Illinois civil lawsuit that resulted in plaintiffs securing a $650 million settlement with Meta under the Illinois Biometric Information Privacy Act.[73] Illinois is one of only a handful of states that have a statute requiring companies to secure consumers' permission before mining their biometric data. The Illinois Biometric Information Privacy Act is broader in scope than CUBI in that it not only requires consent but governs how companies manage and store data. It also allows Illinois residents to bring private actions against companies that violate the law. At five thousand dollars for each intentional violation and one thousand dollars for each violation due to negligence, a company's violation of the law could cost it hundreds of millions of dollars. In another Biometric Information Privacy Act lawsuit in 2022, TikTok paid a ninety-two-million-dollar settlement in a class action alleging that it collected biometric data from users and then transferred the data to other companies.[74] Some companies, such as Clearview AI, have agreed not so sell their artificial intelligence software to other private companies as a result of a legal settlement.[75] To date only three states, Illinois (2008), Texas (2009), and Washington (2017), have biometric data laws. Only the Illinois law provides for a private right of action.[76] Texas and Washington's laws are enforceable only by the respective state's attorney general and not by private lawsuits.

MONITORING EMPLOYEES

Employers monitor employees for a range of reasons, including maintaining productivity, preventing theft or abuse of employer property, and guarding against discrimination or harassment of co-workers. Available computer software has the capacity to determine whether workers access files, print documents, or fulfill online training requirements. Screenshots can be used to determine whether in-person or remote workers are at their designated workstations. Offsite, employee movements and driving behavior are monitored as well. Artificial intelligence can even be used to gauge employee attitudes, morale, and nature and tenor of social interactions with other employees and clients. Although state and federal law protects the privacy of telephone, email, and internet communications, employers have the right to supersede many of these privacy protections by conditioning employment on the voluntary waiver of privacy. Texas employers are not legally precluded from monitoring employees, although the line is typically drawn between personal and work-related telephone calls. Workplace policy typically allows for the "incidental use" of an employer's computers and phones which would extend to personal calls to family members, healthcare providers, and even bank transactions.

Courts have ruled that an employee does *not* have a reasonable expectation of privacy in a company's email account,[77] but suppose that an employee logged on to their personal email account while at work using the employer's computer. Would they then have a reasonable expectation of privacy? As of this writing there are no published Texas court cases that address this matter directly. However, several opinions from other states shed some light on the question. A New Jersey Supreme Court ruling found that an employee had a reasonable expectation of privacy in emails sent to her attorney using her personal password-protected account that she accessed on a company laptop,[78] but attorney-client privilege could be waived or did not apply when an employee's emails to their lawyer were sent on an employer-owned device.[79] An employee was granted relief under Electronic Communications Privacy Act, the Stored Communications Act, and a wiretap law after an employer relying on keylogging software accessed an employee's bank account.[80] Further, employee monitoring would be permitted under a state requirement to report employees who access child pornography on company computers. Such laws provide employers with immunity from liability from privacy claims because they are reporting illegal conduct on the part of employees.[81]

TEXAS STUDENT PRIVACY ACT: PRIVACY AND CONFIDENTIALITY OF STUDENT RECORDS

In the area of public education, privacy laws are often slow to adapt to technological innovation and societal change. Problems arise from the challenges of storing massive amounts of student personal electronic data as well as from students interacting with online instructional software or gaming platforms that use the internet. Federal law offers guidance for the protection of personal data through the Children's Online Privacy Protection Act (COPPA).[82] COPPA outlines the duties of third-party internet providers and website operators in order to protect children's online privacy and safety; it requires operators to issue privacy notices and obtain parental consent prior to collecting, using, or disclosing personal information gathered from children under thirteen years old. In a typical public school setting, COPPA covers a wide range of online services and applications including mobile applications, gaming platforms, smart speakers, student tracking tools, toys, virtual assistants, and any service related to the internet. The Federal Trade Commission is the federal agency responsible for enforcing COPPA.[83]

School districts are also under obligation to the Federal Educational Rights and Privacy Act (FERPA) of 1974, which governs the confidentiality of student records. The law requires that all educational institutions maintain the confidentiality and privacy of student records, ensures that each student has access to their educational records, and provides students with the opportunity to correct error in their records.[84] To maintain privacy and confidentiality of student records all personally identifiable information must be protected. Personally identifiable information, such as a social security number, cannot be released to third parties without the consent of the student or parent.[85] Such information, making a student's identity easily traceable, is considered private and confidential.

The Texas Student Privacy Act (TSPA)[86] focuses on data privacy and cybersecurity in public schools, building upon many of the privacy protections afforded by federal law, as well as the Texas Public Information Act, which contains confidentiality protections.[87] Enacted in 1995 and amended in 2017, the TSPA is intended to protect the privacy of students from any entity that create student profiles for school purposes without first providing notification and securing their consent. The law is directed at "operators": third-party operators of websites, online services, or mobile applications created for school or education purposes.[88] The "covered information" includes name, gender, discipline records, health records, religious affiliation, political affiliation, disabilities, biometric information, food purchases, and geolocation information.[89] It also prohibits the operator of a website from engaging in targeted advertising if it is based on information the operator acquired through the use website and applications created or used for a school purpose.[90]

Further, the TSPA forbids operators from selling or renting a student's covered information.[91] If a school requests the deletion of a student's information, the operator must delete the information no later than sixty days after the request.[92] Since the TSPA privacy provisions are a part of the Texas Educational Code, the Texas Education Agency is the state agency responsible for enforcing the law securing compliance with the law.[93]

The law, however, falls short in guarding against one of the main threats to student privacy: cyberattacks on school databases. Nor does it provide remedies to the victims of hacking and data theft.[94] Schools are one of the main targets for data theft, often more vulnerable to cybercrime than private sector entities because the latter invests more money in preventative measures. In the private sector, the possibility of monetary damages awarded in civil suits incentivize chief executive officers and stockholders to maintain the most up-to-date practices that guard against data breaches resulting from cybercrime. Although it is an uphill battle to recover damages against a private sector business that has its database hacked, it is harder still to win a lawsuit for data breaches against a public school because, as state entities, they are shielded from legal liability by the doctrine of qualified sovereign immunity.

There is a lucrative business selling hacked personally identifiable information online. A child's social security number is particularly valuable because children typically do not have a credit history. This fact makes it easier for the thief to open a line of credit. School districts use cybersecurity software in their district computer networks, but this software does not protect every device; in addition, user neglect and weak passwords leaves data vulnerable. FERPA, last amended in 2001, provides general guidelines for student data security, but does not address cybersecurity measures. Schools, students, and parents are often lulled into a false sense of security when schools issue FERPA and TSPA notifications and guidelines; they believe that their personal information is secure. But school officials are not incentivized to do more than is required under FERPA because mere bureaucratic compliance with the law satisfies the school's duty of care. As mentioned, the doctrine of qualified immunity protects schools from full legal accountability. State law further requires schools to develop a policy to "secure district infrastructure," "determine cybersecurity risk and implement mitigation planning," and notify students and their parents of breaches to cybersecurity within a reasonable time.[95] But the vague language of the law requires only that schools have a policy in place and provide notification to students. Victims do not have access to civil remedies. However, the Texas Cybersecurity Act establishes cybersecurity requirements for all state agencies[96] and creates a cybersecurity council.[97] Provisions of the act that are applicable to hacking into school databases include sections on breach of computer security, electronic access interference, electronic data tampering, and unlawful decryption.[98]

ONLINE IMPERSONATION

As discussed in chapters 1 and 2, the appropriation of another person's name or likeness for commercial or pecuniary gain constitutes a breach of the common law privacy doctrine of appropriation. Misappropriation is typically conducted not with the intent to impersonate an individual but to use that person's fame or reputation to sell a product or service. In contrast, online impersonators are usually not attempting to profit based on a person's reputation or fame but rather to embarrass, intimidate, defraud, or exact revenge on their victim. Impersonation with the intent to do harm is considered an illegal invasion of privacy. In Texas, online impersonation is a crime commonly called "catfishing"[99] which occurs when a person "obtains and uses the name or persona of another person without their consent with the intent to cause harm."[100] Online impersonation is a felony offense involving actions such creating a fake social networking website using another person's name or sending a message or making a post on or through a social media account, email, or text message using another person's name, domain address, phone number, or other identifying information.[101] The "persona" to which the law refers extends to a person's image or general identity.[102] What if a fake profile is created as a cruel joke, satire, or a prank? According to the law there must be intent to cause harm, defraud, intimidate, or threaten.[103] Punishment for online impersonation can range from a class A misdemeanor to third-degree felony, the latter if the imposter sends a message to law enforcement or emergency personnel.[104]

Online impersonation has become more commonplace given the ubiquity of social media, such as Facebook and Instagram, as well as dating and matchmaking sites. Many perpetrators of impersonation are shocked to learn that online impersonation—even as a joke or mean-spirited prank—is a crime. Online impersonation often involves the creation of a fake online persona that is used for nefarious purposes. For instance, in the area of family law, during a divorce, an angry spouse might create a fake social media account in their partner's name to sully their reputation. Often, they will post intimate information or possibly nude photos. Another example would be a person who assumes the name and likeness of a person to create a profile in order to solicit sex or extort money from a hopeful "match" on a dating site. Of course, the widespread availability of artificial intelligence programs now makes it possible to combine a real person's face with a fake nude body. Privacy law has not even begun to catch up to this technology.

A distinction must be drawn between "fake" and "imposter." With a fake persona, the person depicted is not a real person. Imposter profiles impersonate a real victim who has had their name and photos misappropriated without their consent. Social media networks such as Facebook or Instagram have few if any incentives to protect the privacy of individual users because under law third-party providers are not typically liable for messages or photos posted by a user. This fact has long granted third-party social media companies and internet service providers legal immunity from liability for defamation or invasion of privacy.[105]

The language and intent of the law seems straightforward; however, sections of the law have been challenged on First Amendment grounds in state and federal courts. For instance, in *Ex parte Bradshaw*, the Texas Court of Appeals (Dallas) held that the statute prohibiting the act of assuming another person's identity, with the intent to do harm, was not overbroad in violation of the First Amendment.[106] Bradshaw was indicted under the law for intentionally using Joel Martin's name or persona to post messages on a website called manhunt.net, a gay male dating site, without Martin's consent and with the intent to cause harm. Bradshaw filed a pretrial writ of habeas corpus claiming that the indictment was a violation of his liberty protected by the First, Fifth, and Fourteenth Amendments. The trial court denied the writ and the Texas Court of Appeals (Houston) affirmed. Writing for the court, Justice Fillmore rejected Bradshaw's argument that the statute was a content-based suppression of speech simply because the law required the court to consider not merely the conduct of the person allegedly violating the law but the content of speech when deciding if the speaker violated the law.[107] In other words, in its attempt to punish criminal conduct the law also criminalizes what might be protected speech in violation of the First Amendment. Although Bradshaw conceded that the state has the right to prohibit certain forms of speech such as obscenity and true threats, merely because the speech might result in harassment or a violation of privacy does not necessarily mean it loses First Amendment protection.[108] Bradshaw argued that using another's name of persona to *create* a website, post a message, and send a message is an inherently expressive conduct. The state countered that the law unambiguously regulates conduct, not speech. To the extent that it regulated Bradshaw's speech at all, that speech is not a part of the exposition of ideas but is related to criminal conduct. There are few legitimate instances in which the impersonation of another person online would be protected by the First Amendment, such as impersonation for the sake of satire or humor, but the court concluded that falsely identifying oneself online or assuming someone's identity has little or no communicative value.[109]

In *Ex parte Maddison*,[110] Billy Mack Maddison was indicted under the online impersonation law for using Felicia Colburn's name to create a Facebook account with the intent to harm, defraud, intimidate, or threaten Colburn. Maddison created a fake Facebook profile in his ex-wife's name, complete with nude photographs. He then sent "friend" requests to his ex-wife's unsuspecting family and friends. Under indictment, Maddison challenged the constitutionality of the law arguing that it created a content-based restriction that criminalizes protected speech in violation of the First Amendment. He admitted that he may have caused "harm" to his ex-wife when he created a social media profile without their consent, but he believed that the law placed a chill on his expressive conduct, thus limiting what was a creative activity. The trial court agreed with Maddison's overbreadth argument because in order to establish "harm" it was first necessary for a court to examine the content of the speech alleged to cause harm to Colburn. Under the First Amendment, the state bears the burden of showing that the law satisfies strict scrutiny, which according to the court, it did not. "Harm" was so vague and overbroad as to "make it impossible to guess at its meaning."[111]

On appeal, however, the Texas Court of Appeals (Waco) held that the statute was *not* unconstitutional, nor was it overbroad or vague. Further, Maddison could not challenge the constitutionality of the whole statute since he was indicted under only one subsection.[112] Writing for the majority, Justice Scoggins argued that although the trial court was correct in its finding that any content-based suppression of speech must serve a compelling state interest, the online impersonation law unambiguously proscribed taking another's identity without consent for the purpose of harm. It did not target protected speech or expressive conduct. Proscribed harmful conduct is not protected by the First Amendment merely because the conduct involves the spoken or written word. As for Maddison's contention that the term "harm" was unconstitutionally vague which caused a chill on speech for fear of crossing into an "unlawful zone" of expressive activity, the appeals court stated that the Texas penal code clearly and unambiguously defines harm as anything reasonably regarded as loss, disadvantage, or injury, including harm to another person.[113] The District Court's ruling was ordered reversed and remanded.[114]

A third First Amendment challenge to the online impersonation law is *Dupuy v. Texas* in 2020.[115] Dupuy targeted two women by falsely advertising them as prostitutes on Backpage.com without their knowledge or consent. Dupuy had prior relationships with the two women, both of whom rejected him. The first woman he targeted, Amy, grew suspicious after receiving a flurry of phone calls and text messages asking about "overnight services." At first, she ignored the messages but then grew curious, asking one caller about the advertisement and seeking his assistance in navigating Backpage.com. She was shocked to discover that her photos were taken from her Facebook profile. She informed the police that she suspected that a man whom she dated but later rejected had created the fake advertisements. Law enforcement soon discovered from Backpage employees that this same person (Dupuy's alias) had also created a second advertisement for prostitution services for another woman whom he dated named Courtney.[116] Courtney had also rejected Dupuy's attentions. Using Dupuy's alias's internet service provider address, Facebook account, and the cooperation of a local internet service provider, officers identified the defendant as Christopher Dupuy and a warrant was issued to search his residence. Based on evidence seized from multiple electronic devices in his home, Dupuy was indicted and convicted on two separate charges of online impersonation for vindictively impersonating both women with the intent to cause them embarrassment and harm.

Dupuy argued that the online impersonation law violated his First Amendment rights.[117] As in the two aforementioned online impersonation cases, Dupuy reasoned that the statute was unconstitutionally overbroad and vague. If, he argued, the advertisements on Backpage were indeed created by him, then he was engaged in constitutionally protected speech. The statute regulates the content of speech because a court must first examine the content of his advertisement before it can be determined whether he committed an offence. Hypothetically, had he created an advertisement using the women's personae and images stating that they were devout women praying for hurricane victims and to contact them for more prayers, day or night, then he would not have been indicted. So, the conviction would have been content-based—based on what the women were saying. However, as in previous cases, the court rejected Dupuy's argument and held that his speech deserved no First Amendment protection for "communicative conduct in which one individual invades the substantial privacy interests of another in an essentially intolerable manner."[118] Note that in addition to the Texas statute there are also federal laws addressing the act of "false personification."[119]

IDENTITY THEFT

A form of invasion of privacy results from the theft of one's identity. Armed with enough personal, financial, and biometric information, a criminal can ruin a person's life both financially and personally, potentially leaving the victim without money, transportation, or housing. Identity thieves target credit or debit card numbers, social security numbers, state driver's license numbers, and home addresses. Theft can occur as a result of daily online shopping, unsecure Wi-Fi networks, phishing, dumpster diving, or physical theft of a wallet or a package left on the front porch. The most prevalent form of identity theft is fraudulent use of credit card numbers. Identity theft has been a crime in Texas since 1999 when the 76th Legislature enacted a criminal statute that prevents the "fraudulent use or possession of identifying information."[120] Under the law, the theft or possession of identifying information, which is anything that may identify a person, includes but is not limited to (1) name and date of birth, (2) biometric data, (3) electronic identification, (4) government issued identifications, and (5) electronic devices.[121] The use of electronic information consists of the use of a person's home address, bank account number, routing number, card number, or any identification code given to that person.[122] According to the law, the thief must have ill "intent to harm or defraud another" and "obtains, possesses, transfers, or uses" identifying information without consent.[123] Identity theft prosecutions hinge upon the possession of (1) identifying information of three or more persons; (2) identifying information concerning three of more deceased persons, including a stillborn infant or fetus, that would be the identify that person if they were alive; and (3) if the information is obtained, possessed, or transferred, or used without legal authorization. Identifying information includes, but is not limited to, a card, license plate, code, account number, personal identification number, electronic serial number, and mobile identification number.[124] The penalty for identity theft varies based upon the severity of the crime but can range from a state jail felony up to a third-degree felony. Since 1999 all sheriff's offices in the State of Texas are required to establish a unique criminal file called "The Stolen Identity File."[125] Penalties for fraudulent possession and use of identifying information also depends on the number of pieces of identifying information[126] or whether the crime is perpetrated against a person aged sixty-five or older.[127]

Similar to the First Amendment challenges to Texas's online impersonation law, the state's identity theft law has been challenged on the grounds that it is overbroad, suppresses speech, criminalizes thought, and is vague to the extent that the average person cannot understand what conduct is prohibited. For example, in *Ex parte Harrington*,[128] the defendant was indicted for engaging in criminal activity for possessing fifty or more items of identifying information including names and social security numbers. She sought a writ of habeas corpus to set aside her indictment on three grounds: (1) the statute restricts protected speech by affecting the communication of ideas, (2) the law is void for vagueness, and (3) statute unconstitutionally creates what she characterized as a "thought crime." The court rejected all three contentions and found that the statute was a straightforward proscription of possession or use of another person's private identifying information. The conduct that the statute regulates is noncommunicative (the act of theft or possession) even if the conduct includes spoken words.[129] It is unlikely that a person would be convicted under the law because they spoke ill of another or mused that they had planned to dig through the trash to find credit card statements.[130]

INVASION OF PRIVACY FROM THE SKY: DRONES

Unmanned arial vehicles, or drones, are valuable tools with a wide range of applications. Drones are used by nongovernmental actors such as architects, building inspectors, photojournalists, and mountain climbers. Drone use by private individuals, ranging from journalists, researchers, professional paparazzi, and garden variety eavesdroppers, has led to the need for more regulation and civil as well as criminal penalties for drone misuse. Federal regulations focus largely on Federal Aviation Administration (FAA) registration and operating safety rather than potential for the invasion of privacy. The proliferation of drones is a function of their ease of use and safety compared to helicopters, enabling capable laypersons to engage in aerial photography, allowing the capture of clearer images. They are more economically feasible for freelance journalists and small news outlets. Criticisms of drone abuse levied by state lawmakers reflect constituent complaints that they are intrusive, unsafe, a hindrance to law enforcement and first responders, and a means of trespassing on private commercial property and government facilities. In 2013, the 83rd Texas Legislature passed a statute protecting the right to privacy from the "illegal use of unmanned aircraft to capture [an] image . . . with the intent to conduct surveillance on the individual or property captured in the image."[131] The statute was amended in 2015. The law also prohibits flying a drone over "correctional facilities, detention facilities, and critical infrastructure facilities, defined to include oil and gas pipelines, and sports venues." In 2017 the law was amended to include cattle feed lots and other animal feeding operations. Under one section of the law a landowner or tenant may bring a civil action.[132] The state legislature modified the law following incidents of private citizens using aerial drones to photograph and report meat processing plants and stockyards that pollute the environment.

Exemptions were granted for research by universities and colleges and for certain commercial purposes; however, no exemption was granted to photojournalists or for news gathering purposes. As a result, a constitutional challenge to the law was brought by the National Press Photographers Association, which originally fought passage of the bill when it was first proposed in 2013. In *National Press Photographers Association v. McCraw* in 2022,[133] a federal district court ruled that the Texas law violates the First Amendment of the US Constitution in that it prevents journalists from using drones to take photographs as a part of newsgathering and reporting. The court recognized that drones allow journalists to photograph events such as natural disasters, wars, and the manner that police respond to a crime or apprehend a suspect. One member of the National Press Photographers Association, Joseph Pappalardo, a freelance photographer from Dallas, was denied permission to fly his drone over a state-financed construction project. He also argued that fear of liability under the law caused a chill on his speech, thus preventing him from gathering images during the aftermath of Hurricane Harvey, the removal of homeless encampments in the state, and illegal poaching in urban areas.[134] As Papplardo stated, "using a [drone] for journalistic purposes would put [him] at risk of criminal penalties and subject [him] to liability in a civil lawsuit."[135] Press photographers, many of whom were licensed to fly drones by the Federal Aviation Adminsitration, were being threatened with arrest for using drones to photograph and video record such subjects as fires, water treatment plants, a facility that housed immigrant children, and the Texas Rangers baseball team.[136] Fear of liability also discouraged many newspapers from publishing the photos which in turn leads to self-censorship. The National Press Photographers Association argued that the use of drones to capture images should receive as much First Amendment protections as the images themselves, thus challenging the constitutionality of the statute on the grounds that it violated the First Amendment and caused a chill on journalists and photographers.[137]

The district court agreed that the protections of the First Amendment must extend to each phase of the "speech process"; restrictions on the creation of speech, as in photography, curtails expression as does limiting the products of and display of speech.[138] The process of creating photographs and videos captured by drones enjoys as much protection by the First Amendment as do the images themselves. The act of making an audiovisual recording is necessarily included within the First Amendment guarantee of press rights. The surveillance and no-fly provisions of the drone law are both content-based restrictions that regulate on the basis of the subject of expression. The surveillance provision required the enforcing officials to inquire into the contents of the image to determine whether it is prohibited—that is, to ascertain whether the drone photography is permitted if the subject is public property but not permitted if the subject is an individual or private property. The no-fly provision is also subject to strict scrutiny because the legality of the images depend on their purpose: permissible for "commercial purpose[s]," whether the images were meant to generate income by appealing to a market audience.[139] Further, the surveillance provision of the law applies to the identity of the speaker, favoring some speakers and disfavoring others. The same drone image taken legally by university researchers, employees of insurance companies, and real estate brokers would constitute a misdemeanor charge if taken by a journalist. In sum, the unmanned arial vehicle law was ruled to be unconstitutional under the First and Fourteenth Amendments; all officers, agents, employees, and all other persons are enjoined from enforcing the law.[140] The state never plausibly demonstrated how the range of governmental interests, including privacy, that the law advanced were threatened by photojournalism or newsgathering but not by aerial photography for commercial purposes. As we have seen in the preceding chapters, in common law privacy cases, courts have aimed at striking balance between privacy interests and press freedoms.

The concern over drones flying over private property is justified, but so is the concern for press freedom and the ability to report on abuses and law violation by farmers, ranchers, animal production facilities, and refineries. The law was the only statute in Texas directly addressing aerial invasion of privacy, although there remains other penalties for criminal or civil trespass.

As discussed earlier, individuals also have privacy protection from having their images and conversations recorded and disseminated without their consent, especially where there is a reasonable expectation of privacy and when it is done with the intent to harm, harass, or if images are used for the purpose of sexual gratification or a violation of the right to publicity.[141] Having a federal court strike down the drone section in the Texas Privacy Act as an unconstitutional violation of the First Amendment is no small matter. As of this writing in 2023, no new legislation has been enacted addressing these First Amendment concerns, carving out an exception for journalists.[142]

CONSUMER PRIVACY

Telemarketing is at minimum a minor annoyance and at its most extreme an intrusive and predatory practice. Most of us at one time have had to deal with telemarketers either in the form of telephone calls, texts, or the disclosure to telemarketers without our consent of what we assumed to be private personal information including name, age, gender, and contact information. Although it is reasonable to expect unsolicited phone calls, the fact that unknown telemarketers are in possession of our phone number and are able to interrupt our daily schedules and perhaps attempt to pressure a vulnerable person into buying a product or service that they do not want or cannot afford can be an invasion of privacy. In the 2001 legislative session the state legislature passed the Texas Telemarketing Disclosure law which "protect[s] the public against false, misleading, abusive, or deceptive practices in the telemarketing business."[143] It authorizes the Public Utility Commission of Texas[144] to implement a statewide "Do Not Call List,"[145] thus allowing residents to register a telephone number with either of the Public Utility Commission of Texas's two no call lists. The law initially applied to telephone calls but was later amended to include text messages.[146]

The law defines a telemarketing call as an unsolicited telephone call made to (1) solicit a sale of a consumer good or service, (2) solicit an extension of credit for a consumer good or services, or (3) obtain information that may be used to solicit a sale of a consumer good or service or to extend credit for the sale.[147] The code requires companies who wish to "make a telephone solicitation" to obtain a registration certificate from the office of the Secretary of State.

There are numerous exceptions to do-not-call rules that include political campaign fundraising, solicitations from non-profit and charitable organizations, companies with which you have previously contacted to provide goods or services, and where the consumer has not informed the telemarketer they would not like to receive a call.[148] The individual making the telemarketing call is not liable if they make a one-time call to someone who is on the no-call list. The law does not extend to legitimate debt collection.[149]

In 2021 a telemarketing company was assessed nearly $250,000 in penalties for making twenty-eight calls to a single person in Texas. In *Thompson v. Dealer Renewal Service* in 2021,[150] a federal district court in Texas found that the telemarketer failed to register with the Secretary of State as required under Texas law.

In 2023, the Texas legislature enacted HB 4, the Texas Data Privacy and Security Act (TDPSA).[151] The TDPSA is intended to bolster privacy protection of consumer data, extending to a very broad range of individuals and businesses (known as "controllers" under the statute) who collect, store, and sell Texans' consumer data both inside and outside of the state. One of the objectives of the TDPSA is to "maximize interoperability," which means to function with other state privacy laws in instances when data is collected from out of state. Under the law, consumer rights include the right to (1) know whether a controller is processing the consumer's personal data; (2) receive a portable copy, in digital format, of the consumer's personal data processed by the controller; (3) request deletion of personal data provided by or obtained about the consumer; (4) request a correction of inaccurate personal data; and (5) opt out of sales of one's personal data, targeted advertising, and profiling in furtherance of a decision that produces a legal or similarly significant effect concerning the consumer. The Texas Attorney General is granted sole enforcement rights on any violation of the TDPSA.

TEXAS PRIVACY PROTECTION ADVISORY COUNCIL

Before concluding this chapter, it is noteworthy to mention that in 2019 the 86th Legislature approved House Bill 4390 creating the Texas Privacy Protection Advisory Council which is responsible for analyzing laws governing privacy and protection of Texans' informational privacy.[152] Texas Government Code requires state agencies handling sensitive and private information conduct vulnerability and penetration tests of their websites.[153] Personal data is a target for criminals engaged in phishing, extortion, data breaches, identity theft, romance fraud, and internet financial fraud. HB 4390 also requires that Texas residents be notified of a data breach invasion of privacy within sixty days.[154] In 2023, the legislature strengthened data breach notification requirements by broadening the types of consumer data covered and changing the requirement to report data breaches to the Texas Attorney General within thirty days (rather than sixty days) of discovering a breach.[155]

NOTES

1. Texas Penal Code, section 16.02.

2. It is recommended that you read Texas Penal Code, section 16.02, carefully before attempting to record a person or persons. It is also recommended that you contact an attorney specializing in this area of law if you feel that you have been recorded in a manner that violates the law.

3. The Texas wiretap law is found in section 16.02 of the Texas Penal Code.

4. Texas Code of Criminal Procedure, section 18.02. Recording comments or conversations in a public meeting (such as a town hall meeting) without permission is permitted under the state's Open Meetings Act. Texas Government Code, section 551.023.

5. Texas Penal Code, section 16.02.

6. Texas Penal Code, section 16.02(b)(1).

7. Texas Penal Code, section 16.02(b)(2).

8. Texas Penal Code, section 16.02.

9. *Long v. State*, 535 S.W.3d 511 (Tex. Crim. App. 2017).

10. The cases received, regional, national, and even international news coverage. See "Texas principal could get 20 years in jail for planting camera in locker room to catch coach yelling," Associated Press, published July 6, 2012, updated November 28, 2015, https://www.wfaa.com/article/news/local/denton-county/former-principal-convicted-in-locker-room-recording-case/287-306089776.

11. *Long v. State*, 515–17.

12. Ibid, 518–28.

13. Dakota Brewer, "Smile, you're on camera: A discussion of the privacy rights of teachers in the modern day classroom," *Brigham Young Education Law Journal* (2019): 139.

14. Ibid.

15. Texas Penal Code, section 16.02, does not define the terms of the offense but incorporates definitions found in Article 18.20 of the Texas Code of Criminal Procedure.

16. There is no mention of the "one-party" rule in the opinion.

17. Citing the Texas Court of Criminal Appeals decision in *State v. Scheineman*, 77 S.W.3d 810 (2002) and the US Supreme Court's ruling in *Katz v U.S.*, 389 US 347 (1967).

18. *Long v. State*, 535–38.

19. Ibid.

20. *Taylor v. Tolbert*, 644 S.W. 3d 637 (2022).

21. Ibid.

22. *Graham v. Miller*, 2023 WL 1960680 (2023). No. 05-22-00766-CV.

23. Ibid.

24. Texas Citizens Participation Act (TCPA), Texas Civil Practice & Remedies Code, section §27.001, 27.003.

25. Ibid.

26. *Miller v. Talley Dunn Gallery, LLC*, No. 05-15-00444-CV, 2016 WL 836775, at *8–10 (Tex. App.—Dallas Mar. 3, 2016, no pet. h.) (mem. op.).
27. Ibid.
28. Ibid, *11.
29. Ibid, *10 (quoting *Billings v. Atkinson*, 489 S.W.2d 858, 861 (Tex. 1973).
30. Chapter 33.02 of the Texas Penal Code.
31. Ibid.
32. *Collins v. Collins*, 904 S.W.2d 792,797 (Tex. App. – Houston [1st Dist.] 1995, writ denied) (en banc).
33. Ibid.
34. *Clayton v. Richards*, 47 S.W.3d 149 (Tex. App. – Texarkana 2001, pet. denied).
35. Ibid, 155–56.
36. Computer Fraud and Abuse Act of 1986, 18 U.S.C. §1030(a)(2) (2012).
37. Chapter 33 of the Texas Penal Code, section 33.01 (12), makes it a class B misdemeanor to knowingly access a computer without the consent or authorization of the owner. A person can then bring a civil action under section 143.001 of the Texas Civil Practice and Remedies Code.
38. Texas Penal Code, section 33.02(a), (b).
39. *Miller v. Talley Dunn Gallery, LLC*, No. 05-15-00444-CV, 2016 WL 836775, at *9 (Tex. App.—Dallas Mar. 3, 2016, no pet. h.) (mem. op.).
40. Texas Penal Code, section 21.15. Invasive Visual Recording.
41. Texas Penal Code section 21.16(b).
42. Ex parte Nyabwa, 366 S.W.3d 710 (Tex. Crim. App. 2012). See also Ex parte Metzger, 610 S.W. 3d 86 (2021).
43. See Revenge Porn law, Texas Penal Code, section 21.16.
44. *Ex parte Thompson*, 442 S.W. 3d 325 (2014).
45. Ibid, 334–35.
46. Ibid, 338.
47. Ibid, 349.
48. Texas Penal Code, section 21.15. Sec. 21.15. Invasive Visual Recording.
49. *Ex parte Metzger*, 610 S.W. 3d 86 (2020).
50. In *Ex parte Fairchild-Porche*, 638 S.W. 3d 770 (2021).
51. Ibid, *793.
52. Ibid, and see Anayeli Ruiz, "Texas woman awarded $1.2 billion in 'revenge porn' lawsuit," KHOU.com (August 11, 2023).
53. Ibid.
54. Texas Penal Code, sec. 21.17.
55. Supra note 39, Texas Penal Code, section 21.15.
56. 4 W. Blackstone *Commentaries on the Laws of England* *223.
57. See generally Kaspersky.com, "What is facial recognition: Definition and explanation," https://www.kaspersky.com/resource-center/definitions/what-is-facial-recognition; and Samuel D. Hodge, Jr., "Big brother is watching: Law enforcement's use of digital technology in the twenty-first century," *University of Cincinnati Law Review*, 89 (2020): 30.

58. Texas Biometric Privacy Act, Texas Business & Commerce Code, section 503.001.

59. Ibid.

60. Ibid.

61. Ibid.

62. Texas Business & Commerce Code, section 503.001 (West, 2009)

63. Texas Business & Commerce Code, section 503.001 (West, 2017).

64. Jay Greene, "Microsoft won't sell facial recognition to police without federal regulation," NBCnews.com, https://www.nbcnews.com/tech/internet/microsoft-won-t-sell-facial-recognition-police-without-federal-regulation-n1230286; https://www.cnn.com/2021/05/18/tech/amazon-police-facial-recognition-ban/index.html; Jacob Snow, "Amazon's face recognition falsely matched 28 members of Congress with mugshots, ACLU" (July 26, 2018), https://www.aclu.org/press-releases/amazon-facial-surveillance-technology-falsely-identifies-28-members-congress-mugshots.

65. Texas Business & Commerce Code, Ann. § 503.001 (West, 2009).

66. See generally Kelsey A. Santamaria, "Facial recognition technology and law enforcement: Select constitutional considerations," Congressional Research Service (Sept. 24 2020), https://crsreports.congress.gov/product/pdf/R/R46541/2; and State Facial Recognition Policy, Electronic Privacy Information Center (2021), https://epic.org/state-facial-recognition-policy/.

67. *The State of Texas, et al v Google, LLC*, 4:2020-cv-00957.The lawsuit was brought under the Texas Deceptive Trade Practices Act as well.

68. Ibid.

69. Ibid.

70. *State of Texas v. Meta Platforms Inc.*, (2022) (texasattorneygeneral.gov).

71. Ibid.

72. Kashmir Hill and Ryan Mac, "Facebook, citing societal concerns, plans to shut down facial recognition system," *New York Times*, November 2, 2021, updated June 22, 2023, https://www.nytimes.com/2021/11/02/technology/facebook-facial-recognition.html.

73. Illinois Biometric Information Privacy Act (740 ILCS 14/), https://www.ilga.gov/legislation/ilcs/ilcs3.asp?ActID=3004&ChapterID=57.

74. Bobby Allyn, NPR.org, February 25, 2021, https://www.npr.org/2021/02/25/971460327/tiktok-to-pay-92-million-to-settle-class-action-suit-over-theft-of-personal-data.

75. Rachel Metz, "Clearview AI agrees to restrict US sales of facial recognition mostly to law enforcement," *CNN Business,* Mon May 9, 2022, https://www.cnn.com/2022/05/09/tech/clearview-ai-alu-settlement/index.html.

76. Proposed Biometric Privacy laws similar to BIPA have been introduced in Arizona (A 1362), Minnesota (SF 954)), Missouri (HB 1047), Tennessee (SB 0339/HB 0932), and New York (A 1362).

77. *McLaren v. Microsoft Corp.*, Tex. App. LEXIS 4103 (Tex. App. – Dallas 1999).

78. *Stengart v. Loving Care Agency*, 201 N.J. 300 (2010).

79. *Fazio v. Temporary Excellence, Inc.*, 2012 WL 300634 (N.J. Super.) (app. Div. 2012).

80. *Rene v. G.F. Fishers, Inc.*, 817 F. Supp.2d 1090 (S.D. Ind. 2011). See also *Owen v. CIGNA*, 188 F.Supp.3d (S.D. Ill. 2016).
81. See Texas Business & Commerce Code, section 110.002(b).
82. 15 U.S.C §§ 6501–6505; 16 CFR §§ 312.1-.13.
83. Ibid.
84. The Federal Education Rights and Privacy, The Family Educational Rights and Privacy Act (FERPA) (20 U.S.C. § 1232g; 34 CFR Part 99). See *Hall v. McRaven*, 508 S.W.3d 232 (Tex. 2017) dealing with Texas higher education.
85. Ibid.
86. Texas Education Code, section 32.151(3) (2017).
87. Texas Government Code, Chapter 552.
88. Texas Education Code, section 32.152 (West, 2017).
89. Ibid.
90. Ibid, § 32.152(2).
91. Ibid, § 32.152 (3).
92. Ibid, § 32.156.
93. See Texas Education Code, section 39.003(a)(17).
94. See generally Rebekah Luna, "Stranger danger! How hackers break into school databases to steal student data, and what legislatures should do about it," *Texas Tech Law Review*, 54 (Winter 2022): 381.
95. Texas Education Code, section 11.175.
96. Texas Government Code, section 2054.054.0594.
97. Texas Penal Code, section 33; and see Elizabeth Rogers, "New laws are putting Texas at the forefront in addressing cybersecurity as a matter of public policy," State Bar of Texas, https://www.texasbar.com/AM/Template.cfm?Section=articles&Template=/CM/HTMLDisplay.cfm&ContentID=42283.
98. Texas Penal Code, section 33.
99. Texas Penal Code, section, 33.07 (enacted by the legislature in 2011).
100. Online impersonation falls under Title 7 "Offenses Against Property," Chapter 33 "Computer Crimes." Texas Penal Code, section 33.07.
101. Ibid.
102. Ibid.
103. Ibid.
104. Ibid.
105. See *Barnes v. Yahoo! Inc.*, 570 F.3d 1096 (9th Cir. 2009) which held that under Section 230 (c)(1) and €(3) of the Communications Decency Act, the third-party social media company was not liable for harm inflicted on users by other users.
106. *Ex parte Bradshaw*, 501 S.W.3d 665 (Tex. App.—Dallas 2016).
107. Ibid, 670.
108. Ibid, 674–75.
109. Ibid, 678. The court also rejected the argument that the law violated the Dormant Commerce Clause by unduly burdening interstate commerce.
110. *Ex parte Maddison*, 518 S.W.3d 630 (Tex. App.—Waco 2017).
111. Ibid.
112. Ibid.

113. *Ex parte Maddison*, 518 S.W.3d 630 (Tex. App. 2017).

114. Ibid, and see *State v. Stubbs*, 502 S.W.3d 218 (Tex. App.—Houston [14th Dist.] 2016).

115. *Dupuy v. Texas*, 631 S.W. 3d 233 (Tex. App. – Houston [14th Dist.] 2020).

116. Ibid, 236.

117. Ibid, 243.

118. Ibid.

119. Federal laws dealing with "false personification" are found within 18 U.S. Code Chapter 43.

120. Texas Penal Code, §32 .51.

121. Ibid.

122. Ibid.

123. Ibid.

124. Ibid.

125. "Identity Theft Information Guide," Identity Theft Information Guide | Department of Public Safety, accessed December 8, 2022, https://www.dps.texas.gov/section/victim-employment-support-services-vess/identity-theft-information-guide.

126. Texas Penal Code, section 32.51(c).

127. Texas Penal Code, section 22.04.

128. *Ex parte Harrington*, 499 S.W.3d 142 (Tex. App. – Houston [14th Dist.] 2016).

129. See *Jones v. State*, 396 S.W. 3d 558 (Tex. Crim. App. 2013).

130. *Ex parte Harrington,* 499 S.W.3d 142, 148 (Tex. App. – Houston [14th Dist.] 2016).

131. Texas Government Code, section 423.003. Texas Government Code, section 423.002, 423.003, 423.006 together and called the surveillance provisions.

132. Ibid, 423.006.

133. *National Press Photographers Association v. McCraw*, 594 F. Supp. 3d 789 (W.D. Tex. 2022).

134. Ibid, 796.

135. Ibid.

136. Ibid, 797.

137. Ibid.

138. Ibid, 804.

139. Ibid, 806.

140. Ibid, 813.

141. Beyond an invasion of privacy that may result from Peeping Tom drones, celebrities also face violations of the right to publicity. The commercial impact of appropriating a person's likeness rather than the harm resulting from an invasion of privacy itself is the main concern of the right to publicity. See generally Amanda Tate, "Miley Cyrus and the attack of the drones: The right to publicity and tabloid use of unmanned aircraft systems," *Texas Review of Entertainment and Sports Law*, 17 (2015).

142. See "The drone star state: How a challenge to Texas drone law became the latest battleground between the First Amendment and the right to privacy," *Journal of Air Law and Commerce* (Winter 2023): 88.

143. Texas Telemarketing Disclosure and Privacy Act, Texas Business and Commerce Code Annotated, section 304.001.

144. Public Utility Commission of Texas, https://www.puc.texas.gov/consumer/default.aspx.

145. www.texasnocall.com.

146. The state law is enforced in three ways: (1) the Public Utility Commission of Texas may use its authority to investigate violations and impose administrative and civil penalties against violators, (2) the Office of the Texas Attorney General may take actions against violators, and (3) private lawsuits may be brought against telemarketers. In addition, the state's no-call registry parallels the federal no-call list maintained by the Federal Communications Commission (see Telephone Consumer Protection Act, 47 U.S. C. § 227).

147. Texas Telemarketing Disclosure and Privacy Act, Texas Business and Commerce Code Annotated, section 304.001.

148. Texas Business and Commerce Code, section 304.004 (West, 2009). Per Texas Business and Commerce Code, section 304.002148. , a telephone call is defined as "(1) an actual phone call made by an automated telephone dialing system; a transmission to a facsimile recording device; and a call or other transmission, including a transmission of a text or graphic message or of an image" to a cell phone. In simpler terms, under the Texas Telemarketing Disclosure and Privacy Act, a text is considered a phone call.

149. Texas Business and Commerce Code, section 304.058.

150. *Thompson v. Dealer Renewal Services*, No. 4:21-cv-0467-P, 2021 U.S. Dist. LEXIS 223424 (N.D. Tex. November 18, 2021).

151. The act takes effect July 1, 2024, and is added to the Business & Commerce Code.

152. H.B. 4390, Leg., 86th Reg. Sess. (Tex. 2019).

153. Texas Government Code, section 2054.

154. See generally Jordan Elias, "Course correction—Data breach as invasion of privacy," *Baylor Law Review*, 69 (2017): 574; and Jennifer Wilt, "Cancelled credit cards: Substantial risk of future injury as a basis for standing in data breach cases," *Southern Methodist University Law Review*, 71 (2018).

155. The amendment to Texas's data breach notification law (Tex. Bus. & Com. Code Ann. §§ 521.002 and 521.053).

Chapter 4

Privacy in Twenty-First-Century Texas

A Final Assessment

The right to privacy reflects a fundamental human need to be free from intrusion into the most personal and intimate matters; it protects the right to live our lives without undue interference, to associate with whomever we please, and, in the broadest definition of the right, to make autonomous choices with respect to health, sexuality, and reproduction.

This book examined the origins and development of the right to privacy in Texas beginning at a time in the state's legal history when the courts had not yet recognized the common law tort doctrines that allow recovery for invasion of privacy and culminating with the adoption of a robust right to privacy found in judicial decisions and statutory protections. The foundational discussion of the common law origins of the major privacy doctrines in chapter 1 illustrated that many US states adopted the right to privacy as early as 1900, over seventy years before Texas recognized privacy as an independent right. The privacy decisions of the US Supreme Court reflect those common law doctrines as well as the liberties enshrined in the Bill of Rights. Chapter 2 analyzed the Texas appellate court privacy rulings that have had the most profound impact on the origins and development of the right to privacy in the state. In instances where the common law did not meet the need of modern society, legislators crafted legislative solutions in the form of distinct statutory civil and criminal remedies for injuries resulting from wiretapping, unlawful interception of confidential information or images, identity theft, health and consumer privacy, the use of drones to spy and snoop, cybercrime, and theft of medical and educational data. Chapter 3 provided an overview of those statutory protections.

This final chapter is an assessment of the degree to which the right to privacy protects Texans in the second decade of the twenty-first century. A number of questions are raised. What fundamental interests are protected by the right to privacy in Texas? What types of actions and activities are plausibly protected by privacy, and which fall outside the scope of this right as historically understood in Texas? What are the limitations of this body of law? This chapter also offers an overview of some of the most recent state policy changes that will affect privacy.

THE SCOPE OF THE RIGHT TO PRIVACY IN TEXAS

Texas did not create the right to privacy from whole cloth. The state's privacy jurisprudence rests upon several pillars: (1) the earlier decisions of state courts outside of Texas adopted by Texas judges; (2) Warren and Brandeis's 1890 *Harvard Law Review* article, cited as a point of origin in nearly all privacy decisions in Texas (and the United States); and (3) Professor William Prosser's body of work on tort law that influenced generations of lawyers and judges. Prosser's four privacy torts are central to the development of privacy law in Texas: intrusion, also referred to as invasion; public disclosure of private information; false light invasion; and appropriation.[1] Prosser is cited in nearly every privacy case that is discussed in this book.[2] Many of these tort doctrines "diffused" across fifty state court systems as a result of judges citing or acknowledging privacy doctrine adoptions by courts in other states. Even in instances of variation of application of the doctrines in legal disputes by state judges, common principles and theories are woven though the decisions.

It is important to note that seminal US Supreme Court privacy rulings, such as *Griswold*, *Eisenstadt*, *Roe*, and *Lawrence*, have had little to no discernable impact of the development of Texas privacy jurisprudence, which is based on common law doctrines and state constitutional provisions; state privacy caselaw in Texas has never encompassed matters of reproduction or abortion. These federal precedents have been applied in privacy claims brought in federal courts in Texas or when litigants have sought relief in state courts on federal rather than state grounds.

Of course, the success of privacy claims—and thus the breadth of privacy protection—often depends not on the mechanical application of a doctrine or precedent but on the partisan or ideological composition of the courts at a given period in Texas legal history. An interesting finding was that in early privacy claims in Texas judges acknowledged the rulings of the courts of other states as well as the diffusion of these doctrines from state to state, but they were highly resistant to the idea of a right to privacy. In the state's traditionalist and conservative legal culture, the consensus of many judges was that because the common law in the state was a fixed body of law that could only be changed by the legislature, no recovery for invasion of privacy was possible. Eventually this mindset changed, but early on judges feared that adopting any of the existing doctrines would upset settled law and cause a cascade of litigation.

As we saw, privacy did not become an actionable legal claim in Texas until *Billings v. Atkinson*[3] in 1973. The term "privacy" appeared prior to *Billings* but the discussion in these earlier cases referred to a generic right to privacy without amplification or attribution to law or doctrine. The earliest references to invasion of privacy in Texas were not in terms of a right or tort doctrine, but only in the common usage of the term or aphoristically, as in "an intrusion upon one's privacy and modesty."

Privacy caselaw in Texas today recognizes a right based on three of the four common law privacy torts: intrusion or invasion into a person's private affairs, seclusion, or solitude; public disclosure of private information; and appropriation of name of likeness for value or commercial gain. The fourth doctrine, disclosure of false communication about a person, or what came to be known as the "false light" doctrine, is no longer recognized as a viable privacy cause of action. The three tort doctrines in aggregate form an independent right to be free from intrusion into our private affairs and to control over our identity and reputation. Privacy also receives protection from provisions of the Texas Bill of Rights pertaining to arbitrary deprivation of life and liberty, freedom of speech and press, the privilege against self-incrimination, freedom of conscience and religion, and the right to be free from intrusions into the sanctity of the home and person.

Distilling these torts and constitutional provisions into one inclusive theory of privacy is challenging, but a concise definition can be understood as follows: privacy allows for a cause of action for intentional or willful invasion of one's person and home; it protects against intrusion into solitude, seclusion, and the most private and intimate matters. The broad concept of intrusion extends to entering a home without permission, surveillance and wiretapping, video recording of sexual acts and sharing the recording without consent to third parties, and conversations in private as well as public places when there is a reasonable expectation to keep conversations private. Further, privacy allows a person to recover damages resulting from the unwanted public disclosure of private information and from the misappropriation of a person's name, likeness, or reputation for commercial gain or the value associated with self-identity. To recover for breach of privacy, the tortious action must always be intentional—the courts have resisted applying negligence doctrine to privacy law. Privacy in Texas is a negative right—a right to be "let alone." Of course, while in theory the right may seem robust, the actual success of plaintiffs in civil privacy actions is dependent on the facts of each case and the legal philosophy or ideology of the judges hearing the cause of action.

As discussed in chapter 2, the bedrock upon which the right to privacy in Texas rests are four precedent rulings: *Billings*, *Texas State Employees Union (TSEU)*, *Kimbrough*, and *Industrial Foundation*. *Billings*[4] is without doubt the most important privacy decision in the state, not merely by virtue of being the first ruling by a Texas court to elevate privacy to a legal right, but also because it offers the most capacious definition of privacy to date, recognizing a right to be free from the illegitimate appropriation or exploitation of one's personality, the unwarranted publicizing of one's private information and affairs, and the intrusion into one's private life in such a manner as to cause outrage, mental suffering, shame or humiliation.

Billings interpreted the intrusion doctrine to include (to borrow a phrase from *Griswold v. Connecticut*) penumbral privacy interests. The case was decided during a brief progressive period in the state's history that spanned the 1970s and has been cited in 198 Texas court cases; no Texas appellate court would again define privacy as broadly.[5] As the Texas courts grew more conservative in the 1980s and 1990s, many judges adopted a narrow interpretation of *Billing*'s definition of privacy out of concern for an expansion of liability in tort claims and a concomitant litigation explosion. For many conservative jurists, *Billings* was anathema to their legal philosophy of originalism or strict interpretation or just seen as liberal judicial activism.

Three years after the landmark *Billings* decision, in *Industrial Foundation of the South v. Texas Industrial Accident Board* in 1976, the Texas Supreme Court expressly adopted the public disclosure doctrine, recognized as the right to be free from the public disclosure of embarrassing private facts.[6] Using this doctrine, the courts have extended protection to personal information, business records, medical records, and tax records. However, the courts have been less willing to protect disclosures regarding matters such as one's sexual orientation and the results of drug testing.

After *Billings* and *Industrial Foundation*, the intrusion privacy doctrine stagnated; little expansion in terms of scope of its protection took place for another decade. The application of *Billings* in subsequent rulings did allow for existing privacy doctrines to become more securely rooted as precedent, but there is little evidence of courts attempting to expand the scope of protection. Then, in 1987, in *TSEU*,[7] the Texas Supreme Court ruled that a right to privacy contained in the Texas Constitution offered broader protections than the right to privacy under the US Constitution and federal caselaw. The Court argued that the state constitutional right to privacy is an aggregate of provisions of the Texas Bill of Rights, which includes the prohibition of arbitrary deprivation of life and liberty[8]; the freedom to speak, write, or publish[9]; the privilege against self-incrimination[10]; an individual's right to freedom of conscience and religion[11]; and, most fundamentally, the right to be free from intrusions into the sanctity of the home and person against intrusion.[12] Protection against invasion of privacy now came to rest upon two pillars: common law and constitutional. *Billings* adopted the right to privacy as a distinct tort that constitutes a legal injury, and *TSEU* recognized an implied state constitutional right. In many subsequent privacy cases the courts seem to rely on either or both. *TSEU* is cited in sixty-seven cases since 1987.[13]

The appropriation doctrine was adopted for the first time by a Texas court in *Kimbrough v. Coca Cola/USA* in 1975[14] and has been cited in thirty court cases since that date.[15] The court of civil appeals held that unauthorized use of name or likeness for commercial gain is justiciable in Texas and that the definition of privacy was broad enough to support a cause of action for appropriation of name or likeness under Texas common law.[16] Even a legendary football player like Kimbrough has a right protecting against the unauthorized commercial appropriation of his name and image. It is important to note, however, that in order to pursue a successful misappropriation claim, a person need not be a celebrity or even known to the public at large or some segment of the public as long as it is proved that the wrongly appropriated likeness was of value or benefited the person who appropriated it.[17]

As the composition of the Texas judiciary grew more conservative in 1990s, and the last of the liberal Democrats left the Supreme Court, privacy jurisprudence became more cautious and restrained. So it was that in two cases, *Diamond Shamrock*[18] in 1992 and *Cain*[19] in 1994, false light claims that had been recognized as actionable for over a decade in the state by appellate courts, were summarily rejected by the Texas Supreme Court. The Court reasoned that false light invasion duplicated the doctrine of defamation and increased the tension that already exists between free speech guarantees and privacy law. However, support for the false light doctrine persists across a spectrum of litigants, scholars, and practitioners because false light protects two privacy interests neglected by the tort of defamation: control over self-image and self-determination.[20] As Warren and Brandeis argued, a person has a right not only to create their own self-image (a private persona) but to exert control over the image of self that is shared with the public (a public persona). Defamation does not extend full protection to these two dimensions of personhood; it only protects against reputational harm—a lowering of esteem in the eyes of the community. An action that does not necessarily harm reputation may nonetheless harm self-identity and sense of self-worth.

Revisiting the decision to abandon the false light doctrine may be warranted in the age of social media. The doctrine's capacity to protect against highly offensive and harmful speech that falls short of defamation,[21] like the "yellow journalism" of Warren and Brandeis's era, can be freely posted or disseminated online without any viable grounds for recovery for the injured person, unless it can be proved that the action was undertaken with malice and that reputational harm occurred.[22] In addition, as more Texans are harmed by vicious online postings or "ratings" or by the sharing of intimate or sexual photos and videos, there may be a need to reconsider *negligent* invasion of privacy. Texas courts have been reluctant to recognize negligent invasion of privacy for fear of expanding the number of privacy suits resulting from inadvertent or careless acts. Many scholars and practitioners might argue that the refusal to recognize negligent invasion of privacy is a settled matter, but this may not necessarily be accurate. While the authoritative Texas precedent rejecting negligence as a cause of action for privacy torts remains *Billings*, with its firm declaration that negligence does not apply to privacy, the issue of negligent invasion of disclosural privacy has surfaced repeatedly over the years.[23] In a 2001 public disclosure case, *Doe v. Mobile Video Tapes*,[24] the question of whether a person can recover for negligent invasion of privacy for public disclosure resurfaced. The trial court argued that if libel actions can be based on negligent conduct by the tortfeasor so too should invasion of privacy tort actions.[25] However, the appeals court would not deviate from a previous decade of precedent rejecting negligent invasion of privacy. Appellate courts continue to hold tort law requires a workable standard of liability—of culpability—and that intent is the most reasonable one; otherwise, claims would be brought for accidental or inadvertent actions.

THE LIMITATIONS OF THE RIGHT TO PRIVACY IN TEXAS: LOOKING TOWARD THE FUTURE

What are the limitations of the right to privacy? In short, Texas state privacy jurisprudence has never encompassed matters concerning reproduction, abortion, and sexuality as in *Griswold v. Connecticut*,[26] *Lawrence v. Texas*,[27] and *Roe v. Wade*,[28] the latter of which was overturned in 2022 by *Dobbs v. Jackson Health*.[29] Only federal precedent exists in that realm. Texas privacy jurisprudence can best be understood as the right to be "let alone," in the parlance of Warren and Brandeis's *Harvard Law Review* article, and not "privacy as autonomy," which emerged in *Griswold* and its progeny. In the wake of the US Supreme Court's decision in *Dobbs* that the right to privacy does not protect a woman's right to an abortion, for the first time in fifty years there are absolutely no constitutional or legal limitations on the use of state police powers to restrict abortion and abortion-related services or activities. As we saw in chapter 2, Texas judges have acknowledged the autonomy dimension of privacy, but stopped short of granting relief to plaintiffs who allege privacy violations. Some lower state court rulings and dissenting opinions in the 1992 *Morales*[30] sodomy decision supported the concept of privacy as autonomy but refused to strike down the sodomy law. LGBT Texans would need to wait until the US Supreme Court's ruling in *Lawrence v. Texas*[31] in

2003 for the state's sodomy law to be nullified and constitutional protection extended to the sexual privacy of same-sex partners. Further, it is important that the reader understands that even in light of the broad definition of privacy set out in *Billings* and *TSEU*, state courts have rejected the argument that the Texas Constitution and common law create a privacy right coextensive with that recognized under *Griswold* and its progeny. Cases such as *City of Sherman v. Henry*[32] and *Bell v. Low Income Women*[33] recognized that the Texas Constitution protects personal privacy from unreasonable governmental intrusions and interference with personal autonomy, but no Texas court has ever extended privacy to reproductive rights. Any relief from restrictions on abortion or contraceptives has always been wholly dependent on federal precedent. In *City of Sherman*, which involved a claim that the right to privacy confers a right to commit adultery, the Texas Supreme Court ruled that while legal sexual conduct *is* protected under the Texas Constitution,[34] the right to privacy does not include a right to maintain a sexual relationship with the spouse of another person, much less a person of the same sex. Then-Justice Greg Abbott wrote that the decision "does not mean . . . that the government is free to engage in intrusive investigation methods to determine the sexual practices of individuals," but what was at issue in *Henry* was not intrusion into his private life, but more a matter of the "autonomy aspect of privacy—the right to make certain fundamental decisions and engage in certain conduct without state interference."[35] This definition of privacy as autonomy, while recognized by *Griswold* and *Roe*, is definitely *not* a recognized doctrine in Texas, Abbott concluded. This point cannot be emphasized enough in post-*Roe* Texas.

In *Bell*,[36] the Texas Supreme Court ruled that the state constitution's implied guarantee of the right to privacy is not violated by a state law that prohibits funding for abortions unless pregnancy results from rape or incest or places the woman in danger of death. Notwithstanding this finding, the justices, citing *Henry* and *TSEU*, posited a very broad definition of privacy by stating that the Texas Constitution "protects personal privacy from unreasonable governmental intrusions and unwarranted interference with personal autonomy."[37]

Bell, of course, is now made moot by *Dobbs*, which rescinded all abortion rights. *Bell* deserves attention for two reasons: first, it is one of handful of state cases that discuss federal abortion rulings, and second, it declined to decide whether the Texas Constitution "creates privacy rights coextensive with those recognized under the United States Constitution."[38] This means that currently Texans are completely dependent on the rulings of the federal courts for protection of the right to access contraceptives, same-sex marriage, and LGBT rights. If these rights are narrowed by the US Supreme Court, then the state legislature would be free to place further restrictions on matters and activities that fall under the privacy as autonomy rubric. Relief would need to be sought under an alternative legal strategy, possibly using the common law intrusion doctrine, state privacy statutes, state or federal due process or equal protection guarantees, or an appeal to voters. But it is simply too early in the post-*Roe* world to make accurate predictions.

Griswold is still good law, so absent state caselaw that supports the privacy as autonomy doctrine, the relevant question is to what degree has *Griswold* influenced the development of Texas privacy law? *Griswold* is federal precedent and, to reiterate, the right to privacy in Texas is based on state common law doctrines, state constitutional provisions, and, to a lesser extent, statutory protections. The answer to the question then is that in all of the major Texas privacy decisions discussed in this book, *Griswold* is frequently cited in opinions or referenced in a footnote, but the final outcome of the privacy claim does *not* rest on *Griswold* but invariably on state grounds alone. For example, from the time that *Billings* was handed down in 1973, the Texas Supreme Court heard fifty-three cases in which the phrase "right to privacy" was referenced. Of those fifty-three cases, only six cited *Griswold*, and even in those six cases the final decisions were determined by one of more of the privacy tort doctrines. Further, a search based on the general term "privacy" produced 173 results for the Texas Supreme Court, but only seven cited *Griswold*, most notably in *Industrial Foundation*, *TSEU*, *Diamond Shamrock*, and *City of Sherman*. *Billings*—one of the most important Texas privacy cases—was cited 806 times in subsequent cases since it was decided in 1973—does *not* cite *Griswold*. Of all the civil privacy cases heard by Texas courts at all levels, a total of 1,504 cases, only twenty cited *Griswold*. However, no decision was *based* on *Griswold* or any other federal case; the outcome in these Texas cases were based on state grounds.[39]

This book's inquiry has been limited to civil cases, but for the purpose of comparison, a search of the term "right to privacy" appearing in criminal cases alone produced 2,146 results, just twenty-one of which cited *Griswold*. Of criminal cases heard by the Texas Court of Criminal Appeals alone there are ninety-seven right to privacy cases, only six of which cited *Griswold*. The vast majority of these cases deal with search and seizure, typically relying on the Fourth Amendment and federal precedent. The cases not dealing with search and seizure involved issues varying from obscenity, drug possession, sodomy, driving while intoxicated, and (pre-*Roe v. Wade*) abortion, which explains the lack of *Griswold* citations.[40]

As it stands now, any state legislative attempt to place restrictions on access to contraceptives—or related matters other than abortion—would likely be challenged under *Griswold*. If *Griswold* were to be overturned, and the legislature decided to restrict contraceptives, the question would be whether there are state grounds to challenge such a restriction or ban. Is there a state-based common law, constitutional, or statutory basis for a broader concept of privacy that extends beyond the negative right to be let alone to matters of sexual intimacy and reproductive rights? The answer to that question is currently no. This is not meant to imply that *no* Texas judge or court has ever considered embracing a privacy as autonomy approach, but merely that majorities on the Texas Supreme Court or on appellate courts have not.

Although the Texas courts have never adopted a state-based privacy as autonomy doctrine, it is important to point out that other states have and, as we have seen in previous chapters, there is always the possibility that in the future a Texas court might rely on another state's precedent to resolve an intractable dispute related to reproductive rights. The privacy as autonomy doctrine was adopted by a state supreme court as early as 1964 when the New Hampshire Supreme Court in *Hamberger v. Eastman* ruled that the installation of an electronic listening device in the bedroom of two of his tenants violated the seclusion and domestic intimacy of a married couple.[41] In Texas, electronic eavesdropping by a private party would be addressed by the intrusion doctrine or the wiretapping statute. But the interest protected by the privacy as autonomy doctrine in this case was defined in terms of domestic privacy and the sanctity of the marital relationship.[42]

In *Falcon v. Alaska Public Offices Commission* in 1971,[43] the Alaska supreme court adopted the privacy as autonomy doctrine in a case involving a law requiring the reporting of the medical histories of those who hold positions on the local school board. The purpose of the law was to make available to the public the medical histories of all persons seeking or holding office on that body. The court held that the law infringed upon the constitutionally protected zone of privacy which protected the autonomy of both the patient and the physician.[44] In Texas this type of dispute would fall under the tort doctrine of public disclosure or statutory protection of medical records. *Falcon* was later cited by the Pennsylvania Supreme Court which held further that the physician-patient privilege precluded the disclosure of the patient's psychiatric records without the consent of the patient. The unauthorized disclosure of such records, even those of a juvenile patient, is a violation of the right to privacy as autonomy.[45] In 1974 in *Slawek v. Stroh*, the doctrine was adopted to protect a mother against the unwanted claims brought by the father of the child seeking paternal rights. The Wisconsin Supreme Court held that the father's repeated attempts to have paternal rights granted constituted an intrusion upon the mother's right to privacy as autonomy; any action to further the claims of the father constituted a violation of the sphere of privacy surrounding mother and child.[46] The California Supreme Court ruled in *White v. Davis*[47] in 1975 that the privacy as autonomy doctrine prevented the police from posing as college students to infiltrate classrooms, that this action constituted an intrusion on the academic and intellectual freedom of persons seeking an environment in which to think and speak freely. It is notable how the doctrine was adopted in such a wide range of disputes or alleged harms.

The New Jersey Supreme Court adopted the privacy as autonomy doctrine in 1976 in the groundbreaking *Quinlan*[48] case. In doing so, an entirely new body of caselaw now known as the "right to die" emerged. The state supreme court broadened the right of privacy to "encompass a patient's decision to decline medical treatment." In *Quinlan*, the father of a young woman who was in a permanent coma sought judicial action to have his daughter removed from a respirator so that she could die a natural death. Karen Quinlan's attending physicians believed that when a terminally ill patient is comatose or incompetent, the physician must make the critical decisions rather than the patient or the patient's family. The New Jersey Supreme Court reversed the lower court's decision, ruling that Karen Quinlan had the right to refuse unwanted medical treatment. Privacy is broad enough to protect an incompetent person's decision to decline medical treatment in the face of the state's compelling interests in preserving life and maintaining medical standards.[49]

Ever since *Griswold* was first handed down in 1965 the ruling has endured withering criticism, placing the concept of privacy as autonomy on shaky ground, yet it is still good law. Critics of the privacy of autonomy doctrine have derided the term itself, holding up for ridicule Justice William O. Douglas's "emanations" and "penumbras." Others were uncomfortable with autonomy because it is a philosophical term found in moral philosophy treatises, generally defined as the right or condition of self-governance, the ability to move without constraints, free from external control or influence.[50] Once the US Supreme Court excised abortion rights from the protected actions falling under privacy as autonomy, many people, alarmed by *Dobbs*, have expressed valid concerns that *Griswold* itself is threatened by a new conservative majority on the Court. Justice Hugo Black's dissenting opinion in *Griswold* represented the opening salvo. He believed that there was no general right to privacy created by the Fourth or any other amendment that would "give this Court the unlimited power to hold unconstitutional everything which affects privacy."[51] Black unequivocally denied the existence of a right to privacy found in the Constitution. He recognized the "privacy" interest found in the Fourth Amendment but believed that the Court was weakening Fourth Amendment interests by substituting "privacy" for the guarantee against unreasonable searches and seizures protected by the Fourth. Not only could the Court use an expansive interpretation of the Constitution to find rights, so too could a future court use a narrow interpretation to narrow of reject those same rights.[52] Justice Black's admonition is particularly timely in the post-*Roe* reality in light of the cryptic messages in *Dobbs* regarding the substantive due process analytic. The majority in *Dobbs* stated that "*the abortion right, which is not mentioned in the Constitution, is part of a right to privacy, which is also not mentioned*" (emphasis added).[53] However, Justice Alito assures us that *Dobbs* should not be construed to reject other rights based on substantive due process reasoning.[54] Writing for the majority Alito stated:

> [T]o ensure that our decision is not misunderstood or mischaracterized, we emphasize that our decision concerns the constitutional right to abortion and no other right. Nothing in this opinion should be understood to cast doubts on precedents that do not concern abortion.[55]

And in a concurring opinion Justice Kavanaugh wrote that "I emphasize what the Court today states: Overruling *Roe* does not mean the overruling of those precedents [*Griswold, Lawrence*, and *Obergefell*], and does not threaten or cast doubt on those precedents."[56]

However, in a passage that launched a torrent of op-eds and scholarly articles in 2022, Justice Clarence Thomas in his concurring opinion wrote that "[a]s I have previously explained, 'substantive due process' is an oxymoron that 'lack[s] any basis in the Constitution[,]'" and, ominously, "we should reconsider all of this Court's substantive due process precedents, including *Griswold, Lawrence*, and *Obergefell*."[57]

If there is a subtext to the majority's opinion (and Thomas's concurring opinion) it is that the idea that due process contains or is a foundation for unenumerated substantive rights has always endured criticism. Therefore, a healthy skepticism of the legitimacy of this doctrine should not be a shock notwithstanding assurances that *Dobbs* addressed abortion alone. If a hypothetical news headline were to state, "There are threats to substantive due process," this would likely result in collective yawn from most Americans. Few would decide to either celebrate or relocate to another state upon reading such news. However, upon hearing that there are threats to the constitutional right to marry one's same-sex partner,[58] or the right to be free from governmental scrutiny of same-sex sexual intimacy,[59] as well as threats to reproductive rights, including contraceptives,[60] procreational rights,[61] and parental rights,[62] many Americans would most certainly grow alarmed.

RECENT DEVELOPMENTS IN TEXAS LAW

Contraception

As of this writing, *Griswold* is still the law of the land; no laws in Texas restrict adults from having access to birth control and reproductive healthcare through private insurance, state programs, or federally funded Title X[63] clinics.[64] Title X of the Public Health Service is a family planning program for largely low-income Americans that is administered by the Office of Population Affairs, located in the US Department of Health and Human Services. Title X is the only source of federal funding for family planning in the United States. In December 2022 in *Deanda v. Becerra*,[65] Judge Matthew Kacsmaryk, a federal judge in Texas, ruled that the provision of Title X that allows minor children access to contraceptives without parental consent violates parental rights under the Texas family code and religious freedom and parental rights under the US Constitution. The holding originated when a father sued Becerra, the US Secretary of Health and Human Services, because under Title X his daughter could potentially gain access to contraceptives without his consent. The federal judge, a Trump appointee and former pro-life activist and organizer, ruled that by allowing minors unfettered access to contraceptives, Title X interfered with the father's ability to prevent his daughters from engaging in sexual promiscuity and premarital sex, thus weakening his ability to raise children according to his moral and religious beliefs.[66] An appeal of the district judge's order was filed by the Biden administration in 2023 and is pending before the federal Fifth Circuit Court of Appeals.[67] The administration argues that a minor's privacy and due right to contraceptives supersedes Deanda's claim that the Title X program unconstitutionally restricted his parental right to direct his daughters' upbringing. The case is the first major post-*Roe* attempt to ban contraceptives. It is likely that rather than pursuing an outright ban, states as well as private litigants who wish to limit access to contraceptives will pursue an incremental strategy (much like that after *Roe* was decided in 1973) to secure various restrictions in the name of parental rights, health and safety concerns, morality, religious liberty, and the like. The legality of each restriction would then be weighed against the mandate of *Griswold*. If *Griswold* were to be overturned, then access to contraceptives in the state would be subject to a range of legislative restrictions. New litigation strategies based on state and federal law or due process guarantees would need to be adopted and pursued by individuals and advocacy groups.

Abortion

Since Texas is ground-zero for abortion politics, many who read the word "privacy" in the title of this book will assume that the book is about (or should be about) abortion politics. However, abortion politics lies largely outside the primary scope of this book, which focuses on state court decision making in the policy area of privacy. Even when *Roe* was still good law, state abortion cases applied federal precedent and were litigated largely in federal courts rather than in state courts in Texas. Now that there is no longer a constitutional right to abortion, any discussion of abortion policy in Texas must focus mainly on the legislative restrictions imposed by the legislature and executive branches which are no longer fettered by *Roe* and *Casey*. The state may now assert its interest in protecting fetal life, promoting morality, protecting women, or any other reason deemed appropriate by the legislature. This statement should by no means be construed as an attempt to ignore or downplay the importance of abortion law to both sides of the political divide and the burdens that current abortion law imposes on women who are seeking reproductive healthcare, but post-*Dobbs* this is now largely a legislative matter in the state. Many Texans will be satisfied with the status quo, while others will pursue litigation to clarify the vagaries of the state's abortion policies as they relate to reproductive healthcare and emergency medicine; still others, through electoral politics, will seek a political realignment or regime change in the years to come.

Independent of the politics of the abortion debate, and most relevant to the topic of this book, it is necessary to understand in what ways *Dobbs* has limited the expansive definition of privacy that was once protected by *Roe*. That definition influenced not only litigation but the parameters of the debate over the scope of privacy rights. Recall, from our earlier discussion in chapter 1, how the Court's abortion jurisprudence impacted the right to privacy. *Roe* defined privacy as broad enough to (1) encompass a woman's decision to terminate her pregnancy, (2) exert autonomous control over her health, and (3) to be free from bodily restraint or compulsion in the fundamental matters of procreation and childbearing. This definition, the most sweeping understanding of privacy in American legal history, no longer exists as a right under the US Constitution. The question moving forward is how the overruling of *Roe* will impact the privacy rights of Texans.

As expansive as that right was, neither *Roe* nor any other abortion ruling by the US Supreme Court granted an absolute right. Further, after *Roe* was decided in 1973 nearly every conceivable restriction and regulation—short of an actual ban or "undue burden"—was upheld by the US Supreme Court. A reading of cases subsequent to *Roe* reveals that the Court upheld the constitutionality of laws requiring parental consent, "gag" rules, outright bans after the first trimester, preoperative counseling, waiting periods, and mandated sonograms, to name only a few. A woman's right to privacy as autonomy diminished relative to the state's asserted interest in protecting the life of the fetus at different stages of gestation. Consequently, opponents of abortion in the Texas legislature capitalized on an ever-narrowing abortion right long before *Dobbs*.

The current law, passed in 2022 and promulgated in the Texas Health and Safety Code, Chapter 170A,[68] prohibits physicians from performing abortions once a fetal heartbeat is detected (around six weeks of pregnancy) before most women know that they are pregnant.[69] The law creates a cause of action against physicians, but not against the pregnant mother,[70] by providing criminal, civil, and professional penalties for physicians or anyone performing, inducing, or attempting an abortion.[71] Penalties include (1) being charged with a first- or second-degree felony, depending on whether the abortion resulted in the death of the fetus; (2) a civil penalty of at least one hundred thousand dollars, and attorney's fees and court costs; (3) revocation of license or permit of a physician or healthcare professional in violation of the law[72]; and (4) private civil suits related to the prohibited abortion may be brought the provider.[73] Opponents of the law argue that since abortion is the standard of care for many complications related to pregnancy, women's physicians will balk at providing necessary care.[74] Therefore, many lawsuits will focus not on challenging the abortion law itself but on the secondary effects on the ban, such as denied obstetric care.[75]

In 2021, one year prior to *Dobbs*, Texas passed Senate Bill 8 (SB8), also known as the Texas Heartbeat Act. Unlike Chapter 170A of the Texas Health and Safety Code, this law does not make performing or inducing an abortion a crime, but instead allows private citizens to bring civil lawsuits against any physician who provides or induces such an abortion. It also allows lawsuits against anyone who "aids and abets" an abortion in violation of the law.[76] This latter section of SB8 has been called the "bounty hunter" law by opponents, thus allowing the "private suppression of legal rights or the rule of law."[77] The law prohibits a physician from providing an abortion after the detection of a "fetal heartbeat,"[78] with the term "heartbeat" defined as "cardiac activity or the steady and repetitive rhythmic contraction of the fetal heart within the gestational sac."[79] If a heartbeat is detected, a physician may only proceed with the abortion if they believe the woman is faced with a medical emergency. The nature of the emergency must be documented by the physician in the patient's and physician's records.[80]

The law permits anyone (other than a government employee) to file a civil lawsuit against a person who (1) performs or induces an abortion in violation of this law, (2) knowingly "aids or abets" performing or inducing an abortion in violation of the law, or (3) intends to do either of the above actions.[81] Uncertainty surrounds the definition of "aids or abets," so it is unclear what types of abortion-related activities might implicate civil liability. Does the aiding and abetting provision extend to counseling, providing information, or to private conversations? The law provides an example of aiding and abetting as "paying for or reimbursing the costs of an abortion through insurance or otherwise."[82] Again, SB8 does not impose liability on the woman for terminating her pregnancy but extends a wide net of liability over a range of actors associated with the pregnant woman who are alleged to aid or abet the abortion. This might include healthcare professionals, counselors, employers, Uber drivers, parents, and family members. If the person bringing the lawsuit prevails, the law mandates that the court award injunctive relief of an amount not less than ten thousand dollars, as well as court costs and attorney fees.[83]

In can be argued that SB8 violates a woman's right to sexual and informational privacy by creating the necessity of surveilling the abortion patient (or potential abortion patient) by the person who stands to benefit from the bounty hunter provision of the law. Surveillance technology or artificial intelligence programs could be used to track or predict behavior (such as a visit to an obstetrician's office or reproductive health clinic) that might violate a woman's right to privacy under state law. When SB8 went into effect, several lawsuits were filed, including *Whole Woman's Health v. Jackson*[84] in 2021, *United States v. State of Texas*[85] in 2022, and *Davis v. Sharp*,[86] but none were successful in blocking the law, largely because since SB8 prohibits the government from prosecuting those who violate the law, lawsuits challenging the law in federal courts do not have standing because of the lack of state action.

In 2023 the 88th Legislature passed House Bill 3058,[87] which carved out an exception that protects physicians who treat some pregnancy complications and provides a defense to lawsuits and criminal penalties against physicians who terminate a pregnancy to treat the life-threatening complications. This bill also protects pharmacists and pharmacies.[88] Three conditions must be met in order for the exception to apply: (1) a licensed physician must perform the abortion, (2) the patient must have a life-threatening condition and be at risk of death or "substantial impairment of a major bodily function" if the abortion is not performed, and (3) the physician must try to save the life of the fetus unless this would increase the risk of the pregnant patient's death or impairment.[89] The exceptions law extends to providing treatment for miscarriages (spontaneous abortions), ectopic pregnancies (fertilized egg develops outside of the uterus), or in the case of a "previable premature rupture of membranes," which is when a pregnant woman's amniotic fluid breaks prior to viability, which is the point at which a fetus is able to survive outside of the mother's uterus. Treatments for these issues are not considered to be abortions.[90] The law does not make an exception for lethal fetal abnormalities even when it is known that the fetus will not survive.

It is also illegal under the Health and Safety Code to perform an abortion in Texas by dispensing or mailing abortion-inducing medications,[91] such as the two-drug protocol, mifepristone and misoprostol, unless to save the life of the patient or prevent "substantial impairment of major bodily function" of a patient. Medication abortion now accounts for more than half of all US abortions.[92] Mifepristone, which is also known as RU-486—taken in conjunction with the drug misoprostol within ten weeks (seventy days) of gestation—was approved by the US Food and Drug Administration (FDA) in 2000.[93] Mifepristone blocks the effects of hormones that enable the body to remain pregnant; misoprostol then ends the pregnancy. The FDA's initial approval required the drug to be prescribed by a physician following an in-person office visit. In 2016 the FDA modified the rule to allow the drugs to be prescribed via telehealth visit through the tenth week of pregnancy. To circumvent the Texas ban, women order the drugs online, using telehealth services among other means, but in April 2023 a federal district judge, Matthew Kacsmaryk—the same judge who ruled against Title X contraceptives in *Deanda v. Becerra*[94]—revoked the FDA's approval of the abortion-inducing drugs, which have been on the market for twenty years, and also suspended the FDA's 2016 approval modifications. An anti-abortion group, the Alliance Defending Freedom, brought the lawsuit to prevent the federal government from undermining Texas laws and regulations that are "designed to protect their people from dangerous chemical abortion drugs." The Biden administration appealed to the Fifth Circuit Court of Appeals, which then blocked the part of the district judge's ruling that overturned the FDA's initial approval of mifepristone, but left standing the district court's invalidation the FDA's 2016 modifications on the conditions of the drug's access. The Biden administration then appealed to the Supreme Court, petitioning the justices to keep the district court's full ruling on hold while a plenary review continues in the Fifth Circuit. On April 14, Justice Alito issued an administrative stay—an order that keeps Kacsmaryk's ruling on hold until the Fifth Circuit and, possibly, the US Supreme Court make their final decisions.[95] Currently, under the Constitution, states cannot enact prescription drug policies that are in conflict with FDA regulations. When there is a conflict, federal law will preempt state law, especially when state law creates an obstacle to the implementation of federal law, which is referred to as "obstacle preemption."[96] Courts have adopted the doctrine of obstacle preemption to rule that a state's regulation of a healthcare professional's conduct "undermines the public health purposes of FDA requirements."[97] Advocates argue that medicated abortion is the best way of protecting the privacy of women, but that if mifepristone is banned in Texas but available in other states, how will the state determine if a woman obtained them by mail after a telehealth visit with a physician in another state and then took them in the privacy of her home? Would it be a violation of a woman's privacy if the state monitors her physical mail delivery or internet activity with a health provider who is located out of state in order to prosecute the provider? Would the state simply leave it up to private citizens serving as "bounty hunters" under SB8?

LGBT Privacy

As discussed earlier, *Dobbs* narrowed the definition and scope of the right to privacy as autonomy in *Roe* and in doing so may possibly affect the

US Supreme Court's rulings on LGBT rights protected in cases such as *Lawrence* and *Obergefell*. If these rulings are narrowed or overturned by the US Supreme Court, then the state legislature will have more discretion to restrict the autonomy and freedom of LGBT Texans. Approximately one year after *Obergefell* was handed down a Waco justice of the peace named Dianne Hensley decided that she would perform wedding ceremonies *only* for heterosexual couples. Justice of the peace courts in Texas are local courts of limited jurisdiction that hear cases involving traffic violations, some misdemeanor cases, and landlord-tenant disputes. Justices of the peace can also conduct weddings, for which they receive extra fees to supplement their income. There was a great degree of shock and resentment in Texas following *Obergefell*. Almost immediately, many conservative officials including judges began to devise strategies to thwart the ruling. At first, Hensley avoided the controversy by performing no wedding ceremonies at all, as was her option under law, but when she resumed officiating she claimed that the Texas Religious Freedom Restoration Act granted her an exemption based on her Christian faith to perform ceremonies only for heterosexuals. As a consequence, in 2019 Hensley received a public warning from the Texas State Commission on Judicial Conduct,[98] an independent ethics body consisting of six judges appointed by the Texas Supreme Court, five citizen members appointed by the governor, and two attorneys appointed by the State Bar of Texas. The commission stated that her refusal to perform marriage ceremonies for people based on their sexual orientation violated several canons of the Texas Code of Judicial Conduct[99] which prohibit bias and prejudice in the performance of judicial duties, cast reasonable doubt on the judge's capacity to act impartially, and prohibit "willful or persistent conduct that is clearly inconsistent with the proper performance of the judge's duties."[100] The commission found that the judge was selectively applying the law based on her personal religious beliefs. Hensley was entitled to an internal administrative appeal under the code but instead filed a lawsuit in a state district court in 2019 seeking an exemption under the Texas Religious Freedom Restoration Act, arguing that the commission's public warning substantially burdened her religion. The district court and court of appeals dismissed her case because she did not exhaust all administrative remedies (an internal appeal process). The two courts also granted the commission qualified sovereign immunity from Hensley's claims. Hensley appealed to the Texas Supreme Court, which held oral arguments in 2023.[101] That same year, it was reported in the news media that two members of the Texas State Commission on Judicial Conduct were removed by Governor Greg Abbott because he disagreed with the commission's vote to issue a public warning to Hensley. Both members served for nine months even though the Texas Senate had yet to confirm their appointments. Then, prior to a Senate confirmation vote, their nominations were withdrawn by the governor, who has openly campaigned against same-sex marriage.[102]

Recall from chapters 1 and 2 that it was not until 2003 that the Texas homosexual sodomy law was struck down by the US Supreme Court in *Lawrence v. Texas*.[103] The law made it a crime for two consenting adults of the same sex to engage in intimate sexual conduct in the privacy of their home. The law had been challenged on state and federal privacy grounds for over a decade,[104] but appellate courts in Texas refused to strike down the law because *Bowers v. Hardwick*,[105] which upheld Georgia's sodomy law, was the law of the land. However, in *Lawrence* the Court ruled that Texas cannot regulate "the most private human conduct, sexual behavior, in the most private of places, the home." The sodomy law granted to the State of Texas control of a private and personal relationship—whether heterosexual or homosexual. The liberty protected by the Constitution allows all persons the right to "retain their dignity as free persons."[106] Of course, *Lawrence* is still good law, but given the state's anti-gay history, the lingering resentment of *Obergefell*, the narrowing of the right to privacy in *Dobbs*, and the current efforts by the legislature to impose restrictions on transgender persons, we must ask what does the future hold for the privacy and equality of LGBT Texans and how is the right to privacy implicated by recent state policies? Most recently, in 2023, the legislature banned puberty blockers and hormone therapy for transexual children under eighteen years old. The law prohibits to certain children procedures and treatments for gender transitioning, gender reassignment, or gender dysphoria, and bans the use of public money or public assistance to provide those procedures and treatments.[107] The stated purpose of the legislation is to protect Texas families from healthcare providers who are pressuring children to transition or to protect children and their parents from social pressure promoted on social media that may cause gender dysphoria. Opponents of the law charge that it is a flagrant intrusion into the privacy inherent in the patient-physician relationship and into matters best left up to the child and their parents. The state contends that the ban falls squarely in the state's power to regulate medical procedures, promote the rights of parents, and to protect children from practices that are harmful physically and psychologically. In terms of public opinion, more than half (57 percent) of Texans support legislation that would classify as child abuse any gender-affirming care sought by parents from medical or mental health professionals.[108]

Another measure that affects the LGBT persons is Senate Bill 15,[109] which requires college and university athletes to join the collegiate sports teams that align with their sex assigned at birth, regardless of their present gender identity. It also provides protection for whistleblowers who report violations by university athletics program and grants standing to individuals that bring civil lawsuits against a college or university if they believe that the institution is in violation of the law. Proponents argue that the law is not about discrimination but about fairness and safety. The law extends existing restrictions that apply to Texas kindergarten to twelfth-grade public schools into higher education.[110] Proponents of these and other similar laws do not believe that they violate the right to privacy; the laws do not intrude into the homes or private lives of persons, and they do not disclose confidential information. Laws that segregate competitive sports in public schools and colleges based on one's sex that is assigned at birth do not violate privacy. Opponents argue that the right to privacy protects against an intrusion by the government or by private individuals into the one's private life; it extends to an autonomy of self that includes intimacy, lifestyle choices, and the freedom to determine one's private and public persona. If this autonomy of self also extends to the freedom to live a life that expresses their chosen gender, are many of the recent laws pertaining to LGBT Texans a violation of their right to privacy? Whether one understands privacy as the right to be let alone or privacy as autonomy, do such laws violate a person's liberty to present themselves to the world as they wish without fear of monitoring and regulating their name, or the manner in which they dress, speak, or style their hair? Regardless of the motivation behind recent laws aimed at LGBT Texans, the laws empower the government to exert control over the inner lives as well as public lives of a subset of citizens.[111]

Texas Public Opinion on Privacy Rights

Recall from the discussion in the introduction that public opinion polls show overwhelming support among Americans for landmark rulings such as *Griswold*, *Lawrence*, and *Loving*. There are currently no published Texas polls showing support for these court cases, but in light of the recent legislative restrictions on abortion and a federal district court ruling on a minor's access to Title X contraceptives it is interesting to note that 83 percent of Texans surveyed in a University of Texas poll taken in 2022 believe that women should have access to birth control,[112] with similar levels of support among Democrats (91 percent), Republicans (80 percent), and Independents (76 percent).[113] A 2022 Texas public opinion poll on abortion rights found that 39 percent believe that a woman should "always" have access to an abortion "as a matter of personal choice"[114] and that laws regulating abortion should be "less strict." A 2022 poll by the University of Houston Hobby Center following the *Dobbs* ruling found that 50 percent surveyed oppose recent bans on abortion in Texas, while 46 percent support new bans. A total of 80 percent of Texas Democrats oppose new bans, while 76 percent of Texas Republicans support new bans.[115] The Hobby Center poll also found that 52 percent of Texans support making it easier to have an abortion. A total of 84 percent support legislation that would allow an abortion to take place in the event of a lethal fetal anomaly, and 82 percent support legislation that would allow an abortion to take place if the mother's physical health is at risk.[116] One can conclude that current laws may be out of sync with public opinion.

Recent Texas polls show Texans evenly divided on same-sex marriage. A Pew Research Center poll in the state found 46 percent in favor and 46 percent opposed.[117] A survey by the Texas Politics Project at the University of Texas found a similar distribution with 44 percent in support and 42 percent opposing.[118] When Texans were asked if Texas state government is doing enough to protect the rights of LGBTQ Texans, a survey by the Texas Politics Project found that 25 percent said "too much," 31 percent said "too little," 23 percent said "right amount," and 21 percent had no opinion.[119]

Regarding discrimination toward people who are transgender, 40 percent of Texans surveyed by the Texas Politics Project believe that there is "less acceptance of transgender people" while only 22 percent believe that there is more acceptance. A substantial 38 percent stated that do not know or had no opinion.[120] A total of 38 percent surveyed believe that there is "a lot of discrimination" against transgender people, with 25 percent saying that there is "some," and 19 percent saying, "not very much."[121]

We can easily conclude from these polls that a large number of Texans believe in reproductive rights as well as the right to engage in relationships and marriage with whom we please without fear of judgment, regulation, or punishment. This definition of the right to privacy is broader than a negative right to be let alone from nosy neighbors, eavesdroppers, and surreptitious photography; it is a positive right to make choices, pursue life decisions, and engage in personal and intimate acts free from control—to be autonomous.

CONCLUDING THOUGHTS

Many of the legal and political questions that have been raised in the aftermath of the *Dobbs* ruling will remain unanswered for years to come. It is too early to predict with accuracy how abortion policy will be shaped by future legislation and litigation.[122] What will be the effect of the abortion ban on privacy inhering in the patient-physician relationship or the attorney client privilege? What will be the impact of new laws on the confidentiality of health and educational records, employment law, and travel? What impact will the "bounty law" have on privacy in general? Will it affect private conversations among friends, neighbors, healthcare providers, and faith leaders? Does criminalization necessitate the surveillance of women during their pregnancy, or their physicians and caregivers? Will the abortion ban corrode the associational privacy rights of members of reproductive rights organizations?

Bans may implicate employment law, as well: a person might possibly be terminated from a job for obtaining an abortion or by counseling the necessity or desirability of abortion. Even travel may be affected. Several counties and cities in Texas have implemented abortion "trafficking" laws that take the form of travel bans adopted by rural jurisdictions which make it illegal to travel though communities on county or city roads for the purpose of seeking abortions out of state. Theoretically, these bans violate the right to travel under the US Constitution, but in practical terms they would be difficult to challenge if they are enforced not by the state but by private vigilantes. Even if such abortion travel monitors are ordered to cease and desist by the courts, these restrictions might be used to generate the fear that a pregnant woman, seeking an abortion or not, might encounter checkpoints or roadblocks erected by private citizens and anti-abortion groups on country roads and even smaller airports.[123] One can only imagine a woman driving across the Texas state line being flagged down and asked about her reproductive status: "Howdy ma'am, are you pregnant?"

Moving forward, in the absence of a constitutional right, access to abortion will need to be re-framed in terms of a woman's access to medical treatment for pregnancy-related complications, miscarriages, fertility treatments, contraceptives, and even pharmacological treatments for a range of diseases and cancers. Framing abortion in terms of healthcare rather than privacy as autonomy makes the issue less "politically vulnerable."[124]

Although many state supreme courts have interpreted their state's constitutions broadly enough to recognize a state right to abortion,[125] there is little possibility that a Texas court will rule that a pregnant woman's body has common law or constitutional privacy protection that limits the reach of the state's interest in protecting fetal life. That is not to say that a plausible argument for privacy as autonomy should not be made against governmental regulation and overreach. Based on the caselaw, an argument could be posed as follows: a robust fundamental right to privacy exists in Texas based on the common law tort of intrusion into a person's private affairs, seclusion, or solitude. *TSEU*,[126] which is still good law, held that the right to privacy contained in the Texas Constitution offers broader protections than the right to privacy under the US Constitution and federal caselaw—that the state constitutional right to privacy is an aggregate of provisions of the Texas Bill of Rights, which includes the prohibition of arbitrary deprivation of life and liberty[127]; the freedom to speak, write, or publish[128]; the privilege against self-incrimination[129]; an individual's right to freedom of conscience and religion[130]; and, most fundamentally, the right to be free from intrusions into the sanctity of the home and person against intrusion.[131] If we look to the concept of liberty and the right to be free from intrusions into the sanctity of the person, it can be plausibly argued that privacy as autonomy is protected by a constellation of common law doctrines and constitutional provisions in Texas. Liberty from intrusions into our physical being, self-identity, and dignity surely protects against intrusions into life choices such as the decision to prevent the conception of a child, to undergo a medical procedure, and to keep public and private entities from knowing and disclosing our most private thoughts and intimate decisions, such as with whom we associate and our conversations with healthcare providers and spiritual mentors. Privacy also protects seclusion, not only from physical trespasses but also from unwanted access to our bodies.

In her provocative book, *The Common Law Inside the Female Body*,[132] Professor Anita Bernstein argues that once the state enacts legal constraints on abortion, pregnant women are required by the government to remain pregnant against their will. These constraints may have punishment of the woman in the form of civil and criminal sanctions, restraints on her liberty to travel, and limits on access to healthcare. She writes that the right to terminate an unwanted pregnancy is a common law liberty, based on the common law rights to self-defense—in cases of rape, or unwanted penetration—and defense of property ("castle doctrine") that together reflect the principle that invasion of a person's body is a "wrong that maybe fended off, with deadly force if deadly force is necessary."[133] Hers is a negative liberty—a right to be let alone—not a positive liberty—as in privacy as autonomy.

Support for "the right to be let alone" has deep roots in Texas, whereas the application of privacy as autonomy has been left to the federal courts. The states two highest appellate courts—the Texas Supreme Court and the Texas Court of Criminal Appeals—have never extended a state-based right to privacy to reproductive rights, abortion, personal autonomy, or the privacy of LGBT persons. Yes, there have been judges or justices on state appellate courts willing to adopt the privacy as autonomy doctrine but they have been in the minority, such as Justice Gammage in the *Morales* sodomy case as we saw in chapter 2. The last liberal Democrat to serve on the Texas Supreme Court was Rose Spector, who left the court in 1998. Texas judges are elected in statewide partisan elections (or appointed by the governor when seats are vacated due to resignation or death). The at-large or statewide election system for seats on the two highest courts poses a major obstacle to partisan or ideological diversity because a majority of voters who vote for statewide officials, such as the governor or supreme court justices, are conservative Republicans. Democratic judicial candidates do win seats on district and intermediate appellate courts in and around Democratic strongholds in the state, such as Houston, Austin, Dallas, San Antonio, and El Paso, but they are unable to win statewide offices. Thus, the two highest appellate courts will be dominated by conservative Republicans for years to come. Of course, the subject of judicial elections in Texas exceeds the scope of this book.

One strategy that reproductive rights or privacy advocates could pursue is the adoption of a state constitutional amendment protecting the right to privacy. As of this writing there are currently eleven states that have enumerated privacy provisions found in their constitutions: Alaska,[134] Arizona,[135] California,[136] Florida,[137] Hawaii,[138] Illinois,[139] Louisiana,[140] Montana,[141] New Hampshire,[142] South Carolina,[143] and Washington.[144] Adding a privacy amendment to the Texas Constitution would be no small feat. First, there would be political opposition from those who fear that a broad interpretation of a constitutional privacy provision by the courts would undermine state anti-abortion laws and other conservative social policies. Second, a proposed amendment would need to be approved by a two-thirds vote of each house of the legislature before it would be submitted for ratification to Texas voters in a statewide election. Just as the Court's ruling in *Roe* in 1973 launched the anti-abortion, or pro-life movement, the Court's ruling in *Dobbs* in 2022 may have the opposite effect, thus challenging Republican dominance in legislative, executive, and judicial politics over the coming decades.

The right to privacy has recently been bolstered by a 2023 ruling by the federal Fifth Circuit Court of Appeals. Our focus here has been the work of the Texas state courts but the Fifth Circuit, which has the reputation as one most conservative courts in the federal judiciary, handed down a strong privacy ruling in *Amin v. UPS*.[145] The case originated when Joshua Amin sued his employer, United Parcel Service (UPS) alleging that on December 6, 2018, his supervisor, Sergio Castro, denied Amin's request to take a bathroom break[146] while on the job at a UPS warehouse in Dallas. As a consequence, Amin, who was taking antibiotics, was forced to defecate on himself while working at his station in the distribution center. Amin's supervisor Castro told Amin that he already had his ten-minute break and should get back to work or else be terminated. Amin explained that because he was taking medication he needed another bathroom break, but Castro again refused and threatened to fire Amin if he took one step toward the restroom. Castro then followed Amin back to his workstation and said, "from now on you can use [the restroom] right here, where you are." Amin was forced to work in soiled pants. The next day, Castro gave Amin a notice of UPS's intent to fire him.

One of Amin's claims against UPS was based on the tort invasion of privacy, but the federal district court dismissed the case. The Fifth Circuit reversed and found that the UPS supervisor had violated Amin's privacy "by taking what should have been a private matter and exposing it to public scrutiny."[147] The Court acknowledged that that the Texas Supreme Court has long recognized that the Texas Constitution guarantees a constitutional right to privacy *and* recognizes "intrusion upon private affairs" as a tort invasion of privacy. The Fifth Circuit cited the Texas Supreme Court privacy decisions in *Valenzuela*,[148] *Billings*,[149] and *TSEU*,[150] in doing so clearly referencing the fact that Texas courts have cited *Griswold* and *Roe* in those cases. In its per curiam decision, the Fifth Circuit concluded that:

> [P]ersonal privacy is important to Texas's legal framework . . . [and that] . . . The Texas Supreme Court has found that Texas's Constitution guarantees a right to privacy. . . . While the Texas Constitution contains no express guarantee of a right of privacy, it contains several provisions similar to those in the United States Constitution that have been recognized as implicitly creating protected "zones of privacy." . . . We do not doubt, therefore, that a right of individual privacy is implicit among those "general, great, and essential principles of liberty and free government" established by the Texas Bill of Rights. . . .
>
> This right to privacy should yield only when the government can demonstrate that an intrusion is reasonably warranted for the achievement of a compelling governmental objective that can be achieved by no less intrusive, more reasonable means.[151]

The ruling is a strong affirmation by an influential court of appeals of the fundamental importance of the right to privacy, leaving no doubt that major privacy—*Billings* in 1973, *TSEU* in 1987, and *Valenzuela* in 1993—is firmly established in Texas law. There is no doubt of the importance of this ruling, but looking to the future it is uncertain how it will impact privacy litigation in Texas. The case involved a dispute between private parties—not between the state and an individual—so it does not have clear implications for challenging laws directing regulating reproduction, abortion, or other matters related to privacy as autonomy. However, the court points out that privacy protects the person from actions that are intrusive and degrading:

> The [privacy] tort described in the Restatement stands for more than physical or auditory invasions. It encompasses Amin's humiliation as Castro forced him to defecate, a function all civilized humans believe to be manifestly private, in public.[152]

One could argue that many laws recently passed in Texas dealing with reproduction, gender, and other matters bring to mind many of the interests discussed by the Fifth Circuit.

This book, *The Right to Privacy in Texas: From Common Law Origins to Twenty-First-Century Protections*, has examined the origins, evolution, and scope (as well as limitations) of privacy law in Texas based on state court rulings and the statutory protections. While the importance of the US Supreme Court's privacy rulings to all Americans cannot be gainsaid, the vast majority of invasion of privacy claims in the state's legal system are based on state common law torts, provisions of the Texas Bill of Rights, and state statutes.

The day-to-day lives of individuals in their homes, schools, and businesses in Texas are affected far more by these state court rulings and statutes than by the decisions of the federal judiciary. While many people may be outraged by current trends, the right to privacy in Texas *is* robust, allowing for a cause of action for intentional or willful invasion of one's person and home, protecting against intrusion into one's solitude, seclusion, and the most private and intimate matters. It extends to surveillance and wiretapping, to the video recording of sexual acts and disclosure of those recordings without consent to third parties, and to conversations in private as well as public places when there is a reasonable expectation of privacy. Further, Texas statutory data privacy protections are among the most innovative in the nation. Yet, at the same time, the right to privacy in the state fails to protect many of the most vulnerable and often vilified Texans who deserve personal or reproductive autonomy and freedom from government intrusion and overreach.

NOTES

1. See William L. Prosser's classic "Privacy," *California Law Review* 48 (1960).

2. Some scholars have been critical of Prosser as well for stunting the development of privacy. See Neil M. Richards and Daniel J. Solove, "Prosser's privacy law: A mixed legacy," *California Law Review*, 98 (2010): 1887.

3. *Billings v. Atkinson*, 489 S.W. 2d 858, 861 (Tex. 1973).

4. Ibid.

5. *Billings* is cited in 198 Texas court cases since 1973. Westlaw search (under "citing references"), November 2023.

6. *Industrial Foundation* is cited in 175 Texas court cases since 1976. Westlaw search (under "citing references"), October 5, 2023

7. 746 S.W.2d 203 (1987).

8. Texas Constitution, article 1, section 19.

9. Texas Constitution, article 1, section 8.

10. Texas Constitution, article 1, section 10.

11. Texas Constitution, article 6.

12. Texas Constitution, article 1, sections 9 and 25.

13. *TSEU* is cited in sixty-seven cases since 1987. Westlaw search (under "citing references"), November 2023.

14. 521 S.W. 2d 719 (Tex. Civ. App. – Eastland 1975, writ ref'd n.r.e).

15. *Kimbrough* is cited in thirty Texas court cases since 1975. Westlaw search (under "citing references"), November 2023.

16. Ibid.

17. *Topheavy Studios, Inc. v. Doe*, No. 03-05-00022-CV (Tex. App.—Austin Aug. 11, 2005, no pet.). (mem. op.).

18. *Diamond Shamrock Refining and Marketing Company v. Roque Mendez*, 844 S.W.2d 198 (1992).

19. *Cain v. Hearst Corporation*, 878 S.W.2d at 577 (Tex. 1994).

20. See generally Nathan E. Ray, "Let there be false light: Resisting the growing trend against an important tort," *Minnesota Law Review*, 84 (2000): 713.

21. See generally Robin Baker Perkins, "The truth behind false light—A recommendation for Texas's re-Adoption of false light invasion of privacy," *Texas Tech Law Review*, 34 (2003): 1199.

22. Related to this point, Texas does have a "revenge porn" statute, Senate Bill 1135 (2015) which extends civil and criminal liability to the unlawful disclosure or promotion of certain intimate visual material, creating an offense. The law made posting someone's intimate photos to the internet without their permission a crime, punishable by up to a year in jail and a four-thousand-dollar fine. In 2018, the 12th Court of Appeals in Tyler ruled that the law violated the First Amendment, but in 2021 the Court of Criminal Appeals held the law is not constitutionally overbroad because it is narrowly tailored to promote the government interest in protecting sexual privacy. See *Ex parte Jordan Bartlett Jones*, NO. PD-0552-18 (2021).

23. See *Boyles v. Kerr*, 855 S.W. 2d 593 (Tex. 1993).

24. *Doe v. Mobile Video Tapes, Inc.*, 43 S.W.3d 40 (2001).

25. Such as *Boyles v. Kerr*, 806 S.W.2d 255 (1991), overturned by the Texas Supreme Court in 2001; and *C.T.W. v. B.C.G*, 809 S.W.2d 788 (1991).

26. *Griswold v. Connecticut*, 381 U.S. 479 (1965).

27. *Lawrence v. Texas*, 539 U.S. 558 (2003).

28. *Roe v. Wade*, 410 U.S. 113 (1973).

29. *Dobbs v. Jackson Health*, 597 U.S. ___ (2022).

30. In *Texas v. Morales*, 826 S.W. 2d 201, 205 (Tex. App. – Austin 1992), the Third Court of Appeals in Austin ruled that although the right to privacy is not expressly contained in the Texas Constitution, it is created or implied by sections 6, 8, 9, 10, 19, and 25 of the Texas Bill of Rights. See chapter 3 discussion.

31. *Lawrence v. Texas*, 539 U.S. 558 (2003).

32. *City of Sherman v. Henry*, 928 S.W.2d 464 (1996).

33. 95 S.W.3d 253 (Tex. 2002). *Bell* has been cited forty-five times in Texas court cases since 2002. Westlaw search (under "citing references"), October 2023.

34. Ibid.

35. Ibid, 468–69.

36. 95 S.W.3d 253 (Tex. 2002) .

37. Ibid, 265.

38. Ibid, 265.

39. Westlaw search for the term "right to privacy" in civil cases, November 2023.

40. Westlaw search for the term "right to privacy" in criminal cases, November 2023.

41. *Hamberger v. Eastman*, 206 A.2d 239 (1964).

42. Ibid.

43. 570 p.2d 222 (1971).

44. Ibid.

45. *In re B*, 394 A.2d. 419 (1978).

46. *Slawek v. Stroh*, 215 N.W.2d 9 (1974).

47. *White v. Davis*, 533 P.2d 222 (1975).

48. *In re Quinlan*, 355 A.2d 647 (1976) (N.J),

49. Ibid.

50. See generally, Ferdinand D. Schoeman (editor), *Philosophical Dimensions of Privacy: An Anthology* (Cambridge: Cambridge University Press, 1984).

51. *Katz v. United States*, 389 U.S. 347, 374 (Black, J. dissenting).

52. Ibid, 509 (Black, J. dissenting).

53. Ibid, 2245.

54. Ibid, 2277–78.

55. Ibid.

56. Kavanaugh, J., concurring.

57. Ibid, 2301 (Thomas, J. concurring). A discussion of the implications of *Dobbs* on the right to privacy is an article or book unto itself and therefore beyond the scope of our concluding chapter. Much has already been written in the aftermath of *Dobbs*.

58. *Loving v. Virginia*, 388 U.S. 1 (1967); *Obergefell v. Hodges*, 576 U.S. 644 (2015).

59. *Lawrence v. Texas*, 539 U.S. 558 (2003).

60. *Griswold v. Connecticut*, 381 U.S. 479 (1965).

61. *Skinner v. Oklahoma*, 316 U.S. 494 (1977).

62. *Meyer v. Nebraska*, 262 U.S. 390 (1923).

63. Title X (Title X of the Public Health Service Act, 42 U.S.C. §§ 300) is a family planning program, administered by the Office of Population Affairs in the US Department of Health and Human Services. It is the only source of federal funding for family planning in the United States, www.fda.gov.

64. Up-to-date information on availability of contraceptives (December 2023): Know Your Rights: Reproductive Health Care, https://reproductiverights.gov/; Healthy Texas Women: Clinic Locator, https://www.healthytexaswoman.org/healthcare-programs; HHS Office of Population Affairs, https://opa-fpclinicdb.hhs.gov/; FDA Approves First Nonprescription Daily Oral Contraceptive, www.fda.gov.

65. *Deanda v. Becerra et al*, No. 2:2020cv00092 - Document 63 (N.D. Tex. 2022).

66. Ibid.

67. *Deanda v. Becerra*, United States Court of Appeals for the Fifth Circuit, Case No. 23–10159 (2023).

68. Health and Safety Code, Chapter 170A,170A.002, Performance of Abortion.

69. See Charles W. "Rocky" Rhodes and Howard M. Wasserman, "Solving the procedural puzzles of the Texas Heartbeat Act and its imitators: The potential for defensive litigation," *Southern Methodist University Law Review*, 75 (2022): 187.

70. Health and Safety Code, Chapter 170A,170A.002, Performance of Abortion.

71. Ibid.

72. Section 170A.007.

73. Senate Bill 8, 87(R) SB 8 - Enrolled version - Bill Text (texas.gov).

74. See Whitney Arey et al., "A preview of the dangerous future of abortion bans—Texas Senate Bill 8," *New England Journal of Medicine*, 387 (2022): 388; and Maya Manian, "The ripple effects of Dobbs on health care beyond wanted abortion, *Southern Methodist University Law Review*, 76 (Winter 2023), 77.

75. Ibid.

76. Senate Bill 8 promulgates Section 171.208 of the Texas Health and Safety Code which allows private citizens to sue anyone who performs or induces an abortion in violation of the law.

77. See generally Aziz Z. Huq, "The private suppression of constitutional rights," *Texas Law Review*, 101 (May 2023), 1259.

78. Ibid, Section 171.201

79. Sections 171.203 and 171.204 require physicians to test for a "fetal heartbeat" before performing or inducing an abortion. If one is detected or the physician fails to test for one, an abortion may not be performed.

80. Section 171.205 requires the physician to document the emergency in both the patient's and the physician's medical records.

81. Section 171.208.

82. Ibid.

83. Ibid.

84. *Whole Woman's Health v. Jackson*, 595 U.S. ___ (2021).

85. *United States v. State of Texas*, 1:21-cv-00796, (W.D. Tex.).

86. *Davis v. Sharp*, 1:22-cv-00373-RP, (W.D. Tex.).

87. House Bill 3058, 88(R) HB 3058 - Enrolled Version—Bill Text (texas.gov) https://capitol.texas.gov/tlodocs/88R/billtext/html/HB03058F.htm.

88. See House Bill 3058, 88th Regular Session.

89. Ibid.

90. Health and Safety Code, chapter 245. Abortion Facilities (texas.gov).

91. Health and Safety Code, Title 2, Subtitle H., Public Health Provisions, Chapter 171. Abortion, https://statutes.capitol.texas.gov/Docs/HS/htm/HS.171.htm#d; https://guides.sll.texas.gov/abortion-laws/medical-abortions.

92. "Medication abortion now accounts for more than half of all U.S. abortions," Guttmacher Institute (February 2022).

93. Ibid.

94. *Deanda v. Becerra et al*, No. 2:2020cv00092 - Document 63 (N.D. Tex. 2022).

95. *U.S. Food and Drug Administration v. Alliance for Hippocratic Medicine*, Application to Stay the Order Entered by the United States District Court for the Northern District of Texas and for an Administrative Stay, 20230414103258942_Alliance for Hippocratic Med application.pdf (supremecourt.gov).

96. Patricia J. Zettler and Ameet Sarpatwari, "State restrictions on Mifepristone access—The case for federal preemption," *New England Journal of Medicine*, 386 (2022): 705–07.

97. Ibid.

98. State Commission on Judicial Conduct, https://scjc.texas.gov/.

99. Texas Code of Judicial Conduct, https://www.txcourts.gov/media/1457109/texas-code-of-judicial-conduct.pdf.

100. *Dianne Hensley v. State Commission on Judicial Conduct, et al*, Appeal from 459th District Court of Travis County (2022), Texas Court of Appeals (Austin).

101. *Dianne Hensley v. State Commission on Judicial Conduct, et al*, oral argument October 25, 2023 (txcourts.gov).

102. Taylor Goldenstein, "Ex-members of Judicial Conduct Commission say Abbott ousted them over gay marriage case," *Houston Chronicle,* updated December 5, 2019, 6:27 p.m.; Associated Press, "Ex-judicial panelists: Abbott ousted them over gay marriage," *Huntsville Item* (December 5, 2019).

103. *Lawrence v. Texas*, 539 U.S. 558 (2003).

104. See *Texas v. Morales*, 869 S.W.2d 941 (Tex. 1994).

105. *Bowers v. Hardwick*, 478 U.S. 186 (1986).

106. *Lawrence v. Texas*, 539 U.S. 558, 564–567.

107. Senate Bill 14, Texas Legislature Online - 88(R) History for SB 14.

108. Hobby School of Public Affairs, "Texas Legislative Issues 2023 Culture Wars" (2023), https://uh.edu/hobby/tx2023/culture.pdf.

109. Senate Bill 15, Texas Legislature Online - 88(R) History for SB 15.

110. House Bill 25, https://capitol.texas.gov/BillLookup/History.aspx?LegSess=873&Bill=HB25.

111. See generally, Lydia R. Harris, "Identity documents for transgender Texans: A proposal for a uniform system for correcting gender markers in Texas," *St. Mary's Law Review on Race and Social Justice*, 24 (2022): 59.

112. Texas Politics Project, "Should women have access to birth control—overall" (June 2022), https://texaspolitics.utexas.edu/set/should-women-have-access-birth-control-june-2022#overall.

113. Texas Politics Project, "Should women have access to birth control-part ID" (June 2022), https://texaspolitics.utexas.edu/set/should-women-have-access-birth-control-june-2022#party-id.

114. Texas Politics Project, "Availability of Abortion" (April 2022), https://texaspolitics.utexas.edu/set/availability-abortion-april-2022.

115. Hobby School of Public Affairs, https://uh.edu/hobby/txpolicyandpolitics/abortion.pdf.

116. Hobby School of Public Affairs, https://uh.edu/hobby/tx2023/.

117. Pew Research Center, "Views about same-sex marriage among adults in Texas," https://www.pewresearch.org/religion/religious-landscape-study/state/texas/views-about-same-sex-marriage/.

118. Texas Politics Project, "Should same-sex marriage be legal" (April 2023), https://texaspolitics.utexas.edu/set/should-same-sex-marriage-be-legal-texas-april-2023#overall.

119. Texas Politics Project, "Is government doing enough to protect the rights of LGBT Texans" (June 2019), https://texaspolitics.utexas.edu/set/texas-state-government-doing-enough-protect-rights-lgbtq-texans-june-2019.

120. Texas Politics Project, "Is Texas becoming more or less accepting of people who are transgender" (February 2023), https://texaspolitics.utexas.edu/set/texas-becoming-more-or-less-accepting-people-who-are-transgender-february-2023.

121. Texas Politics Project, "Discrimination against transgender people" (august 2023), https://texaspolitics.utexas.edu/set/discrimination-against-transgender-people-august-2023#overall.

122. See Rachel Rebouche and Mary Zeigler, "Abortion law and politics after Dobbs, *Southern Methodist University Law Review*, 76 (2023): 27.

123. Caroline Kitchener, "Texas highways are the next anti-abortion target," *The Washington Post*, September 1, 2023; Jayme Lozano Carver, "A Texas county that borders New Mexico is the latest to consider an abortion travel ban," *Texas Tribune*, September 27, 2023.

124. See Carole Joffe, "Failing, to embed abortion care in mainstream medicine made it politically vulnerable," *Washington Post*, January 11, 2022; and See Maya Manian, "The ripple effects of Dobbs on health care beyond wanted abortion, *Southern Methodist University Law Review*, 76 (Winter 2023): 102.

Ibid.

125. See Robert L. Bentlyewski, "Abortion rights under state constitutions: A fifty-state survey," *Fordham Law Review*, 90 (2022).

126. *Texas State Employees Union (TSEU)*, 746 S.W.2d 203 (1987).

127. Texas Constitution, article 1, section 19.

128. Texas Constitution, article 1, section 8.

129. Texas Constitution, article 1, section 10.

130. Texas Constitution, article 6.

131. Texas Constitution, article 1, sections 9 and 25.

132. Anita Bernstein, *The Common Law Inside the Female Body* (Cambridge: Cambridge University Press, 2019).

133. Ibid, 172–73.

134. Alaska Constitution, article 1, section 2.

135. Arizona Constitution, article 2, section 8.

136. California Constitution, article 1, section 1.

137. Florida Constitution, article 1, section 12.

138. Hawaii Constitution, article 1, section 6.

139. Illinois Constitution, article 1, section 6.

140. Louisiana Constitution of 1974, Article 1, Section 5. Louisiana's Constitution of 1974 protects against invasions of privacy but in 2020 voters passed a constitutional amendment inserting the following words: "nothing in this constitution shall be construed to secure or protect a right to abortion or require the funding of abortion."

141. Montana Constitution, article 2, section 10.

142. New Hampshire Constitution, article 2-b.

143. South Carolina Constitution, article 1, section 10.

144. Washington Constitution, article 1, section 7.

145. *Joshua Amin v. United Parcel Service*, No. 22–10295, (2023), https://www.ca5.uscourts.gov/opinions/pub/22/22-10295-CV0.pdf.

146. See Michael Sainato, "14-hour days and no bathroom breaks: Amazon's overworked delivery drivers," *Guardian*, March 11, 2021, https://www.theguardian.com/technology.

147. *Joshua Amin v. United Parcel Service*, No. 22–10295, 12.

148. *Valenzuela v. Aquino*, 853 S.W.2d 512, 513 (Tex. 1993).

149. *Billings v. Atkinson*, 489 S.W.2d 858 (Tex. 1973).

150. Citing *Texas State Employee Union v. Texas Department of Mental Health & Mental Retardation*, 746 S.W.2d 203, 205 (Tex. 1987).

151. *Joshua Amin v. United Parcel Service*, No. 22–10295, 11–14.

152. Ibid, 12.

Appendix

List of Cases

INTRODUCTION

Billings v. Atkinson, 489 S.W. 2d 858, 861 (Tex. 1973).
Dobbs v. Jackson Women's Health Organization, 597 U.S. 215 (2022).
Griswold v. Connecticut, 381 U.S. 479 (1965).
Loving v. Virginia, 388 U.S. 1 (1967).
Michigan v. Long, 463 U.S. 1032 (1983).
Obergefell v. Hodges, 576 U.S. 644 (2015).
Roe v. Wade, 410 U.S. 113 (1973).

CHAPTER 1

Anderson v. Romero, 72 F.3d 518, 521 (7th Cir. 1995).
Atkinson v. Doherty, 121 Mich. 372 (1899).
Beal v. Doe, 432 U.S. 438 (1977).
Billings v. Atkinson, 489 S.W. 2d 858, 859 (Tex. 1973).
Bowers v. Hardwick, 478 U. S. 186 (1986).
Boyd v. United States, 116 U.S. 616 (1886).
Brents v. Morgan, 229 S.W. 967 (1927).
Buck v. Bell, 274 U.S. 200 (1927).
California v. Ciraolo, 476 U.S. 207 (1986).
Christian v. State, 96 Ala 89, 91, 11 So. 338, 338–39 (1892).
Collins v. Mack, 31 Ark. 684, 689 (1877).
Commonwealth's Attorney for the City of Richmond v. Doe, 425 U.S. 901 (1976).
Daily Times Democrat v. Graham, 102. 2d 474 (1964).
De May v. Roberts, 46 Mich. 1960 (1881).

Dobbs v. Jackson Women's Health Organization, 597 U.S. 215 (2022).
Eisenstadt v. Baird, 405 U.S. 438 (1972).
Entick v. Carrington, 19 How. St. Tr. 1029 (C.P. 1765).
Fairfield v. American Photocopy Equip. Co., 138 Cal. App. 2d 82 (1955).
Fitzsimmons v. Olinger Mortuary Association, 1 Colo. 544, 17 P.2d 535 (1932).
Flake v. Greensboro News Co., 195 S.E. 55 (1938).
Griswold v. Connecticut, 381 U.S. 479 (1965).
Henisler v. Freedman, 2 Pars. Eq. Cas. 274 (Pa. Ct. C.P. 1851).
Hinish v. Meier Frank Company, 113 P.2d 438 (1941).
House v. Peth, 165 Ohio St. 35 (1956).
Hoyt v. Mackenzie, # Barb. Ch. 320, 324–25 (N.Y. Ch. 1848).
Ilsley v. Nicholas, 29 Mass (12 Pick.) 270, 277 (1832).
Ives v. Humphrey, 1 E.D. Smith 1996, 201–02 (N.Y. Ct. C. P. 1851).
Johnson v. State, 63 Miss. 313, 317 (1885).
Katz v. United States, 389 U.S. 347 (1967).
Kyllo v. United States, 533 U.S. 27 (2001).
Lawrence v. Texas, 539 U.S. 558 (2003).
LeCrone v. Ohio Bell Tel. Co., 120 Ohio App. 129 (1963).
Leverton v. Curtiss Publishing Co., 78 F. Supp. 305 (D.D.C. 1948).
Lochner v. New York, 198 U.S. 45 (1905).
McCormick v. Haley, 37 Ohio App. 2d 73, 307 N.E. 2d 34, 38 (1973).
McDaniel v. Atlanta Coca-Cola Bottling Co., 60 Ga App. 92 (1939).
Melvin v. Re, 112 Cal. App. 285, 297 (1931).
Meyer v. Nebraska, 262 U.S. 390 (1925).
Mitchell v. Commonwealth, 88 Ky. 349, 353, 11 S.W. 209, 210 (1889).
Moore v. New York Elevated R.R., 130 130 N.Y. 523, 527–28 (1892).
Munden v. Harris, 134 S.W. 1076 (1911).
NAACP v. Alabama, 357 U.S. 449 (1958).
Nader v. General Motors Corp., 31 A.D. 2d 392, 397 (1969) (Steuer, J., dissenting).
Norris v. Moskin Stores, Inc., 132 So.2d 321 (1961).
Obergefell v. Hodges, 576 U.S. 644 (2015).
Olmstead v. United States, 277 U.S. 438 (1928).
Pavesich v. New England Life Insurance Company, 50 S.E. 68, 122 Ga. 190 (Ga. 1905).
Pierce v. Society of Sisters, 268 U.S. 510 (1925).
Planned Parenthood v. Casey, 505 U.S. 833 (1992).
Planned Parenthood of Central Missouri v. Danforth, 428 U.S. 552 (1976).
Poe v. Ullman, 367 U.S. 497 (1961).
Pritchett v. Board of Commissioners, 42 Ind. App. 3 (1908).

Rice v. Williams, 32 F. 437, 439 (C.C.E.D. Wis. 1887).
Roberson v. Rochester Folding Box Co., 64 N.E. 442 (1902).
Roe v. Wade, 410 U.S. 113 (1973).
Rust v. Sullivan, 500 U.S. 173 (1991).
Sanford v. Murphy, 63 Ga. 410, 416 (1879).
Schuyler v. Curtis, (Sup. 1892) 15 N.Y. Supp. 787.
Semayne's case, 5 C. Rep. 91a, 91b, 77 Eng. Rep. 194, 195 (1605).
Sis v. F-R Publishing Corporation, 113 F.2d 806 (2d Cir. 1940).
Skinner v. Oklahoma, 316 U.S. 535 (1942).
Spahn v. Julian Messner, Inc., 18 N.Y.2d 324 (N.Y. 1966).
State v. Armfield, 9 N.C. (2 Hawks) 246, 247 (1822).
Texas v. Morales, 869 S.W. 2d 941 (1994).
Walker v. Whittle, 83 Ga. App. 445 (1951).
West Coast Hotel v. Parrish, 300 U.S. 379 (1937).
Whole Woman's Health v. Hellerstedt, 579 U.S. 582 (2016).
Wien v. Simpson, 2 Phila. 1548, 158–159 (Pa. Dist. Ct. 1857).

CHAPTER 2

Arnold Palmer, Gary Player, Doug Sanders, and Jack Nicklaus v. Schonhorn Enterprises, Inc, 96 N.J Super. 72 (1967).
Benavez v. Anheuser-Busch, Inc., 873 F.2d. 102, 104 (5th Cir. 1989).
Billings v. Atkinson, 489 S.W. 2d 858 (Tex. 1973).
Bowers v. Hardwick, 478 U.S. 186 (1986), *overruled by Lawrence v. Texas*, 539 U.S. 558 (2003).
Boyles v. Kerr, 806 S.W.2d 255 (1991).
Cain v. Hearst Corporation, 878 S.W.2d at 577 (Tex. 1994).
Cardiovascular Prover Res. Inc. v. Gottlich, No. 05-13-01763-CV (Tex. App. –Dallas 2015, pet. Denied (mem. op.).
Childers v. A.S., 909 S.W.2d 282, 291 (1995).
City of Dallas v. England, 846 S.W.2d 957, 958 (Tex. App.—Austin 1993, writ dism'd w.o.j.).
City of Sherman v. Henry, 928 S.W.2d 464 (Tex. 1996).
Clayton v. Richards, 47 S.W.3d 149 (2001).
Collins v. Collins, 904 S.W.2d 792 (1995).
Colquette v. Forbes, 680 S.W.2d. 536 (Tex. App.—Austin 1984, no writ).
Dallas County v. Harper, 913 S.W.2d 207 (1995).
Diamond Shamrock Refining and Marketing Company v. Roque Mendez, 844 S. W.2d 198 (1992).
Doe v. Mobile Veo Tapes, Inc., 43 S.W.3d 40 (2001).

Doggett v. Travis Law Firm, 555 S.W. 3d 127 (2018).
Express One Int'l, Inc. v. Steinbeck, 53 S.W.3d 895, 900 (Tex. App.—Dallas 2001, no pet.).
Foster v. Laredo Newspapers, Inc., 541 S.W.3d 809 (1976).
Frisby v. Schultz, 487 U.S. 474 (1987).
Fulmer v. Rer, 635 S.W.2d 875, 881 (1982).
Gautier v. Pro-Football, Inc., 304 N.Y. 354 (1952).
Gill v. Snow, 644 S.W. 2d 222 (Tex. App. – Fort Worth 1982, no writ.).
Godbehere v. Phoenix Newspapers, Inc., 783 P.2d 781, 787 (Ariz. 1989).
Hansson v. Harris, 252 S.W.2d 600 (1952).
Henley v. Dillard Department Stores, 46 F. Supp.2d 587 (N.D. Tex. 1999).
McNamara v. Freedom Newspapers, Inc., 802 S.W.2d 901 (Tex. App.—Corpus Christi 1991, writ denied).
Meadows v. Hartford Life Ins. Co., 492 F. 3d 634, 638–39 (5th Cir. 2007).
Milner v. Red River Publishing, 249 S.W.2d 227,229 (Tex. Civ. App. 1952).
Moore v. Big Picture Co., 828 F.2d 270, 275 (5th Cir. 1987).
O'Brien v. Pabst Sales Co., 124 F.2d 167 (5th Cir. 1941).
Passel v. Fort Worth Independent School District, 440 S.W.2d 61, 63–64 (Tex. 1969)).
Pavesich v. New England Life Insurance Company, 122 Ga. 190 (Ga. 1905).
Shelley v. Kraemer, 334 U.S. 1 (1948).
Star-Telegram, Inc. v. Doe, 915 S.W.2d. 471, 472 (Tex. 1995).
State v. Morales, 869 S.W.2d 941, 942, n. 5.
Texas v. Morales, 826 S.W. 2d 201, 205 (Tex. App. – Austin 1992).
Texas Comptroller of Public Accounts vs. Attorney General of Texas, 354 S.W.3d 336 (2010).
Texas Department of Criminal Justice v. Levin, 2019 WL 1575407.
Texas Dept. of Public Safety v. Cox Texas Newspapers, L.P., 343 S. W. 3d 112 (2011).
Texas State Employees Union v. Texas Dept. of Mental Health and Mental Retardation, 746 S.W.2d 203 (Tex. 1987).
Topheavy Studios, Inc. v. Doe, No. 03-05-00022-CV (Tex. App.—Austin Aug. 11, 2005, no pet.). (mem. op.).
United Locating Services, LLC v. Fobbs, 619 S.W. 3d 863 (2021).
U.S. Life Insurance Co. v. Hamilton, 238 S.W. 2d 289 (Tex. Civ. App. – Waco 1951, writ ref'd n.r.e.).
Valenzuela v. Aquino, 800 S.W.2d 301, 305 (Tex. App.—Corpus Christi 1990) *aff'd in part, rev'd in part*, 853 S.W.2d 512 (Tex. 1993).
Watson v. Talia Heights, 566 S.W. 3d 326, 329–330 (2018).

CHAPTER 3

Barnes v. Yahoo! Inc., 570 F.3d 1096 (9th Cir. 2009).
Billings v. Atkinson, 489 S.W.2d 858, 861 (Tex. 1973).
Clayton v. Richards, 47 S.W.3d 149 (Tex. App. – Texarkana 2001, pet. denied).
Collins v. Collins, 904 S.W.2d 792,797 (Tex. App. – Houston [1st Dist.] 1995, writ denied) (en banc).
Dupuy v. Texas, 631 S.W. 3d 233 (Tex. App. – Houston [14th Dist.] 2020).
Ex parte Bradshaw, 501 S.W.3d 665 (Tex. App.—Dallas 2016).
Ex parte Fairchild-Porche, 638 S.W. 3d 770 (2021).
Ex parte Harrington, 499 S.W.3d 142 (Tex. App. – Houston [14th Dist.] 2016).
Ex parte Maddison, 518 S.W.3d 630 (Tex. App.—Waco 2017).
Ex parte Metzger, 610 S.W. 3d 86 (2020).
Ex parte Thompson, 442 S.W. 3d 325 (2014).
Fazio v. Temporary Excellence, Inc., 2012 WL 300634 (N.J. Super.) (app. Div. 2012).
Graham v. Miller, 2023 WL 1960680 (2023). No. 05-22-00766-CV.
Katz v U.S., 389 US 347 (1967).
Long v. State, 535 S.W.3d 511 (Tex. Crim. App. 2017).
McLaren v. Microsoft Corp., Tex. App. LEXIS 4103 (Tex. App. – Dallas 1999).
Miller v. Talley Dunn Gallery, LLC, No. 05-15-00444-CV, 2016 WL 836775, at *8–10 (Tex. App.—Dallas Mar. 3, 2016, no pet. h.) (mem. op.).
National Press Photographers Association v. McCraw, 594 F. Supp. 3d 789 (W.D. Tex. 2022).
State v. Scheineman, 77 S.W.3d 810 (2002).
State v. Stubbs, 502 S.W.3d 218 (Tex. App.—Houston [14th Dist.] 2016).
State of Texas v. Meta Platforms *Inc.* (2022).
Stengart v. Loving Care Agency, 201 N.J. 300 (2010).
Taylor v. Tolbert, 644 S.W. 3d 637 (2022).
The State of Texas, et al v Google, LLC, 4:2020-cv-00957.
Thompson v. Dealer Renewal Services, No. 4:21-cv-0467-P, 2021 U.S. Dist. LEXIS 223424.

CHAPTER 4

Billings v. Atkinson, 489 S.W. 2d 858, 861 (Tex. 1973).
Boyles v. Kerr, 855 S.W. 2d 593 (Tex. 1993).

Bowers v. Hardwick, 478 U.S. 186 (1986).
Cain v. Hearst Corporation, 878 S.W.2d at 577 (Tex. 1994).
City of Sherman v. Henry, 928 S.W.2d 464 (1996).
Davis v. Sharp, 1:22-cv-00373-RP, (W.D. Tex.).
Deanda v. Becerra, United States Court of Appeals for the Fifth Circuit, Case No. 23–10159 (2023).
Diamond Shamrock Refining and Marketing Company v. Roque Mendez, 844 S. W.2d 198 (1992).
Dianne Hensley v. State Commission on Judicial Conduct; et al., Appeal from 459th District Court of Travis County (2022), Texas Court of Appeals (Austin).
Dobbs v. Jackson Health, 597 U.S. ___ (2022).
Doe v. Mobile Video Tapes, Inc., 43 S.W.3d 40 (2001).
Ex parte Jordan Bartlett Jones, NO. PD-0552-18 (2021).
Griswold v. Connecticut, 381 U.S. 479 (1965).
Hamberger v. Eastman, 206 A.2d 239 (1964).
In re B, 394 A.2d. 419 (1978).
In re Quinlan, 355 A.2d 647 (1976) (N.J.).
Industrial Foundation of the South v. Texas Industrial Accident Board, 540 S.W.2d at 672. (1976)
Joshua Amin v. United Parcel Service, No. 22–10295, (2023).
Katz v. United States, 389 U.S. 347.
Kimbrough v. Coca-Cola/USA, 521 S.W. 2d 719 (Tex. Civ. App. – Eastland 1975, writ ref'd n.r.e).
Lawrence v. Texas, 539 U.S. 558 (2003).
Loving v. Virginia, 388 U.S. 1 (1967).
Obergefell v. Hodges, 576 U.S. 644 (2015).
Meyer v. Nebraska, 262 U.S. 390 (1923).
Roe v. Wade, 410 U.S. 113 (1973).
Skinner v. Oklahoma, 316 U.S. 494 (1977).
Slawek v. Stroh, 215 N.W.2d 9 (1974).
Texas v. Morales, 826 S.W. 2d 201, 205 (Tex. App. – Austin 1992).
Texas v. Morales, 869 S.W.2d 941 (Tex. 1994).
Texas State Employees Union v. Texas Dept. of Mental Health and Mental Retardation, 746 S.W.2d 203 (Tex. 1987).
Topheavy Studios, Inc. v. Doe, No. 03-05-00022-CV (Tex. App.—Austin Aug. 11, 2005, no pet.). (mem. op.).
United States v. State of Texas, 1:21-cv-00796, (W.D. Tex.).
U.S. Food and Drug Administration v. Alliance for Hippocratic Medicine, Application to Stay the Order Entered by the United States District

Court for the Northern District of Texas and for an Administrative Stay, 20230414103258942_Alliance for Hippocratic Med application.pdf.
Valenzuela v. Aquino, 853 S.W.2d 512, 513 (Tex. 1993).
White v. Davis, 533 P.2d 222 (1975).
Whole Woman's Health v. Jackson, 595 U.S. ___ (2021).

Bibliography

Adams, Elbridge L. "The Right of Privacy, and Its Relation to the Law of Libel." *American Law Review* 39 (1905): 37–58.

Arey, Whitney, et al. "A Preview of the Dangerous Future of Abortion Bans—Texas Senate Bill 8." *New England Journal of Medicine* 387 (2022): 388.

Ariens, Michael. *Lone Star Law: A Legal History of Texas*. Lubbock: Texas Tech University Press, 2011.

Bentlyewski, Robert L. "Abortion Rights Under State Constitutions: A Fifty-State Survey." *Fordham Law Review* 90 (2022).

Bernstein, Anita. *The Common Law Inse the Female Body*. Cambridge: Cambridge University Press, 2019.

Blackstone, William. *Commentaries on the Law of England* (four volumes, 1765–1769).

Brennan, William J., Jr. "State Constitutions and the Protection of Individual Rights." *Harvard Law Review* 90 (1977): 489–504.

Brennan, William J. "State Supreme Court Judge Versus United States Supreme Court Justice: A Change in Function and Perspective." *University of Florida Law Review* 19 (1966): 225–37.

DeCew, Judith Wagner. *In Pursuit of Privacy: Law, Ethics, and the Rise of Technology*. Ithaca, NY: Cornell University Press, 1997.

Domino, John C. *Civil Rights and Liberties in the 21st Century*, fourth edition. New York: Routledge, 2018.

Domino, John C. *Texas Supreme Court Bob Gammage: A Jurisprudence of Rights and Liberties*. Lanham, MD: Lexington Books, 2020.

Domino, John C. "The Jurisprudence of Texas Supreme Court Justice Robert 'Bob' Gammage: A Legacy in Civil Rights & Liberties." *South Texas Law Review* 55 (Fall 2013): 27–69.

Dworkin, Ronald. *Taking Rights Seriously*. Cambridge: Harvard University Press, 1977.

Elias, Jordan. "Course Correction – Data Breach as Invasion of Privacy." *Baylor Law Review* 69 (2017): 574.

Flaherty, David H. *Privacy in Colonial New England*. Charlottesville: University Press of Virginia, 1972.

Forsyth, Andrew. *Common Law and Natural Law in America*. Cambridge: Cambridge University Press, 2019.

Gajda, Amy. "What If Samuel D. Warren Hadn't Married a Senator's Daughter. Uncovering the Press Coverage That Led to 'The Right to Privacy.'" *Michigan Law Review* 35 (2008).

Gamez, Higinio. "Comment: Son, Get a Haircut or Leave My School? Hair Length Restriction for Male Students Upheld by Texas Supreme Court in Barber v. Colorado Independent School District." *Thurgood Marshall Law Review* 21 (1996): 185–209.

Godkin, E. L. "Libel and Its Legal Remedy." *Journal of Social Science* 12 (1880): 69.

Haley, James L. *The Texas Supreme Court: A Narrative History, 1836–1986*. Austin: University of Texas Press, 2013.

Harris, Lydia R. "Identity Documents for Transgender Texans: A Proposal for a Uniform System for Correcting Gender Markers in Texas." *St. Mary's Law Review on Race and Social Justice* 24 (2022): 59.

Harvard Law Review Association. "The Right to Privacy in Nineteenth Century America." *Harvard Law Review* 94, no. 8 (June 1981): 1892–910.

Huq, Aziz Z. The Private Suppression of Constitutional Rights." *Texas Law Review* 101 (May 2023).

Kaye, Judith S. "Dual Constitutionalism in Practice and Principle." *St John's Law Review* 61 (1987): 399.

Keynes, Edward. *Liberty, Property, and Privacy: Toward a Jurisprudence of Substantive Due Process*. University Park: Pennsylvania State University Press, 1996.

Leslie, Christopher R. "Procedural Rules or Procedural Pretexts?: A Case Study of Procedural Hurdles in Constitutional Challenges to the Texas Sodomy Law." *Kentucky Law Journal* 89 (2001): 1109–157.

Luna, Rebekah. "Stranger Danger! How Hackers Break into School Databases To Steal Student Data, and What Legislatures Should Do About It." *Texas Tech Law Review* 54 (Winter 2022): 381.

Manian, Maya. "The Ripple Effects of Dobbs on Health Care Beyond Wanted Abortion. *Southern Methodist University Law Review* 76 (Winter 2023): 77.

Perkins, Robin Baker. "The Truth Behind False Light – A Recommendation for Texas's Re-adoption of False Light Invasion of Privacy." *Texas Tech Law Review* 34 (2003): 1199.

Powe, Lucas A., Jr. *America's Lone Star Constitution*. Oakland, CA: University of California Press, 2018.

Prosser, William L. "Privacy." *California Law Review* 48 (1960): 338.

Ray, Nathan E. "Let There Be False Light: Resisting the Growing Trend Against an Important Tort." *Minnesota Law Review* 84 (2000): 713.

Rebouche, Rachel, and Zeigler, Mary. "Abortion Law and Politics After *Dobbs*." *Southern Methodist University Law Review* 76 (2023): 27.

Richards, Neil M., and Solove, Daniel J. "Prosser's Privacy Law: A Mixed Legacy." *California Law Review* 98 (2010): 1887.

Rhodes, Charles W. ("Rocky"), and Wasserman, Howard M. "Solving the Procedural Puzzles of the Texas Heartbeat Act and Its Imitators: The Potential for Defensive Litigation." *Southern Methodist University Law Review* 75 (2022): 187.

Schoeman, Ferdinand D. (ed.). *Philosophical Dimensions of Privacy: An Anthology*. Cambridge: Cambridge University Press, 1984.

Schwartz, Bernard. *Super Chief: Earl Warren and His Supreme Court – A Judicial Biography.* New York: New York University Press, 1983.

Schwartz, Gary T. "Explaining and Justifying a Limited Tort of False Light Invasion of Privacy." *Case Western Law Review* 41 (1991): 885–920.

Seigan, Bernard. *Economic Liberties and the Constitution.* Chicago: University of Chicago Press, 1980.

Skeen, Shelly L. "City of Sherman v. Henry: Is the Texas Constitutional Right of Privacy Still a Source of Protection for Texas Citizens?" *Texas Wesleyan Law Review* 4 (Fall 1999): 99–113.

Strum, Phillipa. *Louis D. Brandeis: Justice for the People*. Cambridge: Harvard University Press, 1984.

Tate, Amanda. "Miley Cyrus and the Attack of the Drones: The Right to Publicity and Tabloid Use of Unmanned Aircraft Systems." *Texas Review of Entertainment and Sports Law* 17 (2015).

Tooley, Edward W. "The Drone Star State: How a Challenge to Texas Drone Law Became the Latest Battleground Between the First Amendment and the Right to Privacy." *Journal of Air Law and Commerce* 88 (Winter 2023).

Warren, Samuel D., and Brandeis, Louis D. "The Right to Privacy." *Harvard Law Review* 4 (1890): 193–220.

Westin, Alan F. *Privacy and Freedom.* New York: Atheneum, 1967.

Zettler, Patricia J., and Sarpatwari, Ameet. "State Restrictions on Mifepristone Access — The Case for Federal Preemption." *New England Journal of Medicine* 386 (2022): 705–07.

Zimmerman, Diane Leenheer. "False Light Invasion of Privacy: The Light that Failed." *New York University Law Review* 64 (1989): 364–87.

Index

About the Author

John C. Domino is professor of political science at Sam Houston State University, where he teaches constitutional law, civil rights and liberties, judicial politics, legal history, and Texas politics. He is the author of *Civil Rights & Liberties in the 21st Century* and *Texas Supreme Court Justice Bob Gammage: A Jurisprudence of Rights and Liberties*. His articles on Texas judicial politics and legal history have appeared in such journals as *Justice Systems Journal*, *South Texas Law Review*, the *British Journal of American Legal Studies*, and the *Journal of the Texas Supreme Court Historical Society*. Domino received his PhD from Miami University. He lives in The Woodlands, Texas, with his two children and two dogs.

www.ingramcontent.com/pod-product-compliance
Ingram Content Group UK Ltd.
Pitfield, Milton Keynes, MK11 3LW, UK
UKHW041838031026
15587UKWH00002B/864

9 781666 933116